Artists of the Page

During the time that the pieces of this book were being assembled, the picturebook world lost twelve of its fine artists. Some we had the pleasure and privilege of meeting; others we knew only from the delight their work brought us. With deep appreciation, we dedicate this book to the memory of

Donald Carrick
Fritz Eichenberg
Paul Galdone
Theodor Geisel (Dr. Seuss)
Dayal Kaur Khalsa
Charles Keeping
Errol Le Cain
Arnold Lobel
Ori Sherman
John Steptoe
Margot Tomes
Margot Zemach

Artists of the Page

Interviews with Children's Book Illustrators

by
Sylvia Marantz
Kenneth Marantz

McFarland & Company, Inc., Publishers
Jefferson, North Carolina, and London

Illustration acknowledgments:
    Allan and Janet Ahlberg—courtesy Colin Dwelly
    Nicola Bayley—courtesy Carole Cuther
    Quentin Blake—courtesy Random Century Children's Books
    John Burningham—courtesy Fatimah Namdar
    Babette Cole—courtesy Random Century Children's Books
    Jan Ormerod—courtesy Carole Cuther
    Helen Oxenbury—courtesy Carole Cuther
    Amy Schwartz—courtesy Leonard S. Marcus

All other illustrations are courtesy of the artists.

British Library Cataloguing-in-Publication data are available

Library of Congress Cataloguing-in-Publication Data

Marantz, Sylvia S.
    Artists of the page : interviews with children's book
illustrators / by Sylvia Marantz [and] Kenneth Marantz.
        p.   cm.
    Includes bibliographical references and index.
    ISBN 0-89950-701-8 (lib. bdg. : 50# alk. paper) ∞
    1. Illustrators—Interviews.   2. Illustrated books, Children's.
3. Illustration of books—20th century.   I. Marantz, Kenneth A.
II. Title.
NC965.M34   1992
741.6′42′0922—dc20   91-50951
                                                              CIP

Manufactured in the United States of America

McFarland & Company, Inc., Publishers
  Box 611, Jefferson, North Carolina 28640

Acknowledgments

Travel for the interviews in England was financed in part by a research grant from the Ohio State University.

Our thanks to:

Leslie Simon, for her typing and patience,

All those interviewed and their publishers and editors, for their time and help,

Our grandchildren, for their inspiration and enthusiasm.

Contents

Preface

The interviews that follow need to be read in the context of the way they happened and what subsequently was done with and to them. Here is a summary of these conditions.

How did we start?

Admiration for the under-appreciated talent of picturebook artists had led us to read as much as we could find about them. Some had written extensively about their life and work; others had been analyzed by one or more critics. But many remained a mystery. So when Anita Silvey of *Horn Book* asked us if we would like to interview Anthony Browne on a forthcoming trip to England in 1985, we enthusiastically assented. But we were also apprehensive. This was, after all, not only an intrusion into someone's life, but also a loss, to him, of precious work time. Would he want to meet with us at all? Browne was most gracious and cooperative, and we learned so much that we felt helped in understanding and appreciating his work. We decided to try to do more interviews.

How did we choose the subjects?

The list of illustrators we have interviewed is certainly not a complete roster of "the best," although we deeply admire the work of them all. We have tried not to interview anyone whose work is already well-documented in print. Location also had to play a part; we did not have the time or money to travel to some of the places illustrators choose to live. But if we were able to be there, we seized the opportunity. And if they came to Columbus, Ohio, it was very tempting to interview them here, although we always preferred to visit illustrators where they live and work. Finally, a few people whose work we appreciated chose not to be interviewed. So our list includes an assortment of those who have been masters of their art for years, and some new illustrators whose work has caught our attention. They have in common only their accessibility and our admiration for their work.

How did we work?

Before each interview, we read everything we could find about the artists, and made notes to verify the facts about their lives, backgrounds, training. Then we went through as many of their books as we could find, writing down any questions we had about style, placements, choice of subject, color, etc. We usually asked about their collaboration if they work with a writer, their relationships with editors or agents, the other illustrators they admire from childhood or today, and their feelings about their work. Sometimes we would hear about their work in progress and see examples of the original art for that or other works.

We recorded interviews on cassettes, two if possible since failures have occurred, and then transcribed them onto paper. The interview was then organized by topic, since conversations tend to jump from subject to subject and back again. The text of our questions and comments was kept to a minimum; we tried to focus almost exclusively on what the artists actually said. The final transcription, with an introduction, was sent to the artists for approval. Some simply returned it; others rewrote certain sections they did not feel really represented their opinions, or deleted what they did not wish published. The interviews as published say what the artists want said about themselves and their work. In the cases of the artists whom we interviewed some time ago, we asked for updates on their work since. All were gracious enough to write the additions you will find following the original interview, which may also have been changed by the artist.

The interviews vary in length for several reasons. Sometimes our time together was limited. Some artists have obviously thought deeply about the work they do and are also able to verbalize their conclusions; others simply are better at visualizing than verbalizing, and would rather show and discuss their work in progress. Some would rather talk about politics or education than their art. What we hope we have preserved here is the essence of the artists' expressed feelings about their work.

Although we wanted the artists' words to be the focus of the reader's attention, we felt it would also be good to depict the people who were talking with us. We asked each one to send us some sort of portrait and we urged them to create a self-portrait. The variety of pictures printed herein is the result of our invitation; we have published what they sent. We hope they add to the information and pleasure one gets from the reading of this volume.

Introduction

There's a big difference between easel painting and book illustration. If you take a page out of a book to frame and hang on the wall, you must be disappointed . . . because all the pictures in a book add up to one picture that isn't even there. — Goffstein

It's odd that we have divorced looking and narrative and art. . . . Narrative content is what switches children onto looking at art. — Hughes

In the end the book ought to feel to me like it is an indivisible whole: all the pictures and words linked together with a rhythm of sound and silences, as with music and lyrics. — Young

When I think of a book, the whole thing comes together like a film that is running through my head. The words and pictures come at the same time. — Cole

But the book is the artwork; we shouldn't compare it to the originals. — Byard

One of the parlor games academics play involves trying to define the essence of being human. For us, one of those universal characteristics is storytelling. As far as we can tell, all peoples everywhere tell stories, have always told them. How they tell them becomes grist for the anthropologists' mills as these academics seek to identify and classify and categorize cultures. In a sense, those authors and artists who create picturebooks may be perceived as a universal subculture combining attributes of the worlds of literature and art. They are storytellers who use words and or pictures to inform, entertain and stimulate our emotions. Storytellers who create books with pictures or with pictures in tandem with some words are involved in a

very special activity, one that produces a genre we call "picturebooks" in
order to focus on the oneness of the story, that "indivisible whole" which
Young talks so eloquently about. There are many sorts of books that contain
pictures, that may even be dominated by such visual content, which are
properly called picture books. But the artists whom we have interviewed
are like the magical figure Goffstein talks about who takes all the stuff on
the separate pages and creates a seamless narrative—a picturebook—a
mystical "picture that isn't even there"—except in the imagination of each
person who experiences the book.

As a collection, one that grows by thousands of titles each year among
the English-speaking nations, these picturebooks embody traditional tales
(from Mother Goose to the Grimm Brothers) and provide a stage for the
classics of tomorrow (e.g. *Where the Wild Things Are* or *Jumanji*) to strut
their stuff. Theirs is a most popular art form, one that is crucial in the educational development of all children as well as one that appeals to all ages as
it absorbs and digests concepts from current cultural events and styles and
techniques from the greater historical and contemporary art world. Collec-
tively, picturebooks produce a common core of experience that helps maintain a degree of coherence in a world becoming increasingly tribalized. We
value them as much because of their significant influences as because of
their potentialities to entertain, to teach fundamental concepts about our
societies, and to help encourage constructive human values that are the
bases of all civilization.

Just as picturebooks occupy a special place in the universe of books,
the artists who create them inhabit a distinctive part of the art world. They
are members of production teams housed in the business world, people
with job titles like editor, designer, printer, business manager, and
publisher, to name a few. Each may have some influence on the ultimate
product: the printed book. But, clearly, the keystone of the arch that sup-
ports the overall bookmaking process is the artist (and author where the
artist doesn't assume this function). We are blessed with an extensive cadre
of exceptionally talented artists who keep that process active. What they
have in common is a way of perceiving their experiences as visual narratives
and an urge to tell these stories by means of pictures. Otherwise they are
diverse individuals whose backgrounds represent much of the variety of the
world's population.

Having been involved with picturebooks for some 35 years, we saw this
polymorphous group of artists and wondered about the possible shared patterns in their lives. Most of the words written about book illustrators are published posthumously or tend to be analyses of their works by reviewers or
academicians. We believed that learning firsthand from them about why and
how they go about creating this form of art would enhance our appreciation
of the art itself. We tested this hunch a few years ago by interviewing several

artists whose picturebooks were particularly appealing to us. And the effort paid off. If we found their insights valuable we felt others would also enjoy hearing them. Thus, we scanned our collection for those illustrators in England and the United States whose work exuded qualities of boundless imagination, ability to illuminate the vicissitudes of the human condition, and mastery of whatever media they exploited. As described in our Preface, we prepared ourselves for hours of guided conversations. We hoped to establish a comfortable climate for conversations in order to make it easy for the artists to be candid and expansive in their comments. Our goal was to offer our readers an opportunity to participate vicariously in these conversations. To achieve this goal we worked hard to drop our voices out, as much as possible, when we transcribed the tapes. We wanted their voices to dominate and, if possible, to leave room for each reader's imagination to recreate the conversations as if they were participants. Thus, although the opening paragraphs have a more structured shape, typically the voices eventually seem to stop as if in mid-chat. As in most human interactions, no conclusions were sought. The suggestion remains that the conversations will continue another day. All our lives will evolve and values will be modified and there will be new picturebooks to reflect on.

Although the major focus of this volume is the words of the artists, some attention must be paid to a few other members of the production team merely mentioned earlier (page xii). Giselle Kearley, agent for Charles Keeping after her husband's death, helped us understand the matchmaking frequently needed between editors and artists. At the time of our interview in London she was representing some 30 artists. Often artists "don't realize how much time it takes to keep in touch with people [in publishing houses] to find them a job." Agents make it their business to get to know the many personalities who are the clients for the artists' work in order to create a fit between the buyer's sensibilities and the seller's talents. "Artists working on their own can get things out of proportion, so you must help them put things in the right perspective. With the client, you must be very diplomatic." The artists are pleased to have someone on their side negotiate money matters, and the publishers "want the agent to take the responsibility for getting the work in on time"—a task that often is difficult to achieve because of the personality of an individual artist or the unpredictable nature of the creative process. "We know the client and what they like. If we see something that does not work at all, or a mistake, you have to be careful with the artists, so they don't take offense."

Of course, in describing the successful aspects of the agent's role, it should be clear that not all illustrators employ others to handle the business end of their calling nor do all agent/artist relationships develop the sort of professional intimacy based on mutual respect achieved by the Kearleys and Keeping. Those more likely to have agents tend to take considerable magazine and advertising jobs. But an appreciation of the mentoring capacities of such knowledgeable people, particularly for the new aspirants who need nurturing, helps us better understand the sensitive balancing demanded by the push and pull of the artistic and commercial forces which shape the contemporary picturebook business.

Two other key figures in this lively process are the editor and art director (or designer). As publishers clump together in ever-increasing magnitude on both sides of the Atlantic, these creative people feel pressures to produce books that will be instant sellers. Kearley told us that "Before, you could sell a few this year and a few more next year, and so on . . . [now] they must have a return very quickly." While we heard this somewhat depressing story in many of our conversations, Wendy Boase, at Walker Books, Ltd. in London, was much more enthusiastic about the sorts of projects undertaken by this independent publisher exclusively of children's books. "We're among the few remaining independents and the only one to do children's books exclusively. Our attitude has always been that our bread and butter is our authors and illustrators, and we'll do anything we can for them." Because authors and artists work in relative isolation, many "rely a lot on the editor and art director. We're always on tap here for anyone who needs us . . . . Walker authors and illustrators come first. If they want space to work in they can find it here. Sometimes they feel the need for company."

Because of the success of their sales efforts in such popular outlets as supermarkets (some 2.5 million books sold in one chain in 1988–89) Walker tends to take more risks than many other publishers. "Here, if an editor believes that he or she can make a good book, there's no question that they will be able to do it. You may also take on a new young author or illustrator knowing that their first book is not going to sell a lot of copies, but you hope the second or third book will. This often relates to the art director who may have a vision of the direction in which to guide it. I've seen Amelia [Edwards, art director] bring on so many young illustrators. On the other hand, if someone like Shirley Hughes [see interview] has an idea for a new book, she will bring in a little paper dummy with the story and sketches, and I may suggest that it's a bit wordy here or there and we could save more space for the illustrations."

Chris Kloet, editor for Victor Gollancz Publishing, was equally enthusiastic and informative. In her five years as editor she has doubled (to 40) the number of titles per year. "The kind of books we do has changed as well. I've tried to broaden the base from the odd, exquisite volume they used to be very keen on to do materials for much younger children that are not so obviously geared to parents. There's a different type of picturebook done here that's perceived as being much more sophisticated, that adults respond to, that's very differently marketed. It's very different from the obviously child-oriented book like a Tony Ross [see interview] or David McKee. It's also very different from the European picturebook as decorative fine art: storytelling versus 'fine art.' It has something to do with the fluency of the line. A lot of European books are stuffy. The British try to animate, not to be decorative. Blake [see Quentin Blake interview] is the quintessential British line."

Ms. Kloet shared Ms. Boase's thoughts on the growth of the industry. "People are publishing more and more—too much. It had leveled off at some 3,000–4,000; now it's risen to 5,000 per year. And we're all doing it; increasing our turnover because we feel we have to do more instead of trying to do fewer, better. We are increasingly aware of the need to publish for a wider market. We used to be able to make enough just from the United Kingdom; now we need to go farther . . . . And children's books start slowly. If it's not in paperback it may never reach its potential. It won't be reprinted, and you may think very hard before you publish that author's next book . . . . Other things have become more expensive. Holland is now too expensive so we do all our color printing in the Far East, or occasionally Italy. And we try to share film for printing. If I'm going to take an American book and it's been a year since their printing, we'll hunt up a co-edition and the translation since we have a smaller run. Sometimes they are happy to do this because they know the quality of the work we do is very good."

But the current growth rate and emphasis on international co-publishing is unhealthy. "I think we may be going back, soon, from the whole global thing. We will have become so large because everybody will be publishing for the world market. We'll all be run by a few companies. But things grow and grow until they burst into their component parts, so I'm hopeful that we might get to the stage eventually of much more individual units rather than publishing for a large market."

Within the big picture of the picturebook industry, a complex one that is now booming with an exploding paperback market and the expansion of markets into schools and less traditional supermarket and drug outlets, the production people try to concentrate on the quality of each book. Ms. Boase and Amelia Edwards, art director for Walker, reminded us that "We shouldn't get too involved with sales or marketing. We must channel all our energies into good relations with authors and artists." Yet sales information does infiltrate their lives with such news as the success of a range published exclusively for a supermarket chain. "The trade was very upset at first; they thought this was not a good thing for the book trade because the books were as good a quality as any, so they felt it would be competition [for the book shops]. But we found that, in the case of Helen Oxenbury [see interview], for instance, the sales of her trade books actually rose following publication in the non-traditional outlet. I think this shows that we were tapping a different market. People will get to know authors and ask for them in the book shops . . . it develops a taste for good quality books. In editing and designing the book, there is no difference. You are making the book for children. We don't do different kinds of books for different markets [e.g., supermarkets]."

Another experienced art director, Ava Weiss of Greenwillow Books, expressed a similar sense of responsibility for quality. "It is my responsibility to worry about the graphic looks for the book from beginning to end so that we [the author and Ms. Weiss] will talk about the size as well as the length, even though the length doesn't really vary that much . . . about how much color . . . about the kind of book we think we ought to make out of this idea at the very front end. And then I work along with the artists mostly, all the way through until the book comes off the press. I go to the printer with every single book we publish for the first edition and stay with it until we've got a good press sheet. It is this working along from beginning to end that allows us to keep up the quality. But it is an endless battle to do the very best that we possibly can."

Ms. Weiss, like her UK counterparts, works with experienced artists like Pat Hutchins [see interview] and Vera Williams. "I have to try to figure out what it is that they want in the end in a book so that I can help them realize it." And, like Ms. Edwards, she takes special interest in the young illustrators. "With young artists there is a tremendous gap between what they would like to do and what they can do for reproduction: and everything we do is for reproduction, so part of my job is seeing a lot of portfolios and working with people who have never done a book before and helping them through the growing pains of learning the medium."

Such sensibilities about coworkers motivated Ms. Weiss to tell us that "the nicest thing about the book field is that there are terribly nice people in it, and you can work with people you like." Our conversations with the people in this book corroborated her feelings. We discovered individuals with distinctively different histories and working habits who objectify their fanciful images in relative isolation. They don't form social clubs or frequent the same pubs, nor do most of them seek out the picturebooks of peers. However, they did share an openness to us, a graciousness and willingness to give of their creative time to talk with us about the matters appearing in the rest of this volume. The key attribute that each owns, which is probably what triggered our initial desire to meet them as we experienced their picturebooks, was quickly perceived in person and reinforced in conversation. Each is in some idiosyncratic way "the essential artist."

One

Allan and Janet Ahlberg

A Sampling of Works in Print

The Baby's Catalog Little, 1983, 1986.
Bye-Bye Baby Little, 1990.
The Cinderella Show Penguin, 1987.
The Clothes Horse and Other Stories
  Penguin, 1988.
Each Peach Pear Plum Penguin, 1979,
  1986.

Funnybones Greenwillow, 1981.
Jeremiah in the Dark Woods
  Penguin, 1978.
The Jolly Christmas Postman
  Little, 1991.
The Jolly Postman Little, 1986.
Peek-A-Boo! Penguin, 1981, 1984.

Leicester is more than commuting distance from London, a city much changed by economic shifts and a large wave of immigrants. But the Ahlbergs have found a spot far enough out of the city to seem rural, while close enough for their daughter to feel part of her school community. The view from the informal and comfortable living room is out over fields and trees and toward the remodeled garage-barn that Janet Ahlberg keeps as her studio. There, surrounded by all sorts of visual cues from art reproductions to her latest proof sheets, she draws her characters and designs a special yearly birthday card for her husband. He works separately in a smaller space, perhaps needing less room for his words to grow than she does for her pictures.

They work cooperatively in preparing a late lunch much as they do for books; slicing bread and pouring drinks for us and enjoying the fresh fruit of the season.

Allan was really a grave digger?

Allan: Yes, for a couple of years. Apart from teaching, and my current work, it was the best job I ever had. It was quiet. In the winter I could dig a hole, and . . . I'd be out of the wind and could take out a paperback and

1

Allan, Jessica, and Janet Ahlberg

read. In the summer we would cut the grass with a scythe between the gravestones, and when we were done I could sit behind a pile of grass and read. I had a university education out of that reading.

You met at the Sunderland College of Education?
Janet: Yes.
Afterward you [Janet] went to Leicester Polytechnic?
Janet: Yes, and did some free-lance design and some magazine layout.
The obvious question is how did you get to picturebooks?
Allan: I was teaching. Janet had begun to work doing any design projects she could get, little illustrations in advertisements or newspapers. And she had done some for children's books, but they were instructional books, like how to make things. Then she asked me to write something she could illustrate, because she felt like illustrating fiction. And that's how it happened; I was drawn into it by her invitation.

We did a set of books called "The Brick Street Boys" about a bunch of boys who were mad about English football [soccer].

What do you think were the books that influenced you as a child?
Janet: I used to love the comics. There's something about reading

them regularly, I think, that grips you almost more than a novel. They've got a brash jollity. And there's the joy of having them every week. There was *Rupert,* and many others. And I liked A. A. Milne's poetry, and *Winnie the Pooh,* that wonderful bear.

Allan: I liked the comics as well. Comics are words and pictures dovetailed together. It's very graphic. Often in English comics you have a paragraph underneath the panels as well, or even with *Rupert* a little verse, so you have these strands telling the story.

What was available to you as children?

Allan: They would all be very parochial British comics. These are not like part of the Sunday papers. They are quite separate things sold on Tuesday or Thursday weekly. In fact we liked them so much that when we first started work, the books we did were based on comics. We went to a dealer and bought an enormous number of old comics dating to almost the beginning of the century. We still keep them out to look at. Many of them were done by talented artists, and one of the best children's illustrators we know and admire is a man called Dudley Watkins. His drawing was fabulous and very witty. I don't think he ever did any books, just comics. The American we most admire is George Herriman *[Krazy Kat].* Janet did a forged *Krazy Kat* for my birthday.

But that's a very adult strip.

Allan: I never saw that as a child.

Do you know Little Nemo?

Allan: Yes.

Janet: We have a large anthology of Nemo strips.

What formal art training did you have?

Janet: My parents were both in art. As a child, I liked it. I drew quite a lot. But when it came to choosing in secondary school what to do, I chose the academic because I didn't want to do what they did. But I discovered that was a mistake, after a few years of doing Latin and other things like that. I was awful at Latin. I should have stuck to what I was good at. I had to go back and do my A levels at a college of further education. I had decided to become a teacher. But I was awful at that too. So my father had to pay my fees when I did the course in graphics at the Polytechnic. He was a lecturer there in the fine art department. There was a teacher to whom I owe a great deal, called Andre Amstutz. We work with him now; he's illustrated something Allan has just written, so we're in touch with him and he's a friend as well.

Allan has several other illustrators with whom he has worked, but you haven't worked with any other author?

Janet: Not recently, only way back.

Allan: It all comes down to the logistics of doing a picturebook. They are usually quicker to write than to illustrate. So when I've written one and

Janet is working on the pictures, I'm writing something else. And she can't do it, because she's still doing the pictures for the other. Also, she's not as keen on black and white illustration, so if I've done books of verse or novels, she usually doesn't want to take those on.

You prefer to illustrate in color?

Janet: Yes. I think I'm better at that.

Do you also have a gallery life?

Janet: No. I spend all my time doing books. Also, I don't have a hankering to be a "fine artist." I feel that my skill is as part of a team making books.

Allan: I think the graphic combination of words and pictures is a different thing. You can make a splendid picture and hang it on a wall. Or you can make pictures that combine with words on a page, a page that can turn, and combine into a book — that's quite different. We make books — and that's cover to cover, end-papers, type and printing. The contributions we make are sacrificed to the total. Janet doesn't have any wish to frame pictures to hang on a gallery wall. There are some of our friends in this work that might like to paint landscapes for the gallery wall, and look upon that as a higher achievement.

Janet: That's "real art."

Allen: What we argue is a tangent even to that. I don't think Janet thinks of herself as an "illustrator," even if we use the word. What happens is that we jointly make the book. The book contains words and pictures. We argue about what goes where, and how these elements combine to make the book. If there's a story, it will be in the words sometimes, and then it goes into the pictures, and then in both together. And sometimes the story in the words is not the same as that in the pictures; there's a contradiction there. But she does not illustrate my stories, any more than my words "wordify" her pictures. They jointly make the book.

For The Cinderella Show, *what is the process in making something like this? Does one of you wake up in the middle of the night . . . ?*

Allan: One of the rules is: Never in the middle of the night! But the method varies from project to project. Broadly, the routine would be, when we come to the end of a project, Janet doesn't rest too long; she wants to get on to the next. We have a lot of ideas, sheets of them. Some may be lousy ideas, but we have great numbers of them. We make great lists of general stories. I'll start to play around with them; I write something to push over to her at breakfast, because I work early. Sometimes she doesn't like it, and she has a terrible time with me because I get irritated. Mostly she has a very good nose for what works and what doesn't. Sometimes she laughs and that encourages me to go. Usually the words come first. Then she'll pick it up and play with it, do a few roughs. Then we begin to think: How big should it be, black and white or color? The book slowly takes shape. We begin to think about type and design. We have a friend who is a book designer, so we may talk to him, get several samples of type; then we get galleys, and paste them up. We make a dummy of the entire book. That's what *The Cinderella Show* is. We made the dummy and expected to make it a big four-color book, but didn't. Then we came back to the dummy one day years later and thought, what a waste, we should try to publish it. But we couldn't do it larger; it would have taken Janet four years.

Janet: It came out like that because it's a slight idea and it needed to be small. It would have been too inflated for the modest idea it is.

Allan: But that's how it goes, back and forth, up to where the bar code's going to go, and the blurb as well. Janet's my earliest and probably best editor. So if it's in the book in your hand, we did it. Those bar codes are monstrous; we'd like to shrink them to nothing.

Janet: Sometimes things do get changed and we don't know about it. So we can't guarantee that everything in it is what we've chosen.

Allan: Yes, some American editions are not what we did. When you first start, you have less leverage than we have acquired now. When we did *Peepo* it was translated into American to *Peekaboo*. The title change was necessary because that's what you say in America, but the text is also entirely different. The American publisher thought the text was too long, so I was encouraged to write a shorter version. But I believe the English text is now in the American version.

Are you generally happy with the reproduction of your color?

Janet: Yes. Printing is much better than it used to be in the '70s. We used to have a lot of trouble with things like register, which doesn't seem to be nearly so much a problem now. It's done in Hong Kong or Italy.

Allan: The most recent book was printed 100 miles away, but Hong Kong is more usual.

Will they send you to the press to oversee the printing?

Janet: We probably could go. But I've had trouble traveling recently because of a bad back, so going to the printer isn't easy now as it used to be. When they were printed in England in the '70s and early '80s we always went.

Allan: We have more confidence that they'll at least get the color and the register right. There are even more inexcusable things that happen, like the wrong typeface.

In a recent book, only a few words like "mum" needed to be changed for the American edition. So they changed them and used *a different typeface!* So we've become pretty hard to work with, in a sense, because we assume that everything will go wrong, and everyone will get it wrong. We double and triple check everything and it still goes wrong. Because there are simply so many books going through the editors and printers; it's like a waterfall of books. Our publishers are our best allies in the making of the book. They're the people after our readers who care most—and they do help us. But sometimes they get it wrong.

Janet: They have a lot of pressure on them. They may hate to say no to an end-paper, for example, but they know they can't afford it.

Allan: It's a dilemma. Children's books are a small art and a rather larger business. The art and the business are bound to fight.

Janet: I've always wanted justification for spending my life doing what I'm doing. We know we're not brain surgeons, or politicians. It is good to know that the struggle is worth it, that all the pestering and nit-picking we do is really for some good purpose.

Allan: Picturebooks involve words *and* pictures. To come at them only from the art college can be as distorting as coming only from the university English department. One publisher ran a picturebook competition a few years ago and asked me to be one of the judges. They aimed the competition at art colleges, and they got a lot of packages. But they were like people looking for a good song and going to the college of music; you need a good lyric along with the music to make a song. How you get that duality is a good question. You may not find the words in the art department, and you may not find the pictures in the English department. Many art students approach the picturebook from the point of view of the glamorous beautiful double-page spread. And the words are only a scaffold, or an occasion to generate the pictures. Some of those books get published. There are some magnificent-looking picturebooks for kids that when you sit down to read them are as hollow as empty egg shells. There's no story, no substance—the maker of the book was carried away by the beauty of the pictures.

Janet: You could have a book of just lovely pictures, but without anything else.

What about the difficulty of writing?

Allan: I find it difficult to write novels—easier to write short texts.

Janet: But the short text is very exposed.

Allan: But it's turned out to be something I can do. When some writers write a short text, it's so complete that you have to pry it apart to find a place to put the pictures in. My work's more loosely knitted; I imagine the pictures as I go along. It happens to be the way I work.

Have you ever considered doing a textless book?

Janet: No, I never have. Mainly because Allan gets the ideas.

Allan: If we did, it would still be "written," even if it had no words.

Janet: I suppose you feel you want some words there; you want the satisfaction of text.

Allan: Not entirely. I could well imagine in the next few years doing a book that had no words. All that would mean is that we had an idea and there were no words in it. It got to the top of the pile and got done. But in our picturebooks, the words are not just there for what they tell you in the narrative or informational sense. They have a graphic design presence as well that is independent of what the words mean. So when we put the words down on a page, you can enjoy that page for the way the words are on it as well.

How did you make the transition from some of the earlier books that have a large amount of text to later ones that have much less?

Allan: When I did the first books, I just sat down and wrote things for my own pleasure. I wrote *Burglar Bill, Cops and Robbers,* and *Jeremiah in the Dark Wood.* They were stories of between 2,000 and 5,000 words. It seemed to be a length I enjoyed, and I think I might have carried on like that. Then I did a long story in verse, but the publishers wanted a picturebook text. So I wrote the *Little Worm Book* but they didn't want that either. By this time Janet was waiting to start, so I found something in the Opie's collection of children's playground rhymes called *Each Peach Pear Plum.* I took that and played around with it. Then we waited until the following year when it was published. I didn't think too much of *Each Peach;* I thought *Cops and Robbers* was better. But we noticed that *Each Peach* was receiving much more attention. I suppose that encouraged me to explore the use of fewer [words]. But we still do books with more words and fewer pictures; *The Clothes Horse* is a recent example. *Bye-Bye Baby,* the one we've just finished, has more words—well, a few more! We nearly did a book recently with 5,000 words but it got shoved aside by another.

What research did you do for Peekaboo? *It takes place in another time.*

Janet: I have a wonderful book called *The Army and Navy Stores Catalog* from a store that used to be in London. I have 1939–40, with beautiful engravings of every conceivable household object and prices. I get waylaid every time I look in it. But also I do remember my grandparents' house when I was little. All the things they had were wartime or pre-war. They didn't throw everything away when it became 1950. The people in *Peepo* have Victorian things around also, because they haven't thrown their old things away either.

Allan: The baby in the book is me. It's autobiographical. But the idea of this book started with the hole. To begin with it was going to be the kind of book where first you see just a little bit of an object through a hole, and ask what it is, and then you turn the page and see it all: visual ambiguity. I wrote three or four versions of that, some quite surreal. Then I thought about Peepo, which is a game adults play with babies, and it became a babies' book. If this was a game we played with grandparents, it could have been a book for them! So gradually it became this particular book, which is about the house I grew up in and the territory I lived in. The way Janet did the pictures often has to do with the notion of "reading" the pictures. She enjoys making the details because you know the child will read it and just look around.

Janet: They may be intrigued by the barrage balloon. The publishers wanted that book set in the present day. We had an argument about the necessity of doing that.

Allan: The publishers thought that little children wouldn't be able to make sense of it, and would ask "What's that balloon? What's that picture of Winston Churchill?" But if they ask, you can explain — and, anyway, what is a tuffet?

You sort of quote from Krazy Kat, *from* Hansel and Gretel, *many other traditional sources in the pictures in* Jeremiah, Each Peach, Jolly Postman, *etc. Do you do that consciously, or is it just as part of your background?*

Allan: It's hard to say. When I did *Jeremiah* I was just playing with the traditional beginning "Once upon a time there were three bears . . ." and I thought "Why stop there?" So I added the seven dwarfs, and threw in six gorillas, three firemen, etc. Then I had the problem of telling the story that had them all in it. And the fun, of course. And the reason for all the references is that it gives you so many things to bounce off. Because you can assume your audience knows the story of the three bears you can have some fun with that shared knowledge. It's playing with words to make an entertainment.

Janet: Of course we've always done what amused us. If it didn't entertain me, I'd know it wasn't right, wasn't worth doing.

So you don't write with a particular child audience in mind?

Janet: We're not ignoring the audience. We know it's for other people too, parents as well as children.

Allan: Many children's authors, when asked, say they write for themselves. That may be artistic purity, but there's a lot of truth in it, too. As Janet says, if it doesn't amuse us, what's the point? But I can see increasingly that there is this peripheral vision of the child. As you work, you think, who is this going to please? Our most recent book, we think, has a rather narrow range of children it will appeal to: ages two, three and four perhaps. But it had to start by pleasing us. When we did *The Jolly Postman,* we had the choice early on of putting in only letters that would appeal to six-year-olds. But then we came upon the idea of doing a letter from a solicitor (lawyer) which was more like a university student's joke. So we decided to do a book that had bits for little kids, bits for bigger kids, bits for adults, and let them, like an onion, peel the bits off.

Is it selling to librarians despite its format? They can't possibly check for each piece every time it circulates.

Allan: I gave a talk to a group of librarians after the book came out. I made the assumption that they couldn't stock it. But some of them said they would, and of course they could use it with children who came in.

Did you change your style for Funnybones?

Janet: No. It was just the way that idea needed to be done. That was the only book that I actually initiated the idea for. It just came out needing that crisp cartoon style, the bold graphics.

Allan: Janet did some little skeletons for some reason. And we noticed that she had succeeded in investing them with some charm. So then I sat down and played with her drawings, and wrote. As she said, it's one occasion when we worked back from the pictures to the words. They have to be that very bright color. The whole thing has to do with reversing out the type and the sumptuous effect you get by using lots of black.

How much of your life and your child is involved in your work?

Janet: *The Baby's Catalog* was totally to do with her. It came directly from the fact that she loved catalogs, pictures of almost anything, garden implements, etc. *The Jolly Postman* was definitely brought about by her. When she was about two she liked to see the postman come, and she loved to take things out of envelopes. She couldn't read, of course, but she liked taking letters out and putting them back.

Allan: It truly is the case that the motive that drives us is the pleasure of making. But I'm also aware that there is a business world out there.... We worked for a long time trying to find a way to get the envelopes to be part of the book so you could take things out of them. Our daughter was two when we got the idea, and she was seven when it was published, so it took us five years to write and illustrate, but particularly to find out how to manufacture it. The printer in Hong Kong didn't speak much English, and we didn't speak much Chinese, so we'd send a set of requests, and he'd send a dummy back. But the sequence of envelopes and pages would be wrong. Would we agree to two envelopes together in the middle? No, we wouldn't. So back it went, endlessly back and forth until we finally got it right.

There's a drawing in a book we're doing now that's supposed to be done by a 10-year-old. We were tempted to ask Jessica to do it, but she's talking about an advance and royalties.... She's done two little books of her own that are quite nice. She actually puts bar codes and copyright details in. She even puts reviews on the back.

Janet: She did that on the back of the cover of the program of a school competition she won, Copyright Jessica, Inc. They had to white it out.

Allan: The book called *The Clothes Horse* came from her. It's about common phrases in English which, if you examine them closely, have a sort of narrative buried in them. When she was six or seven, she asked us, "What's a jack-pot?" Janet was explaining it. So I thought I would help, and told her a story about the giant and the pot where he put all the Jacks who came pestering after his treasure. I began to see that language was full of phrases like that. Another was the "night train." Well, the night train brings the night. "Life savings" was another, where a woman saves parts of her life in case she needs them later.

And then you had to figure out how to illustrate it?

Janet: That wasn't too hard.

Allan: It's also nice to make a book that looks different from the book you made before. You don't say that it must be, but it's more fun.

Back to the Worm Book. *Where did you get the idea?*

Allan: It's a string of jokes playing with books published here which are manuals on how to care for animals, like your dog or your goldfish. They employ particular forms of language. So it was a gag to treat the worm that way, and then expanding it to make a sort of microcosm of world history and all that. With the first sentence, "All good worms have a beginning, a middle and an end," there was a promising absurdity. The secret is often the first sentence. It's like getting the first row of stitches on your knitting needles. If you can get the first sentence going, you can probably go. I talked to Janet about it and she did the first little drawings and I wrote against her drawings. With a book like that we accumulate a pile three times higher than we need. Then we throw out the weaker, and boil it down.

Janet: And then nobody wanted it because it didn't fit into any publishing category. It was too small.

Did we see a larger edition in the bookstore?

Allan: That's a new edition. We agreed to rework it for a children's picturebook list. But the little one is better; it should be that size. It was just that it has to fight for shelf space, and the bookstores don't know where to put it. When it finally got published it went into more foreign editions than any book we've ever done; it went to places like Hungary.

Janet: They have worms everywhere. But the printing was awful.

You have been published by a variety of publishers, unlike some other illustrators?

Janet: I had an artist's agent. He took on our first books, the *Brick Street Boys,* and placed them with a publisher. Thereafter we thought we would send everything else to that publisher. But they didn't want the next one we did. We didn't think we should put it in the bin just because they didn't like it, because we thought it was good. So we began to send it around, since we hadn't any money, along with others.

Allan: I'd write a story, Janet would do some sample pictures, and we'd put it in a package like a message in a bottle, and send it out. And publishers would take forever, so we'd wait, and meanwhile I'd do another story, and Janet would do the pictures. We couldn't send that to the same publisher, so we sent it to another. That went on for about 18 months. Some would come back with rejections, and we'd send them out again. Then suddenly, three different publishers accepted three different things within about a week.

Janet: We would have stuck with one if they'd wanted what we did.

Allan: I think it has turned out rather well. We do a lot of books. No one publisher would probably have chosen to publish all we've done over the last 12 years; we needed at least two. Now when we finish something we take it to either Heinemann or Penguin. If one doesn't like it we can try the other.

Do you have anything to say about who gets to publish your work in the U.S.?

Allan: In the early years, we were like any English author; we were grateful if our publisher was able to get it into any American house at all, and if the Americans wanted to turn it inside out we just put up with it. Presently our Penguin books get published in America by Penguin (USA). We seem to be building up a connection with Little Brown (*Jolly Postman*). We would much prefer that Heinemann placed all our books with Little Brown rather than having them scattered around. But we've had to give up worrying about that and anything else except making a good book here at home. And having made it, keeping it that way. In the process of printing and reprinting over the years the paper quality, the printing, and pretty well everything else can go wrong if you don't watch it. You feel like the curator in a museum. So we have hopes for the American edition, but we just have to let it go. If you encounter our work in the American edition only, you may not always be seeing the best we can do.

I thought everything was the same except the publishing info?

Allan: Look at the change to *Each Peach*; the cover here had the title straight in an oval; they curved it. That's not what we designed or wanted.

Janet: It isn't the original intention.

Why would they want to change it?

Janet: So that they could have a hand in the work perhaps? They must have thought it was an improvement.

Allan: At least we were consulted about the changes in *Peekaboo*. They were made so there could be an American edition at all.

Do you feel the picturebook is related more to film than to painting?

Allan: Yes. That's why we mostly talk about the whole book. And there's another related notion: rhythm. You've got words and pictures, big and little pictures, all kinds of rhythms. Some books that we've done are very simple, like *Each Peach*, which has the same rhythm all the time. In our later books we've become more flexible and looser, but with picturebooks you always have the rhythm as you turn the pages. If you have a double-page spread early, maybe you want another later. These questions are not about the narrative or the pictures; they're about the design.

Janet: But they do have a relation to the telling of the story. It's like the timing of a comedian. You pause just at the right place, and then you turn over to the punch line.

Allan: If you want that other double-page spread, and there's no occasion for it, you might have to rewrite to get it in or get rid of the other one. The design tail can't wag the dog book, but it has to be there.

Do you storyboard or dummy?

Allan: Both. You can see the design on the storyboard. But one of the other distinctions of a book is the turning of pages. It's not like the comic strip there. You can reveal things, you can turn back, all sorts of possibilities. The book is a simple (and complex) and *clever* invention. I'm not concerned that it will be entirely overtaken by any other mechanical or electronic forms. There is a simple pleasure just in turning the pages.

Children have to be taught about them.

Janet: We used to leave them in our daughter's cot [crib] at night, so when she woke up she would have something to look at. That gave us another half-hour in bed.

You haven't done board books?

Allan: At the time we might have done them, there was a flood of them. Everybody did them, so we were slightly put off.

Do you use pictures in your work space? Or memory?

Janet: It's not all memory, especially when I know what's in my memory may not be right. If I needed someone in a certain kind of costume, I'd look it up and make sure I had it as right as I could. I'd hate to make a mistake. Recently I've taken more photographs. When I had to do the book about starting school, I went to Jessica's school and did some drawings, but I also took photographs. I took photographs on our holiday last summer of landscapes that I've since used in *Bye-Bye Baby.*

Allan: That was a nice thing that happened with that book. The idea had come to the top of the pile. We were on holiday in Devon, and liked the landscape. It just got sucked into the book. The book didn't call for a landscape, but we decided we could expand that dimension and enjoy it although it's not written into the story. It comes out in the pictures.

Janet: I did a bit of drawing as well. But I'm not good at sitting in fields with white paper. . . . If the weather's good enough for you to be sitting there, the paper's bright enough to blind you. If it isn't, it's raining on you.

Anything you'd like to say about your work?

Janet: Only that we love doing it. But it is a bit strange. The other day we found ourselves having a ludicrous conversation about talking biscuits. It was in connection with a book we're working on. But it's nice that it does end up, we hope, in something worth having.

Allan: We started out both expecting to be teachers. We subsequently shifted to another line of work. And it turned out that the kind of things I write are the kind of things Janet wants to illustrate, and the kind of pictures I would most like to have illustrate my stories are Janet's. So we do argue, but the overlap is an amazingly lucky one.

— Summer 1989

Two

Molly Bang

A Sampling of Works in Print

Dawn Morrow, 1983.
Delphine Morrow, 1988.
The Goblins Giggle and Other Stories Peter Smith, 1988.
Grey Lady and the Strawberry Snatcher Macmillan, 1980.
The Paper Crane Greenwillow/Mor-
row, 1985, 1987.
Ten, Nine, Eight Greenwillow/Penguin, 1983, 1985.
Wiley and the Hairy Man Macmillan, 1976, 1987.
The Yellow Ball Morrow, 1991.

Molly Bang came to Columbus, Ohio, not just as the distinguished author-illustrator participant in the annual Children's Literature Conference, but also to demonstrate a teaching package she has constructed which helps explain the structure of both story and illustration as it involves the students in writing and illustrating their own "hero/-ine adventure journey tales." Although many illustrators interviewed have been involved in lecturing and even in regular teaching, Molly Bang is the only one who has devoted so much time to structured instruction. Her two manuals and the accompanying five filmstrips guide teachers in a course for eighth grade and older. The students use a given structure to write their own "folktales" and then illustrate them using three colors of cut construction paper. The results are quite powerful. The children learn a pattern common to many folktales and novels and to many of the movies they see, and they also learn how picture structure affects our emotions. Since she herself has perhaps the least traditional background and training of any of the illustrators interviewed, she may be best able to have an outsider's perspective on what illustrators do, and how to explain it to other outsiders.

We spent a collegial evening with her in our house exploring the relationship she perceived between her work as author/artist and teacher.

Molly Bang

You went to school in Baltimore. Did you have any special art teachers or classes?

My mother was a medical artist. I drew when I was little. I went to art school when I was six or seven, but then I stopped. Mom and Dad encouraged me to go back, but I refused. I didn't get back into making pictures until I was out of graduate school.

I got my undergraduate degree in French studies, and two master's degrees in oriental studies from Harvard and Arizona.

Were there picturebooks you remember from your childhood that may have influenced you?

Mom and Dad collected books illustrated by Arthur Rackham, and would give them to each other for Christmas and birthdays. I loved looking at Rackham, and I wanted to be a children's book illustrator because of him. I saw him and I said, "I want to do that when I grow up." But I figured I'd do that after I did everything else. There were other picturebooks I loved in my childhood — *Curious George* and *Ferdinand* — but nobody stands out like Rackham. I would look at him again and again.

Was your first trip to Japan in connection with your Oriental studies?

No. After I got out of college, the only thing I could do with French was teach, and I didn't want to be a French teacher. I knew I wanted to learn something in Japan. I didn't know what it was, but I knew I could learn it better there than any place else. I got a summer job and earned enough money to go there; then I taught English there for a year and a half. I took calligraphy once a week, Judo most every day. By the time I left I could fall pretty well. I also learned Japanese, so when I came back to the USA I went to the University of Arizona for graduate school. After that I got a chance to be an interpreter for a team of about 13 Japanese reporters when they were doing the Apollo shot. I was in the press box when the rocket took off. I saw more of the USA then than I had ever seen: California, Houston, Florida, Washington, New York, Huntsville. . . . It was really exciting. Then I went to graduate school at Harvard. It was a year or so later I went to India.

Why are you listed as "Garrett Bang" on your first books?

Garrett is my middle name, and it's the name I used in college and for the first few books.

I quit graduate school because I hated libraries by this time. I figured that what I wanted to do was be a reporter in Japan. I got a job as a reporter for the Baltimore *Sun*, but after two months they fired me. They said I should get my training somewhere else. A couple of close friends reminded me that I had always wanted to do children's books, so why not try that? So I worked for a year building up a portfolio. I illustrated *Peer Gynt* and some stories I made up myself. I took them to Ursula Nordstrom, then editor at Harper & Row, who said, "Why don't you make up your own story?" I went home, took a walk in the woods, and thought up *the Grey Lady and the Strawberry Snatcher*. I worked on that for a year and brought it back to her. She said what everyone else said after that: "It has no words, it's full color and so much too expensive. Kids are not going to be interested in an old lady running around in the woods, and it's weird." On the other hand, it was *The Gray Lady* that got me my first two jobs. When I went to Scribner's, the art editor then, Alan Benjamin, persuaded the editor to look at it. She said, "It looks like you like scary things. If you can find a collection of scary stories that we like, you can illustrate them." Alan then sent me to Ava Weiss, who was then at Macmillan. She and others there saw a Japanese influence, and said that if I could translate some Japanese folktales they would like, then I could illustrate them. So one book ended up being *The Goblins Giggle* and the other *The Men from the Village*.

Did you ever study anatomy in art classes?

No. When I started taking my portfolio around to publishers, they said that I didn't have an "art school style." They knew I hadn't been trained in an art school. I tried many publishers for *The Grey Lady,* but they all said "no way." Meanwhile Alan Benjamin, on his own, took it to editor after editor, with a kindness and consideration I never expected. Finally David Reuther at Four Winds said he would do it, but I would have to do it all over

again, which took me two and a half years. The first version was about 40
pages long, and unpublishable for a variety of reasons. I didn't really know
how books worked, to allow for the gutter. There were five or six pages that
were completely gray. You can't have that in a full color book. So it was finally
the same story, but I think it's a lot more interesting than the original
because I could play with the pages more, to incorporate four pages of action into one.

What medium did you use in Delphine*?*

It's tempera on watercolor paper. *The Grey Lady* is watercolor on construction paper.

Is the horseshoe crab from the Indian Ocean?

No, it's from the east coast of any continent. On the east coast of the
USA they are collected for the blood. There's a chemical in their blood that
clots only in the presence of certain bacteria: Graham negative bacteria.
The horseshoe crab blood is now used as the best hospital test for the presence of these bacteria in human blood. The crabs are bled and thrown back
into the sea; they don't kill them. The crab is on the wall because my father
studied the horseshoe crab and found out about this property of its blood.
He had a crab on his wall with a forked tail like that in the picture, not a
straight one like most. It got lost when the house was painted, so I brought
it back to life there.

Why the white endpapers (in Grey Lady*)?*

I don't know. They would have been nice grey.

What is the fabric that you used for the background of the pictures in
The Men from the Village*?*

That was a gift that was given to me when I left Japan. There's a special
type of weaving done in Kyoto that makes a very beautiful, intricate fabric.

How were the pictures done?

With Japanese ink and brushes, very large ones.

Do you work from real people?

I have always used models for everything, real human beings. But it
was not Japanese who modeled for *The Men from the Village*; it was my
friends and family.

How did you come to do two double page spreads for The Goblins Giggle*?*

They seemed appropriate. I was confined to black and white but otherwise I really wasn't restricted in any way. I have been encouraged to do
what I want to.

The only one I had constraints on was *Dawn*, and that was because they
didn't have enough money to do it all in full color, so it had to be alternating
with black and white.

You didn't use set type for Dawn*?*

No. I wanted to write the words out myself. The editor agreed that that would fit the story better. Most times he felt it didn't, and he objected to it, but in this case he agreed. He hired a calligrapher to do it.

But the Oriental calligraphy in Tye May and the Magic Brush *is your own?*

Yes.

Tye May . . . *is essentially black and white, with just that touch of color. Was that your idea?*

It is the format of the Ready to Read series, but I like it with just that bit of color. I looked at a lot of Chinese art before I did it.

How was it done?

With pencil. But everything the heroine painted was in pen and ink.

How did you get to India?

Both my parents were working there in a medical exchange program. They had been going to Calcutta every third summer. Then they had to move to Bangladesh, when the Communists became powerful in Bengal State and forced all American programs out. So I worked in both places.

You did The Old Woman and the Red Pumpkin *and three other tales from there?*

Yes. *The Old Woman . . .* is done in three colors: red, brown and blue, separated, plus black. I was influenced by a couple of things in Indian art. One was the Jain pictures; that's where the colors came from, although they use gold instead of deep brown. The other was Bengali and Rajasthani folk art.

You have used borders in these illustrations, and then broken them?

I just felt they worked better broken sometimes.

And the books have the decorated endpapers?

Yes, thanks to Ava Weiss, the art director.

Is it from a fabric pattern?

No. The colors are from Jain religious portraits. But they use gold instead of brown. I chose the brown because it is more like skin color, and I felt it was richer.

Are the other books done in India similar in style?

The other book about the old lady, *The Old Lady and the Rice Thief,* is. It is in more color with more detail, but it is not as effective. All the Indian books are out of print.

What did you do while you were in India?

I illustrated my father's annual report. He wanted me to show how water was related to the transmission of respiratory disease. So I drew pictures of how people lived in two different neighborhoods—one where the government had put in cement sewers and electricity and another where they had not.

*Did anyone object to you doing a black folk tale (*Wiley and the Hairy Man)?

No. The first version of the story came from Botkin's *Treasury of American Folk Tales*. I think it's a wonderful story; I wish I could find another as good.

The unusual part of the story is that his mom saves him in the end. That's what makes me feel it's for younger kids. At that age, you need to know that mom is going to stick up for you when things get too hard. You're not old enough to fight the world on your own.

The only problem I have now is very minor; the endpapers have been scrapped in the reprint. I'm sorry because they show the swamp; they set the stage with the fawn and the doe amid the trees.

Do you find any problems using the controlled vocabulary necessary for the beginning reader?

I had a problem with "conjure." It wasn't on the list of commonly used words, but I thought it was too good not to use. So they let me define it in the text. Otherwise the editors didn't give me a specific list of words. I just wrote simply. And I had good editors.

What is the Oriental influence in The Grey Lady . . .?

I was reading some books on Buddhism and Hinduism, and a lot of Joseph Campbell at that time, and Zimmer, who was Campbell's teacher and wrote *The Philosophies of India*. Many people have thought the family was black, but I never thought of them as black. I thought of them as a Byelo-Russian family, the ones who had to escape Russia early in the century. I don't know why. I don't usually think in terms of any specific race. In *The Paper Crane* I did think of the boy and his dad as Armenian; why I don't know.

The Grey Lady has the long Buddha ears; she's the Buddha, the enlightened one. She led him on the path of enlightenment, and converted him from strawberries to blackberries. But it's a switch conversion from one fanaticism to another, not a real expansion. She is not only Buddha; she is nothingness and he is the sun. She doesn't exist except for the things around her, like all of us are defined by the people and things around us.

How did you happen to do Ten, Nine, Eight?

It took me less than five minutes to write. I was away from my daughter for about two or three weeks, and wrote that poem to her. The reason the dad is there is that her dad was with her.

Which comes first when you write your books, the words or the pictures?

Never can tell. Sometimes one and sometimes the other. With *Dawn* the story came first, the pictures later. *Dawn* is an American retelling of the Japanese folktale "The Crane Wife." *The Grey Lady* obviously came as pictures when I took a walk.

How do you feel about the paperback edition of The Paper Crane?

I like the paperback version better. The illustrations are softer, and slightly darker. It's based on a Chinese folktale. In the original, one version is a painted crane, and another has the guest pick up an orange peel, and draw the outline of a crane on the wall with that chalky yellow inside of the peel. I love that version. But I changed it because I started making the book with folded paper, so it seemed more appropriate to make the crane of paper as well.

What is the new book you just finished?

It's about a yellow ball that children are playing with on the beach, and that gets swept out to sea. It has four words in it. It has no visual relationship to my other books. It's done in chalk, which I haven't used before, very large and simple. I just can't do books in the same style as the last one.

Do you usually work large?

No. Everything was to size, except the book I have just finished.

How do you decide how large to work?

I just decided I felt like working big now.

Do you visit schools at all?

I started visiting schools partly for the income. But I felt that I was just an entertainer, and really wasn't helping the kids.

I started volunteering in Falmouth because I volunteered in my daughter's third grade class and then realized I wanted to work with older children. I taught in the seventh and eighth grades one spring—that was the beginning of the manuals. I developed them the following year when I worked in the Cambridge public schools. Last year I volunteered in the third grade again, an hour and a half a day for two and a half months teaching one class how to make pictures. I'll do it again in the spring with second and fourth grades. Schools don't integrate art into the rest of the curriculum, and I want to explore how art can be a daily part of classroom learning.

How about teaching college adults, teachers?

I taught at Simmons for a semester, but I don't think I'm scholarly enough.

You have lived in other cultures: India, Japan, Mali. Is it possible to get intercultural understanding through picturebooks?

They help. When I go into schools, I sometimes use *The Old Lady and the Rice Thief* as a way to introduce the culture of Bangladesh. I read the story and then I go through picture by picture. I think a teacher can read a folk tale from a certain country and work from there with magazines, photographs, and other media.

Can a story and pictures by an artist do something that a National Geographic *article can't?*

When I go through a book, I show them both my sketches and reproductions of Indian art, and the differences in the ways of depiction. We talk about why I did them the way I did, and how they would choose to. The richest part is when the children do their own books and have to figure out how they will represent the scenes and figures.

The ways that various people represent themselves exaggerate different things than I would, like the almond eyes in India and the moon-like white faces in Japan. You see things differently having seen the way people depict themselves and their surroundings. I like to copy the way they represent things and amalgamate that into my pictures.

Do you keep your original work?

No. I've sold some, and given most of it away.

What do you think about the importance of picturebooks for children?

Children look at picturebooks a hundred times more carefully than adults. We adults don't look at things that carefully any more. What they see will affect their lives more because they are so unformed. I think you show the most wonderful things you can to kids.

But I'm finding that a lot of teachers are using picturebooks in higher grades. Older children love hearing folk tales and they love looking at picturebooks. When we make books with fourth and fifth graders, we look at a lot of books with borders, for example, from Persian miniatures to The Book of Kells, to examine how the borders relate to the pictures inside. Then we look at modern picturebooks that use borders as well. When eighth and ninth graders, especially those who haven't had picturebooks in their past, get to look at picturebooks, they are spellbound. We review a structure common to many of them, and they use this to make their own stories. Boys write about a hero, girls about a heroine.

We're all the hero/-ine of our particular life's story. But for eighth and ninth graders the "hero/-ine adventure" is especially apt. Adolescence is a time of intensity and hardship and passion and action—a time of heroism.
—*January 1990*

Three

Nicola Bayley

A Sampling of Works in Print

As I Was Going Up and Down
Macmillan, 1986, 1990.
Copycats series: *Crab Cat, Elephant
Cat, Parrot Cat, Polar Bear Cat,
Spider Cat* all Knopf, 1984.

*Hush-a-Bye Baby and Other Bedtime
Rhymes* Macmillan, 1986.
The Mousehole Cat Macmillan, 1990.
*Nicola Bayley's Book of Nursery
Rhymes* Knopf, 1977.

Nicola Bayley's large, semi-detached Victorian house is in a part of London that is not so crowded, or so hurried. The houses are farther apart, and one emerges from the tube to more open space than the inner city neighborhoods. Flowers grow in the front between the gate and the steps. Inside, one wonders if the Victoria and Albert has set up an annex for its overflow of objects. Paintings, sculptures and objets d'art cover the walls, fill corners and tables, and even sit on the newel post of the stairs. Bayley insists that a lot was already in the house (bought 15 years ago) when she married her husband, but admits that she has added here and there. There is a Felix the Cat collection for her son Felix. "We're both magpies. Luckily we both like the same sort of things." Obviously much research for visual resources for her art can be done on the premises. A life-size stuffed dog makes one look twice before deciding whether to pet it. It held an Easter egg years ago when her husband was a child, in a space revealed when the head is taken off, and is made of cow-hide. It could be a handy model, because "I'm so bad at dogs," she says. "But I'd be stuck with one particular dog. Of course, I'm stuck with one particular cat." And her model drifts by, oblivious to the visitors. She has an "insignificant bleat" compared to a Siamese; "I miss that." Once she threw up a hairball right in the middle of a nearly finished picture . . . "Ghastly."

Nicola Bayley

You were born in Singapore. How much time did you spend there?
    Only a year. I grew up in Hampshire, with a typical British education
in a convent school. Looking back on it, it was quite nice.
    What children's books do you remember?
    Orlando was my favorite. *Babar*, and the *Flower Fairy* books. I never
had Beatrix Potter as a child. I grew into her when I was at art school. I
adored the Pauline Baynes drawings for the C.S. Lewis books, my all-time
favorites. Naughtily I loved them being black and white so I could paint
them in myself.
    After the convent school, where did you go?
    St. Martin's in London, where I did graphics: typography, designing
logos, "commercial art." Absolutely awful stuff.
    How did you choose to go there and do a course that you didn't enjoy?
    It was a battle with my parents to go to art school at all. With the help

of my art teacher and head, I won, but I obviously applied to the wrong places. I was too young for places like the Royal Academy, where I sent my best work. I sent poorer stuff to St. Martin's, so of course I was refused. I collected my better work, and tried again. I got in there for a pre-diploma course of everything: sculpture, photography, one foundation. Meanwhile I had always adored the theater, so I decided to do theater design. But I wasn't old enough or experienced enough to apply to a big theater school. So it was just luck that I got into the graphics department at St. Martin's. That was a three-year course. It was a tutor there who taught me always to keep a sketchbook. At the end of that course I decided I wanted to go on, because I wasn't really anywhere yet. At that time I was doing huge, loose, cartoony drawings. But I was also keeping these little sketchbooks to travel about. Anyhow, when everyone was mounting their projects for portfolios to show, everything I had like that was awful. So literally the night before, my tutor said, "Throw all that out. Cut up your sketchbooks and present that." I did, and there must have been enough there to catch the eye of the people at the Royal College, so I got in. It was a miracle, and a secret, because no one knew I was applying. My family couldn't say no once I got in.

Was your family opposed to your doing art?

I suppose they were being protective. In the '60s and '70s people thought of art school as hotbeds of drugs and sex. And I was coming from a convent school. . . . But the Royal College had a certain amount of prestige, and was considered serious, so that was O.K. It did all gel there. You didn't have those dreadful projects to do. You were left to your own devices more.

How do you relate your work to Quentin Blake's (teacher at the Royal College)?

Blake is one person I idolize. I've adored his work ever since I can remember, even before I knew anything about children's books. My parents always had *Punch* magazine. His cartoons were in there. When I found I was going to be taught by him at the Royal College I was in heaven. I think he's brilliant.

He helped you develop your style even though his is so different?

Absolutely. It wasn't really teaching me how to paint or anything. It was an attitude. In fact, when he told me one of my paintings made him laugh, I thought, "I've got there!" It's a sort of insouciance, that's slightly throw-away, but it isn't really at all.

Did you have a previous more "classical" education in art?

I feel that one of the big gaps in our education here in art school is that we don't have any history of art, not enough academic historical stuff.

How did your style evolve from the large cartoons?

I had always admired Bosch, Breughel, Indian miniatures, other miniatures in the Victoria and Albert, so the interest was always there. And I used to worship and copy Beardsley—no more. But in the '60s it seemed that something loose and large and brightly colored was called for, so I did that. But at the Royal College, I remember thinking that when my friend was in a car accident and couldn't come back to college for mid-year, I was lonely and turned in upon myself. I drew a curtain around my area and became more private, doing my work hidden like a child, at least that's how it seems looking back on it. As the work got smaller and I saw I could do it, it became a sort of challenge to make it even smaller, to see how much I could fit in.

Was there a market for you when you got out?

It was just beginning to flower then. Obviously others, like Burningham, had begun earlier.

You had decided on picturebooks by then?

Halfway through the course with Blake. Half of us in the illustration course thought about doing children's books. Some went into more "fine art." Some went into animation. I even spent one summer doing eye and mouth lip-synch for some film with witches and monsters, with white mitts on and that awful light-box blinding you.

How long have you been working on your new book?

Three years. With gaps. Partly it's due to having my first child. It generally slowed me up. And partly it's because it's the first time I've worked with an author who has actually had any contact with me. I had no contact with William Mayne at all.

How much influence has your editor had on the appearance of your books?

In some cases, like my very first nursery rhyme book, Jonathan Cape let me go off and do it all myself, layout and everything, and I had very little direction. After that, we were really set on the rather rigid text, picture, text, picture. That didn't take much art direction either. It's only since I've gone to Walker that I've really appreciated the work of the art director. Amelia Edwards is a goddess to all of us who work for Walker, an earth mother whose taste is impeccable, a pillar. She leads you subtly and you end up doing your best work. Not only is a book the result of team effort, but all parts are important, even the "feel."

Do you have anything to say about the paper in your books?

It's important but . . . .

What about the covers? British books almost always have paper covered boards.

It must be purely financial. I know that when you're doing a really wizard book a few people start saying "wouldn't it be wonderful to do this in cloth binding and have a proper dust jacket?" But usually by the end that's fallen by the wayside.

Are you satisfied with the paperback editions?

Not always; sometimes they are a bit too orange.

Do you work from real models, sketchbooks, photographs?

A huge mixture of things. Absolutely always from Bella, the cat, from life. And now from Felix. He was a baby in *Hushabye*. And in *Merry-Go-Round*.

Is Felix excited or impressed by your work?

No. He's very blasé about what I do. He isn't remotely interested in any of my books. He likes engines, and machines. Before I had Felix I wouldn't have had a Richard Scarry in the house, but now we're teeming with them. He adores them.

Why did you not have decorated endpapers at first, and then finally do them?

I had never done nice endpapers. I don't know whether it's because it comes at the end of a book, when I'm so tired and rushing for a deadline, with no time to organize it. But other people manage. It's a waste of opportunity not to.

Do you work from actual objects?

This [Oriental] carpet actually set me off on one of my books a while back (*La Corona*). For the *Patchwork Cat* book I had a quilt made from materials I chose because they reminded me of Bella's fur. I had it made in the Log Cabin pattern of stripes. I don't sew well enough to do it myself. For objects like china or jugs there's always something around the house I can copy from. People are my problem; I don't do people well. For the captain in the new book, I used photographs of my father. I use bits of people. For the town in *The Mousehole Cat* (to be published Autumn 1990) itself, I had to go and stay there. It's all exactly the way it is. The house is actually Antonia Barber's [the author] house. Some of it had been modernized, but she told me about that.

Otherwise, things come out of my head, which is why they may come out somewhat inaccurate. I do feel if I was too slavish in getting things "right," they'd stop looking like my pictures, so I usually trust to what I've done in my rough drawings.

How did you decide to illustrate The Mouldy?

I fought to do that text. Mayne sent it to me. I liked it and wanted to do it because it was unlike anything I had done before.

The decorations around the pages, and the little sketches in the corners, were those your ideas?

Yes. I like decorating and embellishing.

How was the transluscence in The Mouldy *achieved?*

Watercolor. With the new book I've cheated a bit; I've used white paint and crayon, but mainly in the past I was very "pure"; if I wanted something light or bright showing through it was always the paper. I don't think you can get anything brighter than the white paper showing through. I wouldn't allow myself to make mistakes that would need taking out. But with this new one I have. I must be getting old. I just don't think it's quite as pure as it should be, as perfect an object in the end as I quite like my pictures to be. It's a matter of pride, of my spirit.

Where did The Mouldy *flower forms come from?*

I can remember sitting on the train to Brighton on the way to visit my mother. I had just been given the text, and I had a notebook where I made notes on how I visualized Talitha, the daffodil fairy. It all came straight out.

You could have used the same decorated frame for each page, but you didn't.

Well, there was a different amount of text on each page, so they had to balance. And it was more rewarding, in a way, more in keeping. That's why I won't settle for the same band of waves on every page in my new book. If you're going to do them, I think they have to be different on every page. Otherwise I think you're selling the reader short. It's like the picture on the cover of a book. If it's also the same as one inside, I think you're cheated.

Are there other authors you'd like to illustrate?

The one I would really like to do is Ambrose Bierce. I did two of his in college.

But your work doesn't have that sardonic malevolence.

There must be something of that in me that wants to get out. The trouble is those stories are so dark and strange, that you could hardly see the pictures. I worked very small in college, so the tiny pictures were stuffed with things. That gave them such a dark look that from a distance they looked like a little square of black paper.

You had an upper-middle-class background. Do you think that comes out in your work?

Apparently it does. One stinging review very early on stated how very middle-class my pictures were. There wasn't enough gritty kitchen sink in them for the children who like that sort of thing.

Have there been other social pressures on your work?

I can remember doing, very early, an aerial view of a zoo. A few months later I was asked to color a few heads of the people in black. I hadn't even thought about it. It wasn't that I didn't want any black people at the zoo. Now of course I would think about that. When I did the second nursery rhyme book, I can remember very consciously having a black baby sleeping under a tree.

Do you go out and talk to children about your work?

Never. I used to talk to groups, when I first left college and didn't know how to say "no." But it is a nightmare for me. It may be because when I was asked to talk to some students at Manchester Art College, I got there and the whole hall was full. I hadn't prepared a talk; I had brought my portfolio and expected a sort of seminar. That has haunted me ever since. Quentin Blake can go and amuse a roomful of people with his drawings, but I can't. I know my limitations.

Does a medieval manuscript or Book of Hours represent value in your evolution as an artist?

I certainly had access to reproductions of illuminated manuscripts in my training. Very early I also bought with my own money a very big reproduction of one.

How much time do you need for a book generally?

I'd say nine months. A very significant time. Less than a year, anyway, and more than six months.

Are there more cat books coming?

Not for a while. I could do cat books forever, but I'm already pigeonholed. Even my close friends say I should give the cats a rest.

—*Summer 1989*

Four

Gavin Bishop

A Sampling of Works in Print

A Apple Pie Oxford, 1988.
Chicken Licken Oxford, 1987.
The Horror of Hickory Bay Oxford, 1987.

Mrs. McGinty and the Bizarre Plant Oxford, 1987.
The Three Little Pigs Scholastic, 1990.

The city of Christchurch borders a cove of the sea and spreads onto the plains which stretch to the foothills of the mountains on New Zealand's southern island. Gavin Bishop and his family have returned from a day of skiing in those mountains. We are driven up to the rambling Victorian house from the still-green parkland of the city. The terrace offers a spectacular view of the lights of the city. The Bishops, both very busy teachers and artists, have found the city limits rising up the sloping streets to pass them as they have lovingly restored the high-ceilinged old house.

How do you find time for your illustration work? Don't you find high school teaching too demanding?

I did find the juniors, those about 13 or 14, very demanding. But the others, those of 15 or 16, aren't like that. They have elected to take the course, and that makes all the difference.

I would prefer to do something else, and I must admit I have applied for other jobs, but in a place like New Zealand, the only other places I could go to and use the skills that I have would be an art school, and the idea of hiring someone who specializes in illustration would be utterly unheard of in both the university art schools here in New Zealand. They're not

Gavin Bishop

interested. They're interested in international art. The other possible spot for me would be a teacher's college or a polytech, as in Britain, and there are only a very few of those positions. So I've been teaching in high school for years, and simply can't get out of it even though I can teach pretty well what I want.

How do you manage all this: family, illustration, teaching?

I don't work at the books every day, or every week. I have bursts. Sometimes I'll have something going, and I'll get stuck on it so I'll put it aside.

Other artists play down what I do, the picturebook. There did seem to be in New York City, when we were there, an awareness of picturebooks, and shows in galleries.

Do you get an opportunity to travel abroad regularly?

No, but I have been overseas several times and I was fortunate in 1983 to receive a New Zealand Literary Fund travel grant which enabled me to get to the Bologna Book Fair. Last year I went to New York for three weeks and I also had a bit of time off teaching when I did a seven-week full-time Maori language course. I had to be able to show that it would help my teaching.

How did you begin to do picturebooks?

It's one of those things I had always meant to do. We did a lot of illustration in art school, because we were quite fortunate to have a lecturer who was a very well known illustrator, who used to do a lot of work for a highly respected weekly magazine here, called *The Listener*. Years ago it used to have its articles illustrated with art rather than photographs. He used to encourage us a lot. Years later, when the library association established a prize for illustration by a native New Zealander, they named it after him. It's for illustration, but has turned out to be mostly for picturebooks.

Are there any picturebooks in particular that you remember from when you were a child?

Not any respectable ones. You can't go back very far in the history of New Zealand picturebooks, and what you find is mostly very poor.

How then did you begin to do picturebooks? What influenced you? Your oldest child is 15. Was there any impetus from having your own children?

No, I would have done it even if I hadn't had any children. We used to go out and buy picturebooks, even when we were in art school. We used to walk through the bookstore, where the picturebooks were right on the aisle. We always stopped and spent some time there, and quite often we would buy a particular book, especially if we liked the illustrations. We wouldn't have time to read the story. Sometimes we'd get home and find that the story was dreadful, but we would buy them for the illustrations. It was in those days that we discovered people like the Provensens. It's interesting to see that they're still going on. We were absolutely captivated by them then. And that was something that I always kept tucked away in my mind as something I would like to do.

Then when Oxford University Press was trying to establish a children's list here, they said, "Why don't you write something?" When I started, I just wrote and wrote. I didn't even know whether I was doing a picturebook. Then I thought perhaps I should do some pictures. I had to make a lot of changes, and do some pictures several times because they turned out to be the wrong size or the wrong shape. I also did some illustrations for other things. Finally I saw how to design a real picturebook.

When I tackled *Chicken Licken*, I tried to find as many old versions of the story as possible. I wanted to do something dynamic. I looked through various texts in the library, and found one from Joseph Jacobs, that he had collected in Australia. I popped Goosey Poosey out and put Chicken Licken in as hero.

Would you change your work in response to children's reactions?

I like them to respond well, but I don't put much store by their ideas. I think that as an adult I should generally be able to come up with ideas that are more interesting than the average child. My publisher here is Oxford University Press. *Chicken* has sold very well in England.

What's a press run here?

Five thousand for domestic consumption. They would print about ten thousand and count on selling the rest in Britain and Australia. *Mr. Fox* was printed in paperback and they ran 35,000. *Mother Hubbard:* I've given the whole story a setting of a single day. The endpapers are the wallpaper of her bedroom and the half title page has her waking up at three o'clock in the morning; you can see the clock. And she looks down the corridor and the dog is barking. Mr. Hubbard is asleep beside her. She gets up and the story begins. There's also a cat all the way through as well as Mr. Hubbard. The children I have read this to have found it hilariously funny. I wanted to show how people can be a slave to their pets. In the last verse here she says "your servant" and that sums it up. My original idea for Mother Hubbard was to make it extremely slapstick with all sorts of English vaudeville types and pantomime, seaside holiday style. I started out that way, but it just didn't work. She became coarse and crude, but then I knocked several stone off her weight.

One of the best spin-offs I've had came from the New Zealand Ballet. They commissioned a children's ballet and asked me to do the story, the costumes and the stage designs [August 1986]. The ballet director had seen some of my children's books and asked me if I'd be interested. I said I'd love to. I'd done quite a bit of theater work, especially at school. The New Zealand Ballet is a small company, but it's very good, so it's exciting to see it performed by such marvelous dancers. I've got an idea and I'd like to do another one.

How do you find time to do it?

Well, I have to go a bit soft on teaching for a while, and set up some projects that will last the students for a few weeks. I don't find teaching so draining any more, only in fits and starts.

Did you realize that the story of *Mrs. McGinty and the Plant* all takes place right here in Christchurch? The Sure-to-Rise factory is actually a baking powder factory and that house there is just a few doors from where I teach and the whole area is just like that. [We drove that way the next day and saw it all. It does look as it is depicted in the book, but with Bishop's personal twist.] When I did this book, it never occurred to me that the Sure-to-Rise factory would have anything to do with the monstrous plant. It was just something I thought would be rather funny. But now everyone who sees it says, "I like the joke about the baking powder factory."

Are you satisfied with the reproduction of your original art in your books?

All the colors of all of my pictures are brighter in the books, and softer in the original. When it comes back from the printer I usually can't believe what they've done to it. It's printed on a kind of art paper, a coated stock.

Do you act as your own art director?

Sort of. The editor I work with is a very experienced editor. She worked in England for Oxford University Press and was a managing editor here. She now free-lances for Oxford at home and has another press. She's very knowledgeable.

I think to keep down the cost they allow just a couple of proofs, and that's it; unless it's *really* bad, they'll let it go through.

It varies from book to book. There was a problem from Hong Kong with all the covers curling up in the book shops. *Hickory Bay* was sent back and 4,000 copies had to be redone. The copies of *Mrs. McGinty* fortunately flattened out.

How did you happen to do Bidibidi? *It's really an illustrated book.*

That was the book I really cut my teeth on, the first piece of work I'd ever done. It's a bit ill-resolved, I think. Perhaps sometime I'll have another go at it.

The one the children like most is *Horror of Hickory Bay*. It's set at a place near here. I was looking for a sinister quality. Some ventriloquist dummies have that really cheeky, naughty quality. What comes through in the dummy is obviously a part of you, an alter ego. There were even comic books with the Archie Andrews character, doing things they wouldn't dare do themselves, sort of smart-alecky, for fun. I used Alexandra (his daughter) as a model for this girl in the story. At that time she looked like this little girl. She's grown a lot taller and skinnier since then. She chose to play the violin then.

My next will be *A Apple Pie*. Very calm and straight [said with a twinkle in the eye]. They wanted me to do something for the very youngest children. I didn't see that many ABCs. And I didn't want to do just another ABC or 123.

Do you folks in the picturebook business here meet each other often?

No, it's a solitary work.

Can you identify those artists who most influenced you?

It's people like Gorey, Raymond Briggs, Quentin Blake, Maurice Sendak, that have made a difference. Looking at their work, seeing what they've done to solve the same sorts of problems that I've come up against. But there's no one in particular that I keep going back to for reference.

How about people in the general art world?

Albrecht Dürer, and even Gustave Doré. Their use of line.

I notice you have some Oriental calligraphy around. Is that an influence?

I was inspired by Japan when we first went there. It's a core I can always call upon. But I'm not aware of any form in particular that has a strong influence on me. Sometimes I do a drawing and I feel as if I haven't got complete control and have no idea what I'm doing. But then I have to look at it weeks later to see. Sometimes I find something that I think is so exciting that I just can't think beyond it. Then I start out designing a book and I'm going to try to make it as much like that idea as I possibly can. But then once I start that book it gets farther and farther away from that original wonderful idea. Sometimes I get so despondent by the time I finish it I don't like it at all. It seems nothing like that wonderful idea I had originally.

Do you do a lot of thumbnail sketches first?

No. I do a full-size dummy. I like working full size, book size, as soon as possible. I like to have it all sitting there in front of me. I find I can work out problems and ideas much better if I can actually physically do them. This is even true in the garden. I have to go out and actually do it. My dummies have become rougher and sketchier, however.

So you also have to take your original vision to a publisher, who can tell you to take it back and change it.

Quite often it pays off, because a lot of the ideas you start out with are isolated, and it takes something from outside to see the unevenness. You need someone to knock those edges off. I like that sort of help.

There's no single strong direction that picturebooks are taking here, so I've been very fortunate to be able to do what I want to. But I am limited in my range. If I make it more exportable it would be so bland. I can't do that.

—*Summer 1986*

Update

The picturebook business does seem to be booming in Australia. It's not bad here in New Zealand if the number of new books being published is anything to go by, but the small population limits the business here and certainly makes it impossible to make a living from local sales. I get to visit at least five different towns a year throughout New Zealand as a guest author at Young Writers conferences. These are run by groups of primary school teachers, and young students good at writing are invited to attend, to promote writing and reading.

It is with great delight that I can tell you that Scholastic in New York is publishing my *Three Little Pigs* this spring. Admittedly I would be more pleased if it was a story of my own, but this is a wonderful start. It is very traditional as far as the text goes, but the pictures are very definitely set in a Canterbury summer; very dry, drought-like conditions allow for a slightly surrealistic quality. Not your usual European setting. It should go down well in your Midwest. It's fairly quiet, non-violent, but the two pigs still get eaten and so does the wolf, and so they should or the story just would not work.

I am still teaching for a living, but I am now at Christ's College, one of the oldest schools in New Zealand, a boys' school like an English "public school" (Harrow, Eton, etc.). It makes a nice change from the hurly-burly of the coeducational state school system.

At the moment I am completing a book for older children based on the life of a great-aunt of mine, a Maori woman from the Waikato in the North Island, who married a Scotsman in 1860 and followed him down to the south of the South Island. After a long and hard life she died at 93. It is a story of dispossession and the breaking up of a family. She and the rest of her family all left their Waikato home and were dispersed all over New Zealand in an attempt to escape the Land Wars of the 1860s. I have done a great deal of research for it, have visited all the places mentioned in the story. It is called *Katarina*, and although I don't think of it as a picturebook, it does have pictures on every page executed in pencil/graphite with soft watercolor washes. They look in some ways like old lithographs. For me it is one of the most important pieces of work I have done. I think it should be well received here in New Zealand, especially if it is published with the support of my grandfather's tribe, Ngati Mahuta in the Waikato. There is a lot of interest here at the moment in bi-culturalism and the many new historical accounts . . . of colonization of this country. . . .

Next I begin work on 13 episodes for the TV series of *Bidibidi*. TV N.Z. in Dunedin are producing it as a wildlife series for young viewers. They are using puppets against backgrounds painted from scenes in my book. The series will be screened in November and December with the final episode showing on Christmas Day. There is talk of marketing it for international sales so you may be able to watch it.

As soon as I finish the scripts I begin the illustrations for a book by an Australian author, Jeffrey Leask, called *Little Red Rocking Hood*. It sounds a bit corny, but is actually a lot of fun, and should be a hit with the pre-teen set at whom it is aimed.

The other project I have worked on was another ballet, *Te Maia and the Sea Devil*, an hour of non-stop action. It took place on the west coast of the South Island on a beach and then under the sea. There were wonderful dancing crabs and sea gulls. The hero was a young girl who saved her father and mother from the clutches of the Sea-Devil. I enjoy designing for the theater but generally avoid it because of the enormous amount of time involved if you get roped into painting all the sets and props.

My family is fine; the girls are growing up very quickly. Cressida, our oldest, is 19 next month and in her second year at university. Charlotte is 15, and Alexandra is 12, in her first year of high school, and still plays the violin, but to get her to practice is sometimes a struggle. Vivien is still teaching full-time; it looks as if we will both be teaching for some time yet.
—*1990*

Five

Quentin Blake

A Sampling of Works in Print

All Join In Little, 1991.
The Bear's Water Picnic by John Yeoman. Atheneum, 1987.
Esio Trot by Roald Dahl. Viking, 1990.
The Giraffe and the Pelly and Me by Roald Dahl. Farrar, Straus, 1985.
Hard-Boiled Legs by Michael Rosen. Prentice-Hall, 1987.

The Marzipan Pig by Russell Hoban. Farrar, Straus, 1986.
Monsters by Russell Hoban. Scholastic, 1990.
Mrs. Armitage on Wheels Knopf, 1988.
Quentin Blake's ABC Knopf, 1989.
The Story of the Dancing Frog Knopf, McKay, 1985, 1990.

Quentin Blake's pied-a-terre in London is reached from a tube station by crossing a very busy commuter-filled road. But once you turn a corner, the three- and four-story houses face a quiet park, and the traffic is far away. From his upstairs apartment he can look out over the greenery and work, or wait for inspiration at his house on the coast at Hastings. The apartment has the security required in a large city, but the Morris-like wallpaper and the eclectic furnishings, with assorted etchings on the walls, are almost lost in the clutter of work in progress, work already done, and a wall of shelves filled with Blake-illustrated volumes in a multitude of languages and editions.

With all that has been written about you, why did you bother with us?
There really hasn't been that much. A book of mine has just come out, so there may seem like more has accumulated at this time. Also several people at once may have just got around to me. My own book will be out, but who knows when.

35

Quentin Blake

We will try to ask questions that have not been already covered in the many articles about you.

Perhaps I won't know the answers.

Art teachers here also don't accept this as "real art"?

My job was in post-graduate teaching. I think more goes on about picturebooks on lower levels. The Royal College of Art (RCA) has what used to be a three-year and is now a two-year course in a special illustration department of about 30 to 35 students. That's 10 or 12 a year. Of those, maybe one or two might work in children's books. There are a number of reasons. I have had some very good students, like Nicola Bayley and Colin McNaughton. But there are not many. Some simply go and do it, rather than going on to post-graduate study. It may be also that some students who feel they are gifted want to be an "artist," a genius really. So unless they feel a real urge to do picturebooks they aren't going to. A lot of illustrators started out as painters, but weren't making any money. But we found we were interested in books. The emphasis has shifted, not in the attitude toward books, but toward illustration. So in fact what we are getting in illustration departments, which are much stronger than they used to be, is a lot of people with a stronger bridge between fine art and illustration.

Still, a "fine artist" is the best you can be in the popular conception. But there's less compartmentalization, I think. Part of that has to do with the improved printing technique which gives so much color [to] printing. I think the Royal College of Art has also had an effect because of the way we've always treated it, that each of the people is an independent artist finding out what he can do. Which means that blurs the distinction. Once that has begun to happen, it becomes fashionable in magazines and company reports. At one time a painter/designer might have done those; now an illustrator may. And illustrators are also showing their work in galleries, quite similar work. (I've done painting that is different from my illustration; it's something that goes on in private.)

Another thing that I think is back of it is the return to figuration in art in general. There are people in illustration who have been doing that all the time. Also there's the interest in expressionism. Those things all work together. But a lot of the time they haven't worked together toward the kind of illustration that's called "narrative." They tend to be more decorative, emotional, tasteful. So it is still hard to find people who actually do narrative illustration.

Are there courses in your college in industrial design, graphic design?

There have always been strong graphic design courses, a product of the '50s and '60s. That comes from the RCA, which was set up afresh after the war in 1948. It had become a sort of painting college. But then what has to happen happened; it was accused of becoming too much a painting college, and must relate to design and industry. So we got courses in almost everything. They set up a department that was originally going to be called "commercial art" or "publicity design" which became graphic design. There weren't departments called that in England before. Illustrators came to be a subsidiary part of that; and then, later, became independent.

The many illustrators that have emerged recently in England would come out of those departments rather than fine arts?

It depends on their age. If they're young, they will be from illustration departments; a few may be from graphic design. Some may be painters, which is the more traditional way.

What has happened in the '70s and '80s is that the graphic design departments flourished and were very strong, and rightly. Then illustration came as a second wave. Maybe after the design departments became very organized and Swiss, and photography surged forward, they decided they'd like a little something hand-done. In fact I think the illustration departments benefit from that. They've taken a lot of people who might otherwise have been painters. It's part of the nature of graphic design that it looks more hand-done than it used to.

Your own painting is more non-objective than your illustration?

They are highly abstracted but you can see what they are; they're nudes. They are moody, with non-naturalistic colors. There's a lot of brush-marks. I keep them elsewhere.

How did you come to illustration?

I didn't actually have an "art training." I read English at Cambridge. When I became a part-time art student at Chelsea I did painting and life drawing, not illustration. Because I felt that I was supposed to be doing these drawings for magazines, which I was doing, and I felt I really didn't know anything about drawing. You can get by for just so long. I had to know what these bodies were doing and where the knees came. So I had started doing illustration already, and I was beginning to develop a style there, the scratchy style, and at the same time I was studying painting and that developed as a different activity, because it started later rather than the usual other way around. Then I started teaching at the college, about 20 years ago, and more or less stopped painting. I kept on drawing to some extent, but stopped painting. Teaching and doing books was all I could cope with.

You teach studio; how to teach?

We run small studios, with part-time staff. They are really criticism sessions, one-on-one, tutorials. These are post-graduates who don't need much instruction in technique, because some of them were better than the tutor. Each would be working in a different way and need individual or small group guidance with general criticism. It was like a tutorial editorial meeting.

You would set a project?

In the beginning perhaps a group project. After that we tend to go into individual projects which might be proposed by the student or by the tutor when he sees the way he thinks that student seems to be or ought to develop. Then there are projects that come into the college from outside, either as a commission or a prize. You can't control those in advance; some you do and some you don't. For example, for a long time there's been a prize given by the Folio Society for a set of 8 to 12 illustrations to one of a number of books that they put forward. It still goes on, judged by us in the college and them, and a visitor from outside. The prize was for new work, so it became a project built into the academic year. They don't publish the actual book, but they now not only show the prize-winners, but actually commission them to do work for them. There's a food magazine called *A La Carte*, that gave a page a month last year with copy to be illustrated by a student. You can't handle too many of those, but they add zip to the program.

Do you feel there is a British style of illustration?

You see them from outside. They all look different to me. It's only a guess, but I think one thing is that it may be that they don't feel that the climb to the top is such a long climb as it probably is for your people. There are more schools, and more of you. Maybe they feel that in the American situation you have to have a tougher approach, whereas our people feel that if they're good at it they can slip through to the front without having to fight their way. Or something in the water. . . .

Do you see many picturebooks, from here or abroad?

Some. It tends to be the ones that stray in front of me.

If you were tutoring someone who was doing illustration, would you bring books "out there" to their attention?

Yes I would, to some extent. You don't have to have a complete collection. But I can remember when Nicola Bayley was a student, she was doing that tiny work. We knew she was good, but we didn't know what would happen with her. So somebody said to her that it might be good to have some black and white work in her portfolio. She never had done any. I suggested she have a look at Edward Gorey's work. She came back the next week, and it didn't look like Edward Gorey, but like Nicola, but it worked. It was extraordinary; you so rarely suggest something and see the result directly like that. Sometimes there are people that you need to suggest that they have a look at how the book works, or how Bemelmans puts his work on the page, for example. It tends to be scattered references for the particular student.

How about the outrageousness of some of your works, like those for Roald Dahl?

The *Witches* is scary as well. To me the scariest thing in the book is not the witches at all, but the fact that at the end of the book he didn't turn back to a boy.

Is there a community of illustrators here?

I'm not sure. I think a lot of illustrators of children's books know each other better than I know them, because I'm involved in another network, which is the art schools. A lot of the illustrators I know are colleagues or people I've taught; they're generally not children's book illustrators. I like being in a wider context. I think they see each other more at children's book functions, schools, conferences. There is an Association of Illustrators started to bring together people who might get lost, who tend to be the young illustrators making their way. That has flourished as a kind of center. They used to have a magazine.

You have a "castle" on the coast?

It's just a very old building. But this flat is really it. I've been here 10–12 years, and it's been wonderful. The college is 20 minutes' walk away. It's made my life possible. If I had to travel far, I couldn't have coped with it all.

You'd like to do more illustration for adults?

I think that a lot of the elements in illustrating picturebooks and in other illustrations are the same. There are special interests and approaches that you have to have for children's. But a lot of it—the way you draw, the liveliness of the drawing, the disposition and sequencing of the pages, the atmosphere, responding to what the author wrote—all that is true of children's and adult books. Sometimes people talk about it as if it were a completely separate activity. The thing I object to is people saying that it's just a thing you do for children, not for us. The difference is in some of the things that go into an adult book that might not go into a child's. What I felt about the adult books was that it might enable some adults to look at and read them where they wouldn't read a children's book. Partly because it would also reinforce the links between the two, and partly because you would get some atmospheres that I'm not likely to get in a children's book. It would spread my range a little further. Once somebody says, "You do funny drawings," there's a tendency for the range to narrow rather than widen. So if somebody is doing a paperback of jokes, they think surely I can do it. One can make a living that way, where there would be no variation in tone.

One of the nice things about the Dahl books is that although there is a strong element of humor in them that I respond to, they're not all quite the same. You don't actually know what he's going to do next. It calls for a shift of approach. It did for me to begin with, because he's not the same sort of person that I am at all. But there's a lot to get a hold of in his work. You feel as if you're shifting ground and thinking "Yes, he would like that." Whereas it's possible to be a sort of straight cartoonist-illustrator doing the same thing each time. When you get another author, an adult author, it gives you a slightly different interpretation.

One of the most difficult things about illustration, I think, is every time you start a new book you think how bad the drawings are that you did to begin with. It's as if you went back several stages in your development while you are finding out what this book is about. It's nice to do the sort of adapting you have to do for each new book.

A Holocaust book . . . would you do that?

Yes I would. I don't say I would do it better than someone else might, or as well as I generally do. I did one illustration for an extract from Russell Hoban's *Riddley Walker* for the *Times* education supplement, for example. I really thought I would like to illustrate that book. Of course Russell knows how to be funny under the most extreme circumstances, but it is certainly not a humorous book; it's sparse and odd. I wouldn't like to do it all the time, but I certainly would like to do a book of that kind. Probably I ought to have struggled a bit more in that direction. But in the beginning, as Tomi Ungerer has said, "I did everything that I was offered."

The books that you have both written and illustrated have been humorous books?

Yes, they'd have to be. I don't write enough. I don't think I could write and illustrate a dark book. I could illustrate if someone else wrote it. But who knows.

You have stated that the illustrator is like the actor . . . takes the text and plays it. . . .

I feel that very much. I think it helps to explain it. If someone is acting in a play or directing it, that is an interpretation, and yet it is also a direct creation as well; it's both those things somehow. It's the same as when you see somebody in a play: You know it is the actor, but you also know it's the person in the play; somehow you hold both those things in your mind at the same time. You know it's Laurence Olivier, but it's also Coriolanus.

Your version of Sarah Plain and Tall? Huckleberry Finn?

I did it for the French. The English edition was the same as the American edition; unillustrated. But the French published it in a paperback edition that was to be illustrated, so they needed an illustrator. I can't remember how they got hold of me, but I had done other things for them. As for *Huckleberry Finn*, I was having lunch with one of the previous editors of Puffin books. He said they were going to do a series of classics. They needed four, and if the series didn't develop, they were going to do them in a slightly different, more substantial way. He said he was sorry there weren't any funny ones. I said I didn't mind. And of course, *Huckleberry Finn* is funny, terribly funny, but not only that. I said I'd have a go at that, if he didn't mind. And he hadn't invited me to talk about that at all, but some other book.

How did you take nonsense words like Hoban's "Womble" and objectify them?

Although they are nonsense, they have another element. "Womble" is about things that wobble. He didn't tell you how the game worked. So I didn't want to make it a real game. I don't want you to be able to see exactly how it works. But I want it to look as though it might work. So you keep that sort of vagueness about it. I thought the whole book was kind of Edwardian. That was the atmosphere I got, although it didn't say that in the book. So they're old-fashioned games, like croquet or spillikins. "Muck" was actually played in the mud, a kind of old-fashioned rounders. For "Sneed-ball" he even mentions one or two items to include.

Where did you get the idea for the Dancing Frog?

One of the interesting things about the business is that you get to see how other people work as well. It came about, I think, because of two or three things crossing: I gave a talk a long time ago to a conference of librarians, and they said it would be nice if you gave a talk where you actually draw something as well. I was talking about how I approach illustration: that it was artificial in some ways because whatever style you have, realistic or not very, you can control so you can adapt to the book you're doing. So I wanted to be able to say "if I had to draw a frog just to tell you what a frog looked like I could draw a very naturalistic one" . . . although it wasn't very because I had to draw it very quickly. But to take the other extreme, you sometimes have in the book a person or creature doing something they don't actually do, so you have to imagine what that's like on no real evidence. You also have to adapt whatever you're drawing so that you can show what that is. But there was no book there; it was just a little demonstration. So that was the frog. But where the story came from; it got crossed over from ideas I had from knowing students who had the problems that you have if you're a girl and want to be a professional artist. There are tensions of allegiance. Somehow a little bit of that got into it. I also wanted to put in the idea that your parents and grandparents lived in a different period, but in fact they had the same kinds of problems as you and they were as interesting as you are. You don't want them to be packed away. So that got into it. In the first version of the book one of the other things it started from was Josephine Baker. The American publishers said they wouldn't publish it unless she was a) not black, and b) has more clothes on. I could see their point of view if you don't know who Josephine Baker is. . . . My idea of her was that she was a very dynamic artist, and her own person; but in fact if you saw a girl in a music hall with practically no clothes on dancing in a jungle scene, you might not get that message at all. But I was sad, because I could remember my father telling me about going to see the Folies Bergère, where he saw a black girl dressed only in bananas. Who else could it have been? So there was another piece. But how all those things got stuck together I don't know, but they did.

This is a heavier text than your usual?

I was imitating an author. I think it was the influence of other authors I've illustrated. It's more like a story written by somebody else. It was an attempt to change the mood a bit.

A single publisher in the U.K.?

No. I deal with the publishers of the authors I illustrate: Jonathan Cape, Deutsch, Gollancz, Walker, though Cape is always the publisher of the texts I write myself. The Hoban book for Gollancz called *Monsters* is fascinating because in it a boy draws monsters and one seems to come to life at the end. What interested me was that I faked the boy's drawing. I couldn't see how else to do it, because I look over his shoulder. But how could I reconcile my way of drawing with his? How could one of his drawings be in one of my drawings? So the drawings just appear as works of art, like plates in an art book, as he did them. It was fun to do. I almost didn't come back. Some people have actually drawn like children. I disapprove of that, I don't see any point in it. Mine are just facsimiles. As a technique, there are too many things you need to do. And just because children draw like that doesn't mean they see like that. They're referring to their mental concept. You have to get back to it. Once you do, you discover that children's drawings are sequential, they happen in time. It was fascinating. I'm afraid that is a lack of elegance in the book, in that the title page is the first page you come to; there are no endpapers. But it had to match the rest of the series.

Who decides your endpapers, in Bear's Water Picnic, *for example?*

I do. There is something I always want to keep control of: the tinting of the color of the endpapers. I don't like them too strong. What happened was because that's 32 pages, self-ends, you could have a picture on the endpapers. You actually have to give up 6 pages to get printed endpapers, because page 1 is stuck down and so is the last. ABC needs 26, so it works.

How did you choose what to use in the ABC?

There were two principal criteria: As far as possible I felt it should be kept simple in words, so a very small reader could read it. I couldn't resist "cockatoo," but apart from that they're fairly simple. But of the simple words available I wanted those that would give me an incident. I didn't want to draw just the thing; it had to have an implied narrative. Otherwise it would have been like all the other alphabets we have already. I never had done one, and might not have now, but my publisher suggested it. They hadn't done one in a long time, since Burningham's. That is richly textured. We wanted something different that would still work. I like it when you get the incident but also it implies the moment after, or you can say what's going to happen next.

What is your work method?

From a very rough dummy right to full size.

Are you happy with the way the press has dealt with the color reproduction?

Moderately. The first proofs were disgraceful. But they're now quite good. They're done in Italy.

In that book and another done about the same time I was using colors which they find quite hard to do, a sort of blue-green and mauve, for an edgy feel. Green that's a little bluish has a sort of zing to it, tends to come out as mint green. So I think it's not as good as it could be. They would probably say I'm mad to use those anyway.

You dedicated the ABC *to your friend John?*

Yes. Partly because he's my oldest friend, and partly because we did an ABC years ago, and he's letting me "do" the alphabet, so we can't reprint the other one.

Who chose the type?

We just sat there and talked about it. Something like that size appeared on the roughs. We looked at faces and chose. . . .

I guess I'm a 20th century Rowlandson rather than Cruikshank, who became more of a chronicler later in life. I like aspects of both of them. I guess I have also been influenced by the wonderful Japanese animal drawings on the old scrolls. There are so many influences; sometimes it's hard to say where things come from.

—*Summer 1989*

Six

Anthony Browne

A Sampling of Works in Print

Alice's Adventures in Wonderland by Lewis Carroll. Knopf, 1988.
Bear Goes to Town Doubleday, 1989.
Changes Knopf, 1990.
Gorilla Knopf, 1985.
I Like Books Knopf, 1989.
Kirsty Knows Best by Annalena McAfee. Knopf, 1987.
The Little Bear Book Doubleday, 1989.

Look What I've Got! Knopf, 1988.
Piggybook Knopf, 1986.
Things I Like Knopf, 1989.
The Tunnel Random, 1990.
The Visitors Who Came to Stay by Annalena McAfee. Viking, 1984.
Willy and Hugh Knopf, 1991.
Willy the Champ Knopf, 1986.
Willy the Wimp Knopf, 1985, 1989.

"*I can't tell you how the idea of a book develops, just that there are a lot of ideas inside me, and I have to wait for one to force itself out. That's the only way I can do it. Nobody could commission me to do a book. Something will happen, usually in the middle of the night. It fairly quickly slips into place once it starts happening.*"

In Anthony Browne's book *Hansel and Gretel* (Watts), the girl and the boy sit at a table watching television, and the jumble on the wicked stepmother's dresser includes a bottle of Oil of Olay. One of Browne's young heroes goes through a mirror to encounter dogs walking men, while an innocent white bear cleverly eludes hunters in woods where teacups and shoes grow amid the greenery. Browne has also created Willy the Wimp, *a book with every child's alter ego hero,* and Gorilla *(both Knopf), in which the gorilla fulfills a lonely girl's wishes.* Why this fascination with simians — and lonely children? Most of all, why the almost frightening transposition of a classical fairy tale to a setting in the contemporary world? We went to interview Anthony Browne to get the answers to these and other questions.

We had to battle the tide of arriving commuters that engulf London each

Self-portrait by Anthony Browne

morning before finding a quiet compartment on the train. The Ramsgate train from Victoria Station went through Gillingham and Faversham to Birchington-on-Sea, leaving the masses of buildings and people behind. Past the fields appeared glimpses of the gray-blue sea and, finally, a small, ivy-overgrown station where no one else alighted. A very unneurotic-looking young man with ample dark hair and mustache, informally dressed in a work shirt and jeans, proved to be Mr. Browne. He drove us in his small car through the fields of rapeseed and cabbages on narrow, single-lane roads to a brick farmhouse where he rents studio space. A fire burned in the grate; a large, uncluttered desk held painting supplies; and the walls displayed some familiar posters. By contrast, piles of books, magazines, and portfolios on the floor and half-filled cardboard cartons suggested the tentativeness of the occupancy. He brewed fresh coffee, and we began to chat. *

How did you begin your career?

At Leeds Polytechnic Institute I did graphic design and hated it. I wanted to be a painter. I found that illustration was treated as a kind of second-class art. At the college I attended, we were meant to be advertising

---

**Originally published in* The Horn Book Magazine, *November/December 1985.*

executives—people who could organize, illustrate, present their work, tell other people what to do, and not do the physical work—while I actually enjoyed drawing.

I turned against graphic design in general; I just wanted to be a painter. I used to like Francis Bacon. My father died when I had just started art school at Leeds, and I got this morbid interest in death and insides of people's bodies. I used to spend a lot of time in Life Class, and quite often instead of drawing the outsides of bodies, I did what little I knew of the insides—gruesome imagery. So that's what attracted me to medical art. I totally avoided what I thought was commercial.

In Manchester I got a job, which was pretty well paid, as an assistant lecturer in medical art. I enjoyed it, and it exorcised that gruesome fascination with the insides. Eventually, lecturing became repetitious. Nobody, understandably, was interested in my work as paintings or drawings. But medical art was great training; it was much better than actually being in art school, because I wasn't being judged on the quality of the paint or design or balanced composition—just on whether the artwork did the job. I had to explain something visually that was very difficult to explain any other way.

I nearly went to teacher training college. When I first left Leeds, I applied to Goldsmiths. I only spent a morning there studying teaching theory. I went back and taught a day a week at the Art College in Leeds. After I left medical art, I taught realistic drawing, which was the most difficult job I ever held. I spent a lot of time in the library feeling guilty about how much money I was being paid and designing greeting cards for Gordon Fraser. The cards continue to be a major source of my income.

How do you create your artwork?

I use watercolor, semi-moist and concentrated liquid—no tubes. The artwork is usually the same size as it will appear in the book. When I was a kid, I drew what would now be called surrealist jokes—but I thought of them as funny things going on and labeled them with arrows. My artwork hasn't changed that much. It has so often been said that Magritte is an influence on my work that I decided to come out of the closet with blatant references to him. Surrealism is, or at least was, such a common influence on art students in England that his images have become almost ordinary because they've been exposed so much. There have been so many imitators.

Do you sense any stylistic influences from your childhood reading?

There weren't many picture books around as far as I can remember. I know very little about contemporary American picture books other than Maurice Sendak and *Harold and the Purple Crayon* (Harper). I kept getting American reviews of *Bear Hunt* (Atheneum) saying that I'd copied *Harold and the Purple Crayon*, and of course I'd never heard of *Harold and the Purple Crayon*. I admire Rackham now—but I don't consider him to be an influence.

When I first designed books, I adopted a page design in which I used a small picture on one page and a large one on the facing page. Well, that was a period I was going through. I have not used that design recently. *Willy* has opened things up. I think I got a bit conscious that I was tending to put a formula around things. *Gorilla* certainly used that design. I became aware that I was tending to use it automatically. I got away from the design a little with *The Visitors Who Came to Stay* (Viking). Where I had a big picture and a little picture, I still used the form, but the little picture was an object.

Which of your books has given you the most trouble?

My worst seller is *Hansel and Gretel*. Julia MacRae had just rejected an idea for a book, and she said, "Is there any traditional story you'd care to do?" I mentioned "Hansel and Gretel," so she said to have a go at it. I produced a picture of the father and stepmother taking the children into the woods, and I don't really know why I put them in contemporary clothes. I can rationalize it and say that I remember this story and identify with it, although it bore no relation to my childhood. I had a very secure childhood. I can only think that I remember the story very vividly. So it's not actually set in the 1980s; it's really set in my childhood in the 1950s. I can't pretend that I made any conscious decision to make the story more relevant to children today by putting it in modern dress, but maybe there was some of that feeling underneath. Spain was the only foreign publisher to take *Hansel and Gretel*. Germany has difficulty with *Hansel and Gretel* because of the oven.

I read as many versions of "Hansel and Gretel" as I could find. I amalgamated them. I suspected the book was going to be controversial because I was bringing the pictures up to date. Therefore, I thought I'd not meddle too much with the story. I was very conscious, I think, of not wanting to do a pretty book in contrast to other versions. I've occasionally used a pretty style for greeting cards, but it's not really me. *Hansel and Gretel* was my most difficult book because I knew I was going to be judged purely on the illustrative qualities of the book, whereas before I was doing both story and illustration. Because I was illustrating a traditional story, I knew I was making myself vulnerable on a technical level. So I spent more time on these illustrations than I had in any previous books.

Starting with a picture on the title page of a small bird in a heavily barred cage, vertical lines are used for chair backs, bed frames, willow fabric, trees, windows and, of course, the cage that Hansel is kept in by the witch. The bars theme was quite deliberate but not in the early stages of the book. Many of the things that occur in the pictures are not in the dummy. Sometimes they aren't even in the preliminary drawings. A lot happens once I actually get to work. I tend to work consecutively; I start with the first picture and go through the book. As things happen in the story, the pictures develop. I don't think I was aware of the bars when I did the first picture.

Actually, the picture of the father hugging the children on their return was a very difficult picture to paint. I tried to show it from all sorts of angles, this side, that side. It's also a difficult ending for the book. If one were to alter the ending, I think one might get rid of the idea of the stepmother having died. Sometimes she goes away. I'm not sure what kids' reactions are. *Hansel and Gretel* was greeted with some of the best reviews and the worst. One reviewer wondered, "Why not put the Social Services in there?"

In your acceptance speech for the Kate Greenaway Medal for Gorilla *you detailed some of your experiences with gorillas. How do you relate* Gorilla *to your own feelings?*

Gorilla is about the relationship between a child and her father. My father was the kind of man who never actually found a career. He did lots of things. He was a boxer; he taught art for a while; he was in the army; he tried rugby. He died when I was 17. I really didn't know where the story came from, but I think it has something to do with my father. He was a big man, and I was always a small boy. He was very keen on sports and encouraged my brother and me to be good at them. And yet he also drew and made delicate little models. I think that in some way the contrast of his strength and masculinity with his delicateness and his encouragement of our efforts to draw and write poetry has something to do with *Gorilla*.

I wasn't thunderstruck; there was no searing light when I saw my first gorilla. Particularly, I remember seeing Guy, who was a very large gorilla in the London Zoo. I used to go and spend a lot of time looking at him.

I was doing a school program for Thames Television. I'd finished the artwork for *Gorilla*, but it hadn't been published. They wanted me to write and present a program about children's books. They saw the *Gorilla* pictures and said, "Wouldn't it be great to have some shots of you in a cage with a gorilla?" I thought it would be very exciting and a little bit frightening. They said, "Oh, you'll be fully insured. Don't worry about it. We'll make sure it's O.K."

The keepers suggested that I go into the cage with a couple of females a few times before the filming so they could get used to me. It was wonderful — one of the most wonderful experiences I've ever had! I went in twice for about a half-hour at a time. I was wrestling with them and carrying them on my back, sort of play-fighting. It was scary, but incredibly exhilarating.

Then we went one day for the filming, with the camera people there. It seemed different. As soon as I went in, one of the gorillas came up and seemed to be sniffing my calf. I patted her on the back as I would a dog, because she was an old friend. Although I'd only been with them twice, those were such memorable experiences that I felt I really knew this gorilla. Then suddenly she sank her teeth into my leg, and I've never known pain like it. It was the shock as well. It seemed as though a friend had turned on me. It was like a dream when a friend's face suddenly turns into something horrible. Here I was with the microphone, and the expensive film running, supposed to be describing what it was like to meet my first gorilla.

It turned out that the owner of the zoo had some sort of argument with the television people about how much he was going to be paid. He decided to feed the gorillas just as I was going into the cage. I was in there for twenty minutes before they could see how badly hurt I was. I kept looking down at the leg, but I was so embarrassed, I didn't want to say, "Please can I get out?" They rushed me to the hospital eventually. It wasn't quite what we had had in mind.

How do you feel about the books you didn't write yourself?

The Visitors Who Came to Stay is the first book I've illustrated that's been written by somebody else—Annalena McAfee, a friend of mine who lives in the village. Some people consider the book a follow-up to *Gorilla*. I certainly don't; I don't think it's as good as *Gorilla*. It was quite difficult to convince Annalena that a story could be told in the pictures as well as in the words.

Knock Knock is the new book I'm working on, the second one I've illustrated written by someone else. I feel better about the process this time. It's a book aimed at younger children. It's not written by somebody with any great pretentions to be a writer, but she's run a children's book club for some time and knows a great deal about what works with children. There is a lot of chanting: "Knock, knock. Who's there?"—using the idea without the jokes. I wanted to put in some jokes, but she, I think quite rightly, said that the book was aimed at an age group that wouldn't appreciate them.

For the book I'm working on some drawings of children, and drawing them doesn't come very easily to me. Working quickly for first sketches I probably sub- or unconsciously use material from Burningham or Oxenbury. The text has a simplicity and a repetitive chant, which I find quite appealing. I don't think I would have come up with the chant by myself. The little girl always has control of some potentially frightening images. She can always say, "But I won't let you in." It is also quite difficult to do some of these creatures which are potentially frightening.

I like to have something in illustrations that might not be spotted the first time, so the child can go back and discover things in the pictures. That technique makes the books something one would want to go back to.

After the interview we had a hearty "ploughman's lunch" of bread and cheese at the Bell Inn, where Browne seems to be a regular. Lunch was punctuated by greetings from locals and enlivened by many conversations in a dialect we could just about follow. The original artwork for all previous books was back in the studio, where the family was already packing up to move to a larger house. How could we impose on Mrs. Browne while she was coping with a two-year-old and the baby along with the boxes? "No problem," he said, and it seemed to be no problem. She was young, attractive, and incredibly calm and hospitable under the circumstances. While the baby slept and then woke and quietly devoured her food, young Joseph—complete with a Super-man shirt and cape right out of Gorilla—*received a Superman flight through the air from Dad and a reading from a favorite book. We savored the paint-ings along with the warmth of the family scene, so pleasantly and humanly cluttered, so nonsurreal, so different from what Anthony Browne's books and the pictures seemed to show.*

Back through the fields and the town and past the home-to-be with studio space, we shared views on the plight of education and other woes of our respective countries. "Don't forget to change at Faversham." It was back to teeming London with the fresh sea air in our lungs and the memory of open spaces, the pictures, and the peace.
—1985

Update

I suppose *The Piggy Book* came from two sources, the first being in my wife's family. . . . My brother and I were brought up a bit like Simon and Patrick. My father, though, was surprisingly non–Mr. Piggott-like, consider-ing his generation. But my mother treated us in a similar way for the first 14 or 15 years of our life, and that's difficult to break out of. I would, of course, wouldn't I? I like to think that I succeeded. Mostly.

The Tunnel was not, in fact, based on my own children, Joseph and Ellen, but more on my own experiences as a younger brother. There was indeed a tunnel, one potentially much more dangerous than that in the book. I think the book was about the two sides of one person, as much as it was about sibling rivalry.

As for *Alice*, this was, and still is, the book I feel most vulnerable about. I was, of course, influenced by Tenniel, but tried to get away from him by concentrating on the dream aspects of the book. It's a very surreal story, so it seemed only natural to interpret it in the visual language of the surrealists. I didn't want to "just" illustrate the story; that's been done over 100 times. I wanted to reflect Carroll's jokes, puzzles and wordplays with visual puns, and to try to bring in and involve children who may be put off by the Vic-torian quality of the text and Tenniel's illustrations. Sounds a bit presump-tuous, I know, but to even try to illustrate the book is a bit presumptuous. I have mixed feelings about the book; I do about all of my books; but generally I think it's okay. Some things maybe I would change, but I did want to wrest the book back from adults (I didn't want to try to imagine

Carroll's psychological state for instance) and put it firmly back on children's bookshelves.

Hansel and Gretel does not look at its best in paperback, but I am pleased to see it get a wider audience in America. It's one of my favorites, and one that disappeared almost without trace in the hardback edition in the U.S. in 1981.

I have, thankfully, given up doing greeting cards now, a decision I made whilst working on *Alice*. I had been doing them for about 14 years, and increasingly found that I was just rehashing old ideas, and it began to feel unhealthy. It's my success in the States that has enabled me to give up the financial security of doing the cards, and for that I'm extremely grateful.

I still visit schools and libraries, more than I want to, but I know it does me good. It's often uplifting to see their enthusiasm for my work, and sometimes helps prevent me from getting things out of proportion. Their comments and criticisms are very honest.

I am particularly excited at the moment because I've been showing slides to kids in Australia, England and America of my forthcoming book *Changes*. I've been thrilled by their reaction. It's a book that's been quite a departure for me. Usually I plan everything out like a film, on a storyboard. I don't exactly know how each picture is going to look, but I've a rough idea, and of course I know the story and how long the book is, etc. In *Changes* I knew how the book started: with one image of change, but I didn't know where it was going. I knew lots of things were going to change throughout the book, and that they were going to keep on changing. But I didn't want it to be a fantasy book. Quite soon, however, the ending and the reason for the changes came to me and the whole project slotted into place so I knew the ending and the beginning but I didn't know what would happen between the two. The book had to develop finished painting by finished painting, without a dummy and without knowing whether the book would be 10 pages long or 100. It was very exciting, and it worked! I'm actually pleased with it, a rare occurrence.

I'm still very pleased to be living in a small village. My work seems increasingly to be taking me abroad to France, Holland, Australia and the U.S., which provides a welcome contrast. It's wonderful to see the talents of my children develop in music and art particularly. And Jane has emerged from 17 years of visually creative hibernation to produce two picturebooks. I'm astounded to see the progression of her drawing and painting and I eagerly await what she does next.

—1990

Seven

Ashley Bryan

A Sampling of Works in Print

All Day, All Night: A Child's First Book of African-American Spirituals Atheneum, 1991.

Beat the Story-Drum, Pum-Pum Atheneum, 1987.

The Cat's Purr Atheneum, 1985.

Climbing Jacob's Ladder: Heroes of the Bible in African-American Spirituals selected and adapted by John Langstaff. Macmillan/Margaret MacElderry, 1991.

The Dancing Granny Atheneum/Macmillan, 1977, 1987.

Turtle Knows Your Name Macmillan, 1989.

Walk Together Children Macmillan, 1989.

Ashley Bryan came to the Children's Literature Conference in Columbus, Ohio, to tell his tales in his own special way. Beyond his stories he is known for his distinctive illustrations on African themes. Until recently a professor of art at Dartmouth College, he now spends much of his time traveling and telling stories. We were fortunate to be able to spend some hours over dinner with this gentleman with the mesmerizing voice as he told us of his own growth as an artist.*

Even as a child you drew. But when did you decide on making art your career?

I was encouraged to draw throughout elementary and junior high school. When I was in high school, I wanted to do many things, but drawing and painting subsumed almost everything else. After graduation I took the exam for the Cooper Union Art School and was accepted. My work there

**Originally published in* The Horn Book Magazine, *March/April 1988.*

52

was interrupted by World War II, and when I came back from the army, I completed my art studies. I then started over as a philosophy major at Columbia University. I took a book binding course there and got so excited with the art of binding that I bound twenty or thirty books in a term when other students bound two or three.

When did you become involved with creating books?

It just seemed natural. I created my first book in kindergarten. As we learned each letter of the alphabet, we drew a picture for it. The teacher gave us construction paper for the cover and taught us to sew those pages together. That *ABC* was my first book. I was author, illustrator, editor, publisher and binder, and I also got rave reviews for these limited editions, one of a kind! Because my efforts were so well received at home, I made books as gifts for family and friends. By the time I was in fourth grade, I had "published" hundreds of books!

How did you actually get started on your first children's book for a publisher?

Someone brought Jean Karl to my studio in the Bronx. I had always done drawings for the books I read, so I had endless illustrations on my work table. When she came, I thought she came to see paintings. But my illustrations were on the table, and she studied them. I had done extensive work on African folk tales because I was involved in a project with Kurt and Helen Wolff at Pantheon, and I had completed a whole series of plates in color and in black and white. She didn't say much then, but when she went back to her office, she sent me a contract to illustrate selections from Tagore. Later she asked if she could use some of my illustrations for a book of African tales. I said, "You bet! But I don't like the way they are written." She said, "Tell them in your own way, Ashley." Jean has kept after me over the years. As soon as I do one book, she is immediately encouraging me to do another. Even in semiretirement she continues with my work.

Now that you are a professor emeritus, do you miss the contact with students?

·   No, because everywhere I go I feel that I am still teaching. Through my programs in black culture I'm trying to push past the resistances and the stereotypes and open audiences to feelings that can change, or be included in, their lives. The same energies are still being called upon. When I did the talks along with teaching, the time for my own artwork was limited. I find I can do other things only if my own work is going well.

Have you also maintained your life as a painter?

I have always been a painter. When I lived in New York, I exhibited my work. When I left for Dartmouth in 1974, I decided I would eventually live on a little island off the coast of Maine where I had always spent summers. That is where my studio and exhibition areas are. People come during the summer to see my work. I've had a few exhibits in the past few years

Ashley Bryan

at university galleries and at an Afro-American museum in Philadelphia, but they are rare.

If we were to visit your studio in Maine, what would we see on your easel?

You'd see a painting of some part of the garden around my house. I paint from the changing patterns of color, as flowers bloom or fade, against the background of the fields stretching down to the ocean. When I first came to the island about 40 years ago, I did a lot of work by the shore, but in the past 15 or 20 years, I have hardly gone past the garden.

I work with oils on canvas, outdoors, in the spirit of the impressionists. But I don't work from the essential feeling of light at a specific time; I work from a sense of rhythm. I can work on a painting over a period of a week outdoors with the changing qualities of light. When I establish where I'm going rhythmically in a composition, what I have seen in the course of the day feeds into the composition and makes the ultimate painting. In a week I may feel that I've gone as far as I wish on a canvas and start another.

When do you create your books and how do you create your illustrations?

I generally paint during the day, and in the evenings I work on other projects, books being one of them. My illustrations for the African tales *The Adventures of Aku; Beat the Story-Drum, Pum-Pum;* and *Lion and the Ostrich Chicks* (all Atheneum) are often referred to as block prints or silk screens, but they are all painted. I paint them in this manner because I can get almost a 100 percent relation from my original to the reproduction in the books. The artist is always after that faithfulness. In some techniques a 15 to 20 percent loss may occur in the reproduction, and the artist has to be prepared to accept that. These illustrations are based on my study of African art; the sculpture, masks, and rock painting, and they are absorbed into the style that is my own. If reviewers ask, "Is that Masai?" they have missed the point, because I am not copying any specific group. Just as in my retelling of the African stories, I want something in my art that reflects African art without being necessarily authentic. In *Walk Together Children* and *I'm Going to Sing* (both Atheneum) the illustrations are block prints. I was inspired by the early religious block-printed books. The spirituals are religious songs, and over a thousand have been collected since the end of the Civil War. Since there were no books introducing these songs to young people, doing selections of them is one of my major projects. I'm planning to do a hundred songs in the style of the medieval religious books. Each of the two that I've done contains 25 songs, so I've two more to go!

I enjoy the stages leading up to the final book: the earliest idea sketches, the paintings in stages, and then, finally, the tracing on the board for the finished painting. The color separations are then done for me. Sometimes more of a richness exists in paintings in the rough stages than in the finished plate. What readers finally view will seem immediate, if the excitement of the process, the back-and-forth battle for corrections, is in the completed work.

I do a lot of sketching. Many ideas for my illustrations come from my sketchbooks. For example, in my books of the spirituals you can see illustrations of my grandmother and the children I have drawn on a playground, adapted from my sketchbooks. I always have a sketchbook with me.

Do you have input into the design?

I generally do the design of my books, although the book designer puts them together. We choose a type then, working with the galleys. I decide where my pictures will go. When I hand in the art, it is usually in the book size. Then the designer makes the adjustments.

In The Dancing Granny *[Macmillan] how were the illustrations originally done?*

That story from the Ashanti was collected in Antigua in the West Indies, on the island my parents came from. My grandmother stayed behind, but she finally came to visit after World War II, when she was past 70. She picked up the latest dance steps from the great-grandchildren and outdanced them all! I drew upon that.

The illustrations for *The Dancing Granny* are brush paintings. Generally my illustrations are the same size as those in the book, but the Granny originals are a third larger. They were based on my study of Japanese brush painting. I particularly like the work of Hokusai — his sketchbooks of scenes from daily life. I have done a lot of drawing from dancers, and I really like to draw from life. I went to my sketchbooks for help. I did hundreds of brush paintings of the dancing figure and assembled them in the layout. I wanted the book to move in the rhythm of the figures dancing. When they were reproduced, the variation in dark and light in the brush strokes was, unfortunately, lost. But the spirit of the dancing figure is there, and the book remains popular.

How do you feel about encapsulating a story into this frozen form when folk tales generally change and evolve with the teller and the circumstances?

The oral tradition lives today, and it lives in books as well. The problem is how to give a written story that texture and vitality and drama — the back and forth play of teller and audience of the oral setting. I try things that will give a vitality of surface, a textural feeling, a possibility of vocal play to the prose of my stories. So I take risks in my books. I do a lot of things that people writing prose generally do not do: close rhythms, rhyme, onomatopoeia, alliteration, interior rhyme — the poet's tools, what you usually avoid when you write prose because it stops the story. But I want to stop readers to slow them down; I want readers to hear the sound of the printed word.

Do you try out your ideas on anyone before you publish them?

I read to friends and to children, sometimes in the little one-room schoolhouse on the island. I always read aloud to hear how my work sounds. If something is not clear or not rhythmically right, they help me. But I do a lot of revision through my own ear. It's very important to me that the sound and the play of the voice are meaningful and accurate in terms of the listener.

The Cat's Purr [Macmillan] in its basic form is the story of why a cat eats a rat. But as I developed it, I realized that there are stories of why cat eats rat, but no one has ever figured out what makes a cat's purr. There was a drum in the story, and I asked myself why. I made the drum very small, and gave it the sound when stroked of purrum, purrum. When I went to children with that sound, they said, "That's a cat; you can't fool us." So the story became why the cat purrs.

How do you do your oral presentations?

I always read from poetry first, because my prose is based on the experience of hearing poetry read aloud. In the schools in the Bronx, where I grew up, we always read poetry aloud. We were given several weeks of practice before being called on to recite. It was felt that poems, like songs, were meant to be heard. The soul of a poem is experienced in hearing it. Today we have very little experience in hearing selections from the treasury of English and American poetry read aloud. It's a miracle that anyone likes poetry at all. Would people love songs, the German lieder, Italian and French art songs, if they never heard them sung but only heard them from sight-reading notes printed on the page? So when I read a story, having read poetry, the audience is prepared for the play of voice that carries over from poetry to story.

What poets do you warm up with?

Langston Hughes for one. I feel the black poets tend to be overlooked, so I focus on them in my readings—also Gwendolyn Brooks, Nikki Giovanni, Paul Laurence Dunbar, as many as I can include. I read from them because a lot of the sound, the rhythm, the cadence that I'm after come[s] from the black poets. I try to make clear the fact that almost all poetry is meant to be heard.

Do you think that there is a possibility that through the narration or illustration in a picturebook one can enter into or better understand another culture?

We generally enter into a people's culture through their art. Before visiting the Ivory Coast recently, I talked to friends who had studied the Baoule culture. I saw photographs and films of villages they had studied. I saw their sculpture, weaving, pottery, and I read their stories. So when I visited the Ivory Coast, the visit to the Baoule was even more meaningful. Their art had given me an insight into the center of the people's lives, a deep respect for their beliefs and for the way they live—because they fashion their art form from their soul and for their needs.

Do you travel to collect the stories for your books?

No. My stories are mainly collected in libraries, because I'm working from hundreds of tribal languages. Much of the material that I work with was collected by missionaries and anthropologists in the late 1800s, often with the desire to get a written alphabet, and they used stories as a way of developing a vocabulary. The forms are generally very stilted in the direct English translations from which I work. Sometimes they use only four or five sentences to tell the story, but the story-motif is documented. I take off from there.

Why specifically do you go to Africa?

As a black American, I have African roots. Retelling and illustrating African tales has kept me close to African sources. So it's only natural that I'd want to visit Africa. Long before my first visit, I'd read African tales and studied African art and history. The visits were wonderful! I was in the African setting, observing and meeting Africans and drawing all the time. So the visits have deepened the commitment to my work.

The artist working today has the world cultures at hand. In my work as a black American artist, it is the African root that nourishes whatever other world culture I may draw upon.
—1988

Update

Now that I have retired from teaching full-time, I do occasional lectures as professor emeritus. I regard my teaching time as my visits with groups throughout the country. Most are scheduled between February and May. From June to the following February I do my work at home, on Islesford.

I retold the Japanese legend *Sh-Ko and His Eight Wicked Brothers* to companion the fine brush paintings of my friend Fumio Yoshimura. *Turtle Knows His Name* is a Caribbean tale I retold and illustrated with glowing watercolors for a glowing relationship of Grandma and Grandson.

Now I'm completing a child's first book of African-American spirituals. It is in full color, a different visual approach from my other books of spirituals. Piano and guitar arrangements are being set by a musical friend. It should be ready for the Spring 1991 Atheneum list.

I deliver the Arbuthnot Honor Lecture this month in New Orleans. Then I will be part of the Educated Eye Preconference at the American Library Association Conference in Chicago in June before I return to my painting.
—*April 1990*

Eight

John Burningham
and Helen Oxenbury

A Sampling of Works in Print

Burningham

Come Away from the Water, Shirley Harper, 1977.

Granpa Crown, 1985.

Hey! Get Off Our Train Crown, 1990.

Humbert, Mr. Firkin and the Lord Mayor of London Crown, 1989.

John Patrick Norman McHennessey: The Boy Who Was Always Late Crown, 1988.

Mr. Gumpy's Motor Car Harper/ Penguin, 1976, 1983.

Mr. Gumpy's Outing Holt/Penguin, 1971, 1984, 1990.

Time to Get Out of the Bath, Shirley Harper, 1978.

Where's Julius? Crown, 1987.

Oxenbury

All Fall Down Macmillan, 1987.

Clap Hands Macmillan, 1987.

Helen Oxenbury's ABC of Things Delacorte, 1983.

I Can; I Hear; I See; I Touch all Random, 1986.

Say Goodnight Macmillan, 1987.

Tickle, Tickle Macmillan, 1988.

Tom and Pippo series all Macmillan, 1989.

We're Going on a Bear Hunt by Michael Rosen. Macmillan, 1989.

Hampstead Heath is on the fringe of central London. At the bus and tube stop is a small village of sorts, with pub, grocery and other amenities. But just beyond begins the Heath itself, a vast expanse of meadow, trees and open space that is doubly refreshing for being in the city. Climbing the hill along one edge, one passes detached and semi-detached houses as well as an apartment block. The number on the gate of a large double Victorian house defines it as the home of the authors and illustrators of some of the most popular books available for the very young child: the husband and wife team who write and illustrate separately as Helen Oxenbury and John Burningham. Behind the high-ceilinged, comfortably

59

Helen Oxenbury

furnished house is a deep grassy yard with outbuildings and a small pool complete with hungry golden carp. The work spaces are upstairs, while the shaded yard gives space to relax on a pillow and have a cup of tea where the birds sing.

Burningham has just returned from a trip to Japan in connection with a new picturebook with a strong pro-environment message that is being jointly published in Japanese. It is called Hey, Get Off Our Train. *This is his second trip to Japan in the last few months; interest in his work is strong there, but jet-lag is wearing. He has found remarkable interest and enthusiasm there for the picturebook in general, and his work in particular. Oxenbury feels this interest in general is less in the U.K. We begin conversing over tea before he arrives. The afternoon will continue in this stop-and-go fashion as telephones and family business carry off one or the other, or both, for periods of time.*

Do you go out to talk at schools or libraries?

Oxenbury: Yes, but it really takes time from your work. It takes a day to worry about and get ready for it, the day you do it, and a day to recuperate.

How did you happen to end up in art college?

Oxenbury: I was encouraged at home. My father was an architect, so art was around. He used to do illustration. He used to draw our toys for us with watercolors. Nobody objected when I wanted to go to art school. I guess they thought that after a few years I'd give it up and get a proper job, like a secretary.

Your board books for the very young child have really filled a gap. . . .

Oxenbury: That's why I did them. Because I couldn't find much, if anything, for our 10-year-old when she was that young.

Do you see changes in the children's book publishing field?

Oxenbury: I don't think that any of the huge conglomerates can be as good as the small units. The authors and the artists "get in the way of the business" when there's a takeover. There are only a few small independents left.

Have you personally felt any pressure on your work because of this?

Oxenbury: No, because I have been with Walker from the beginning. They have been my main publisher. I started with Heinemann years ago, and I see the frustrations there, but I've never had that personally. I've been lucky. But God knows what it's like for people who are just starting. It must be very difficult and very frustrating.

The trouble is that it kills innovation. They daren't experiment, they can't take on people that maybe will sell and maybe not. They can't take risks.

Are you working on a book for older children now that your daughter is older?

Oxenbury: Yes. Goodness knows what I'll do when she's 13 or so! My two older children are in their 20s. I didn't actually stop doing picturebooks when they were past that age. But I certainly won't write back to the beginning again. Now I'm using more text; it's more meaty. There are fewer illustrations, black and white drawings. I don't think I can do any more of those very early books.

You have changed from your earlier style in The Quangle Wangle's Hat, *etc.*

Oxenbury: I just can't look at my older books. I wish they would quietly die, but they keep coming back in another cover. I do remember they were done with tremendous enthusiasm; I loved doing them.

Were you commissioned to do the Lear or was it your idea?

Oxenbury: No. It was my idea.

Did you want to do any others?

Oxenbury: That was the one I thought visually spoke.

In 1964, you said you enjoy making children's books. But you said they were bothersome to write: "An endless struggle." Do you still feel that way? [John arrives.]

Burningham: [Pouring himself a cup of tea.] That still applies. I

John Burningham

wouldn't say I enjoy it. But there are things I have to do. Every time I think
about giving up, I have an idea I just should do.

*In talking about the lithographic process, you say that the color
lithography form of reproduction has many limitations. What are some of
them?*

Burningham: I feel the limitations more strongly now. In four-color
lithography what you have now is a series of dots. There is a sameness about
that reproduction process, although it's extremely clever. It will never give
you what the traditional lithography or letterpress gave, the pure color applied to the paper. The new lithography is extremely boring. It's never what
you have put on the page; it's just a very smart con. On the rare occasions
that I've used the pure lithographic process, it's a wonderful thing to see,
but it's too expensive to do in large numbers. When I started out doing
posters, we used to do 12- or 13-color stone lithography, and the results
were phenomenal. I think we'll get back to that. I think that the way the
publishing world is going with multinational takeovers, and where you have
possibly five buyers throughout the world that are going to ensure the

success or the failure of a book, you will find what we have found with roof-thatchers. Just as the last is about to die out, a group of young people materialize that want to be taught how to do it. So I think that publishing is destined to go through a very dead and uncreative phase. And then we'll be back to a very small craft-type press that will produce what people actually want. They will do this only with tiny overheads and very small profits. For people like us it doesn't matter; we probably gain from these conglomerates, because we're established. But God help the fellow who comes along with a new idea. One must never get depressed because it always changes.

You are not satisfied with the quality of the reproduction of your art work in your books?

Burningham: It's satisfactory only in terms of the process that is used. It's not the same as using real color, real ink on paper. It has a blandness. This has happened in every field, except perhaps ceramics. Fabric design has suffered because you have manufactured dyes and colors instead of vegetable dyes. A reproduction of a William Morris fabric is anathema to what they were originally. The same thing is happening to Islamic carpets. It will never be the same. No matter what the original medium, you always have a sense of disappointment when you see the proofs of a book. You know the limitations of the process, and whether or not they've done it well.

Oxenbury: They never seem to be able to do five or six color; I wonder if we'd be less disappointed with that.

Burningham: When you flick through a magazine with photographs of the Himalayas, or some monastery, and someone else has been another place, what you're being shown is a kind of sameness. This didn't happen years ago when color photography was in its infancy. Is this because one is so jaded? Things that should have tremendous impact don't. I can only put it down to a bland quality. Perhaps it's a limitation of the medium.

Does Borka *have an edge that* Where's Julius *lacks?*

Burningham: I can't criticize the process, because the four-color process has improved enormously. But it has that bland quality that to me gets visually boring.

Does the paper stock affect that quality? You see a difference in fine quality art books.

Oxenbury: Those books also use more than four colors. That makes a difference.

Burningham: It's better. But there's a lack of excitement in the huge amount of reproduced material. They've put enormous effort into it. It may just be me, but I find it very difficult to get interested in it. When I've gone to Japan, I've been given books with absolutely brilliant printing of some 16th century Japanese printmaker. I'm sure they're 10- or 12-color lithographic printing, but it's just another bit of art in a book.

Is that why you're talking about a book for adults rather than children?

Burningham: It'll be the same thing, when it comes to reproduction. I designed a lamp in the form of a tower block for somebody. We had it silk-screen printed. In each window there's a different image. Those were done in about seven colors. This was tremendously exciting, to see the quality of the color.

Are you doing black and white work for this reason?

Burningham: Yes, black and white is good. Even black and white photography is more interesting than color photography.

Oxenbury: The last book I've done, *We're Going on a Bear Hunt*, is alternate black and white and color two-page spreads, and I love the black and white.

Burningham: It's particularly interesting on its cover. It will be in color in the U.S.A. because they insisted. They say it won't sell in black and white. They may be right. It's the sales people who can't bear black and white. They say, "Everything's in color." In actual fact you get swamped up on the shelf in a sea of color. This should stand out in contrast, but they can't see that.

How did you feel about doing Wind in the Willows *when it had been done by Shepherd and so many others?*

Burningham: I didn't know the story. I'd never had that book as a child. If I had, I'd never have agreed to do it. In fact, when Penguin asked me to do it, I said, "Send me the text, but blank out the pictures." But now having seen them, I don't think Shepherd's drawings are all that good, although I admire his work enormously. And I didn't like the Rackham. And now that I've done it, history will judge, but there's nobody else who's done it whose illustrations I look at and say "Wonderful!" Whereas with Shepherd's drawings for *Winnie the Pooh*, anyone would have to be insane to try those. They are masterpieces. One wouldn't try to do *Peter Rabbit* either. Potter learned to draw with a great quality that I'm afraid many people these days don't have. There's nothing like starting out with mushrooms and ending up with rabbits.

Oxenbury: I find her texts very difficult for children to understand.

Burningham: But I didn't like them as a child.

Have you had questions about the death of Grandpa?

Burningham: As far as children are concerned, they accept it very matter-of-factly. Grandpa is just gone. They are making an animated film of it. It's a very good film, I think. When they see it, adults are often close to tears. But not the children.

How do they convert to film?

Burningham: If you are going to do a half-hour film, you have to have massive amounts of animation. The people doing this film have the essence of my work but they've extended it. Because they put the same amount of effort in the right direction, they've made a good film. I've made various comments, from time to time, but they've taken off from what I did and made something that's their own. They've done 45,000 drawings.

Does film influence the way you work?

Oxenbury: I did film sets, for example Judy Garland's last film. But in terms of the story board, yes.

Burningham: I think it depends on the project. Some things lend themselves to film; you even know you've got a potential film. Other things are not right for it.

Most of Helen's work is very realistic, based on real life.

Oxenbury: I do the things I know.

Was doing the Around the World *book fun?*

Burningham: Three months of intensive travel, panicking about what you could possibly do to make Fiji look different from Tonga, when you were there for a day, instead of enjoying yourself and not getting up tight about doing a book? It ended up as an anti-travel book. And people thought I was so lucky to go to all those places.

You had an unconventional education. Did you have any conventional art education aside from Summerhill?

Burningham: I spent a lot of time mucking about in the art room. But there was no real direction. Obviously anyone who's running an art room will say, "Why don't you try this?" or "You shouldn't be doing it like this, but like that." But that was it.

According to an early article, you work differently. John works and works over something, while Helen tries it, and if it doesn't work, throws it away and starts again. Is this still true?

Oxenbury: Yes. I don't like looking back at my old books either. I haven't looked at any for a long time. I really ought to have a look. I think my style is very different now. It has simplified.

Burningham: I think that I work much more like you work now. I spend less time mucking around. I'll throw it out. There's a drawing of a crane in *Train* which is probably 20 drawings that I did and rejected.

How did you find the train for the book?

Burningham: It was very difficult to do the train, because I couldn't find a long shot. If you take photographs, they lie. When I got to Japan, the television station had a film of it, and a model. I thought "If only I'd had this earlier, I would have had the spacing and other details I had struggled with." The animals were much less of a problem.

Is there pressure from outside to have words or color?

Burningham: It's just a general attitude of "What do we need to sell the book?" Lots of color, lots of this or that. That's what I think is so good about that *Bear Hunt*. It's gone against all those marketing rules.

Hey Get Off Our Train *is larger than you've worked in a while, isn't it?*

Burningham: Yes. I did feel more comfortable with more space in that because I wanted to get the elements; which you can't really do small.

Do you work to scale?

Oxenbury: Yes.

One irritation you speak of is the lack of appreciation of the art in picture-books versus "serious art" popped in frames. How do we overcome that?

Burningham: You can't overcome that until and unless you produce something with a frame around it and put it in a gallery. But actually I think that's changing. The market in original children's book illustrations is becoming quite a big business. I don't know if it's because fine art has such a high price so this is a way of getting hold of original art. Edward Ardizzone's work, for example, is now worth a lot of money. It started with people like him. But it is irritating to hear "Oh, you do children's books. What fun." It does rile me, because it's been going on for years. That's usually followed by "I have an idea for a children's story. . . ." If they knew what blood one sweated trying to simplify, the constant pruning of what you have to put in the drawing and what you have to put in the text to get what you want. . . .

Since most children's books are bought by adults, you end up working in a medium that is bought by people for children, but also for themselves, so in order to be a success a book has to work across the board.

[Helen leaves to get Emily from school.]

How do you feel about reviews?

Burningham: I have found over the years that if one has had any intelligent reviews it has been in the States. Normally the review just tells you the story of the book. Occasionally I have had very perceptive and intelligent reviews. But very few. I wish there would be just a page where the reviewer would just say, rightly or wrongly, that this is a good book or a bad book and why. I think that's what reviewing should be.

You have made a distinction between illustrated books and picturebooks. What is the meaning of difference to you?

Burningham: Every project has a different problem attached to it. You have to elect how to approach it. Are you going to have a lot of words or few words, how much color . . . ? By adding the words you add nuances, but it's a marriage. . . . In a book like *Wind in the Willows* the pictures add a quality of character but there's so much in the text already that the pictures can't add that the balance is off. It's very rare that I take a text on to illustrate. But in a way it's a treat. Because you are at liberty to read through and decide what it is that you can contribute to something already described. You are faced with trying to define the characters. In the case of *Wind in the Willows,* since I didn't know the story, I found some of the characters in Shepherd not very successful. The water rat is a very hairy creature, and you can't get any eye expression in that case. So Shepherd's is a real water rat, and my rat is a rat-type rat. I decided not to be totally true. I didn't feel that the hairy face is the right way to do it. I felt I was able to get more into the black and white pictures without it. The trouble with that book was that it wasn't a good enough hardback. The color pages were double backed and tipped into the wrong places. They should have been single color pages that went into the right place in the text. The hardback hardly sells. But the paperback, which has only the black and white illustrations, does very well. It looks good.

Have you ever thought of doing a book together with Helen?

Burningham: It could happen. I've got nothing against it. But we are each always working on our own problems.

The art world elitism doesn't represent part of your world?

Burningham: The book and film world do much more.

Do you see a parallel between Jacques Tati and Mr. Gumpy?

Burningham: Interesting that you should mention him. I think he was somebody who in *Mon Oncle* showed the way everything was going to go in the future. It pioneered the use of sound. I'm a great admirer of Tati. But again, he's known as the man who made the funny films, rather than the one who had tremendous foresight and insight into the horrors of technological society. Had he written a thesis he would have been then taken by the literati in a different way. Again, it's the frame around it and the glass of sherry.

How do you perceive your evolution? Change in style?

Burningham: I think that the early work has great qualities of naiveté, which in some ways I'd like to return to. It has a sort of absurd freedom which maybe turned into something else because I'm always trying something new; I don't believe in repeating myself. Those early books are Cinderella stories, the little lost thing that finds salvation. I think the later books explore many more interesting relationships between adults and children and authority. And the latest is on the environmental theme. So hopefully I'm developing with the time.

—*Summer 1989*

Nine

Carole Byard

A Sampling of Works in Print

Africa Dream by Eloise Greenfield. Harper, 1977.

The Black Snowman by Phil Mendez. Scholastic, 1989.

Cornrows by Camille Yarbrough. Putnam, 1979.

Grandmama's Joy by Eloise Green-field. Collins, 1980.

Have a Happy . . . by Mildred Pitts Walter. Lothrop, 1989.

On the lower end of Manhattan island, right on the Hudson River, looms a large brick building that once housed a factory. Some years back it was converted into apartments and studios for artists, the open floors divided into a maze of corridors and the whole interior painted white, including the rolled steel ceilings. There Carole Byard has a studio downstairs to create in two and three dimensions, and shares an apartment rich with images on the walls, painted or printed by her and her friends. Only some are reminiscent of her picturebooks. One wall is laced with the shapes of musical instruments from Africa, while African carvings are visible on other surfaces.

Do you still teach at Parsons? How do you find the time?

Yes, but only one day a week. I have 16 term papers to read before tomorrow. This is an art history course called "A closer look at three artists during troubled times." It looks at the life and times of Kaethe Kollwitz, a German woman artist; Charles White, an African-American; and Valerie Maynard, an African-American woman, during a span of almost a hundred years, so I can incorporate social conditions and history with their lives and work. These artists created work that spoke to everyday people, and have a political perspective in their work. It gives students an opportunity to learn

68

Self-portrait by Carole Byard

more than the usual art history of names and dates. I bring people who knew them or are specialists in their work. I had a man named Harry Henderson who recently completed a book on African-American artists with the late Romare Bearden. Harry and Romy had interviewed Charles White. Valerie Maynard, who is the only one living of the three, is a friend of mine. I taped interviews with her, and let her tell her story. I have exhibitions of their work in class. The students really respond. About 90 percent of my students are white, and about 8 percent are Asian. And unfortunately, a small percentage of black students. Most have never had a black teacher. We get into race relations when we reach the '60s, and most of them have no idea of what happened then.

Then doing pictures for books is only a small part of your life.

In some ways, yes, if you go by how many books I've illustrated. I've done only 12 or 13 in about 20 years.

How did you come to book illustration?

I really wanted to do it. I went to art school to be a "fine artist." But the school encouraged all students to take courses that would help them survive. For me it was between advertising and illustration, and I chose illustration. I found it not that different from what I was doing; I was working from models anyway with my fine art, and this was working from models with the point of view of the text. I realize how important it was for me to do that for me personally, because I work in a realistic way. Most of the books I saw with black kids in them are cartoon-like. I felt that I wanted our kids to see themselves in books looking like real people, like we really look. That was important to me.

You have worked for many different publishers?

When I first got out of school I tried pounding the pavements with my portfolio. I was looking for any kind of illustration work, but I really wanted to do books. I got a lot of compliments, but I didn't get anywhere. So I got an agent, a black literary agent who handled a lot of popular black writers. He also represented the legendary Tom Feelings, whose work I loved. Within a month the agent had two books for me. One was *Willy*; the other was *Nomi and the Magic Fish*, for Doubleday.

Did you do your own color separations?

Yes. School had prepared me for that. *Under Christopher's Hat* was also pre-separated.

For the most part you illustrate other people's stories?

Yes, so far. I do have a desire to do my own story. But one of my problems is that I want the perfect children's book. I've written stories, but I haven't felt that that's the one. I have some things that I decided I didn't want to do, and have never shown to a publisher. But I just might. It's one thing to come to the text and go straight to the visuals, to create the characters and make decisions about what everything looks like and how it feels. It's another to deal with the text and the other too. But I think the time is close. I want to do books that I really like. I sometimes get manuscripts that I feel are not right for me or don't really move me. Especially these days, I wouldn't want to take a job I didn't like that could take a year to complete.

One of the things I like is that I don't know the writers. I like to come to it fresh. I have only met most of them after the fact. I learned from experience that I don't enter into a contract with a writer; they have to sell their story to a publisher. And that it does me no good to start illustrating a book before all the typing is done. People will say they want me to illustrate their book, but they have no idea what that means to me. I just can't unless I really like it and they have a publisher.

Why the single color in I Can Do It By Myself?

They gave me one color to wash over . . . I had to choose. I did that story over in color recently (just before *Black Snowman*) for an educational publisher (Scott Foresman) doing a series of stories kid-like. It won't be a single book; it's in a collection of nine stories.

Do you find charcoal a medium for which you have an affinity?

It's something I was using in high school before I came to New York. I definitely used it a lot in art school. We did a lot of drawing from models and in museums. I like using it in my fine art work as well. I do a lot of charcoal drawings as finished pieces. It was natural for me to use it for my illustrations. At the same time what happened after *The Sycamore Tree* is that I got a lot of black and white work. Now everybody is doing color, and it was nice to do *Black Snowman* in color. It's the first one I've done in color if I don't count the one I redid. I did covers in color, but the editors felt my black and white work was strong, and they saved money by printing black and white. I use a variety of soft and hard pastels and pastel pencils. *Willy* is charcoal with three color pastels, pre-separated.

Who had the idea of two-page spreads in The Sycamore Tree?

I did that myself. I set the book up. I like to work with double-page spreads. For me, when you open a book, what you see is both pages. It's hard for me to do a little thing here and a little thing there.

Do you use kids as models?

Usually I have kids in the neighborhood or my godson.

What experiences have you had with so many different editors?

I have never had any conflicts. I have enjoyed the materials I have illustrated. Almost always they have been books that I felt needed to be done. Particularly the books that have Africa or African influences are more interesting to me because I like doing people and natural settings outdoors. I really don't like drawing telephones and automobiles. So you won't see a lot of city books. If I do, I will make it a more intimate story of people interacting. The editors I have worked with have usually called me because they have the kind of book they think I'd be interested in, and they know my work already. It will probably be a story about relationships between people, like *Grandmama's Joy*. They let me do what I like.

How do you decide about the pictures in a book like Have a Happy . . .?

I read the text, and I read it, until I get a sense of where the pictures should be. I think "this is a moment, and this is . . ." I make a dummy; I lay out the text and cut the manuscript. Often I decide the size of the book. I try to get a big book when I can. Today they are making them a lot bigger than they were, let's say, in the early '70s. I used to try to get as much space as I could. When I bring in the dummy, it has all the art where it is going to go in the text. In some cases, like *Cornrows*, the text was already laid out on each page, but there was still space for me to do it the way I wanted. It must have felt right to me, because I don't remember any conflict. I like to put the pictures in the books.

That book really took time. I resigned from my teaching job at the time. This was a case where the writer, Camille Yarbrough, knew my next-door neighbor and was looking for an illustrator. She came to see me. She started looking around at my work while I was reading her manuscript. I thought to myself, "I really love this story! It's almost as if I wrote it myself." So that time it worked. And she never interfered once I started.

You don't work to scale?

No. I work bigger, two times actual size if possible.

What control do you have over the final product? Do they show you proofs?

No. I could go with them to the printer. I did with *Cornrows*, and I'm glad I did, because it was awful at first. They had a lot of trouble with *Black Snowman*. The first printing came out really dark, so they sent it to another place. Some of it is on, but some of it is not.

You work on a paper very different from the semi-gloss they print on. Does the change bother you?

Yes it does. It changes the color intensity, and brightens up some things. I know things are going to be changed, and try to keep that in mind and work accordingly.

Did you use models?

Sometimes I use kids who are my godchildren, or kids who live in the building. For *Have a Happy*, since there aren't that many young black kids in this neighborhood, I asked a friend of mine with two boys if they would pose, and she found someone with a little girl. I had my dummy already, and knew what I wanted them to do, so I did a lot of sketching. I showed them the dummy, and they did a little of what I wanted and a little of what they wanted. In this case I also took Polaroids on the spot, because there were four kids who didn't know each other well, that I had to get to relax and interact. I got most of what I needed in one day. It was like directing a film.

You don't do a storyboard. Do you think in terms of filmic sequencing?

I certainly think in terms of what has happened and what comes next, where I'm placing this illustration and who was in the last one, and what is the right moment, and what is the weather like. I try to give variety. And if you line the pictures up, you can almost follow the story, beginning to middle to end, without the words. I try to think about the parts that I feel are really important to the story; that I would want to see if I were a child. I would want to see that moment when the snowman touches Jacob in the *Black Snowman*, and the other important times in his awakening. When the snowman picked up Peewee, it was important to me to show Jacob's disbelief in that moment when Peewee was so happy. Almost in the next scene the snowman is working his magic on him. That was the original cover scene which I did over for the cover with space for title information, but they changed it because they felt it was too mysterious or scary. I feel that kids today are very involved with things that are alien or different, and would not be frightened, but intrigued. The cover they used is cut and pasted from scenes inside, and you can see the edges. I was disappointed in that. I also wanted to change the title. When I read the story to kids and asked them for a title, they usually would say "The Magic Kente" or "The African Snowman."

Do you often read to kids?

When I want to get a feeling of what they think of a story, of how they like it. I do it here, not in public.

Do you go "on the road" to give talks?

I have gone to colleges in Michigan, Philadelphia, and others, and to speak to groups of librarians at conferences. I like to talk to kids in schools too, if I can make it. Black History Month is when they all want you to come.

I keep all my original art work, sketches, working drawings. I do a slide show showing the transitions of a piece from concept to sketch to printed book. I like to show students the original art so they can get a sense of what I'm doing, like a small exhibition. *Cornrows* is about my biggest work [size of art]. I have some original illustrations in an exhibition in a gallery that just opened. But the book is the art work; we shouldn't compare it to the originals.

You are involved with groups of black artists. Is there a parallel group of black illustrators?

I don't think so. A few years ago I got the idea that maybe we ought to be in touch. I admired John Steptoe's work so much, but never got to know him. But I never did anything about it. Recently I got a call from Pat Cummings. She told me about a group she had started of people of all races in the business, and invited me to a session where someone makes a presentation on aspects of the field, like reading the royalty statement, etc. We need that sort of thing.

How do you see the difference between your "fine art" and your work for picturebooks?

I find a need to separate them for myself. I guess part of it comes from the idea in the art world that they are two separate things. I sometimes refer to the fine art as "my work," and the books as "my illustration." To me, that means that other people are involved. That's the major difference. Also, with my own work, there is more of an opportunity for me to change. With illustration, it's almost locked into realistic imagery. I haven't put any focus on development of a different kind of style. I feel the need for it to be the way it is. My fine art work has changed a lot by comparison.

Is the evolution in your studio work a function of the media you are using?

Only in a way, because now I am doing more sculpture than before, also using different materials. For example I'm painting, but with earth like the dirt and clay that I dig up in various places, and I'm using branches, rocks and natural fibers, for sculpture and installations in rooms and outdoors, as well as paintings on canvas.

On the question of illustration vs. "fine art," I never gave up either one for the other. I have felt it important for my allegiance to be with my fine art. It probably would have been simpler just to illustrate, because people are asking you to do it and you get paid. My "fine art" was really the opportunity to express what I wanted to do, so the illustration has been supportive of that. Also the books I have illustrated have for the most part had to do with things that concern me anyway, exploration of Africa or providing positive images for black kids, or positive black images for everybody. Both things have been for me political positions. In the books I have illustrated there were opportunities to deal with people's hair, clothes, homes, how people live. I find that to be very important and meaningful. The same way in my fine art, this painting on the wall is called *Self-determination*. This piece is *I want to take you higher*. These are the themes the books deal with, that I can also deal with in my fine art. The brown and blue lithograph is called *From somewhere within*, a sort of self-portrait, a way of letting the creative energy flow. The linoleum print was originally done for *Black Enterprise* magazine for an editorial illustration about aging and senior citizens. Sometimes I have pieces like that that bridge the gap for me, illustrations that can stand independent of the text. I wouldn't put that in an exhibition with other pieces, but I have it hanging here. Sometimes there isn't that much of a difference. Other times, I guess because of the nature of the business, people in publishing are really not that interested in the fine artists. And people in fine arts are not that interested in illustration. Younger art students today have different attitudes about that; they are more open. They don't see that line drawn as clearly. I think they came up from seeing special effects and different ways of seeing. In my classroom they are interested in what I do as an illustrator as well as a fine artist. Next semester I go to Minneapolis College of Art and Design. I have put together a lecture that deals with both, bridging the gap from the books to the sculpture.

I have separated it also because I have found that on my resume it doesn't help to have a string of books listed if I'm sending it out to a gallery. The people in publishing don't scoff at the fact that you've exhibited. But they are most interested in what I'm going to do with a book.

So I've had to weigh my time as well. I took a job four days a week in Baltimore in 1984, because I wanted to have more teaching experience, and get out of the city but still be close to New York. It was a wonderful high school, with all the equipment and facilities for talented students, but I got so involved with the job that I had no time for illustrating or fine art. I finally realized that there is only so much you can do in one lifetime, and I would have to focus. I got more involved in my drawings and didn't do any illustrations for a long time, except for little stories in *Cricket* occasionally.

What role do you think picturebooks play in the lives of kids?

I think children really identify with visual images. They observe and take in a lot, and they get a lot from these images. Picturebooks are especially important now, because of all the electronic images and the role TV plays in the child's view of the world and other people, and who they are. Picturebooks at least allow for more interpretation, more time to go back and forth and look things over. But for me a lot of it was wanting kids to see themselves as real people, to appreciate how they look, to have real people they could identify with in these books, not just cartoon characters, that was important to me. Also, I try to show closeness, feelings, emotions, to reinforce the positive things that happen in people's lives. I think that picturebooks are so valuable. In *The Sycamore Tree* when I did the two-page spread with the tree and the woman, I was thinking about the kids who have a book to themselves when they are by themselves looking. They've seen the book before many times. But I have about 22 little people hidden in the tree. Sometimes I do things like that for those kids, so they can see something they didn't see before. Books were very important to me when I was a kid. I had an aunt who loved books, my Aunt Kitty. She would go to the library and take books out for me and my brother, and read them to us, and then leave them there for us to read. My mother died when I was very young and my father raised me and my brother. My grandmother lived with us and took care of us while my father worked, and then when she had a stroke we took care of her for three or four years. Other relatives helped too, but in the summers I took over. She was a wonderful person whom I loved very much. She was blind and in a wheelchair, so one of the things I did was read to her. I really enjoyed that journey with her.

I think picturebooks are also learning tools for kids. A lot of kids flip through and really want to look at the pictures, maybe too often.

About organizations of black artists, and life in New York as a black artist, is it still difficult in the art world as a black artist?

Yes. Particularly in the fine art world. Things are changing. There is a lot of focus today on multi-cultural efforts and cultural diversity. There are more shows that include other ethnic groups, there are more with Hispanic, Asian, and black artists. But in the end, when they start looking at who is at the top in the art world, they would never include people of color. People who think of art as an investment look at who is in the museums. . . . Howardina Pindell, a black woman artist, really gathered statistics. She looked at the shows the galleries and museums put on over a five-year period and at what percentage of those shows had even one work by a person of color. Her findings were pitiful. She asked for information on the shows and people sent it to her. They didn't realize what that information compiled would look like when she published it. Once it was out things started changing a bit. There were other groups that also put on pressure, groups with guerrilla tactics, some who make signs of protest about racism and sexism in the arts. In the past year or so what was always understood has been coming out. Now the artists of color are getting together, like *Coast to Coast,* women artists of color. Right now I'm curating a national exhibition to open here in January of 1990 for the Women's Caucus of Art and the College Art Association conferences — the exhibition will travel. There will be over a hundred women of color from across the country exhibiting in the show. When we first came together as volunteers on the steering committee we found we had so many life experiences in common. Most of us have had friendships or affiliations with white artists, but we have rarely had them between blacks and Native Americans, or Asians and Hispanics, etc. When we came together there was so much we didn't know about each other, and so much we shared, particularly the racism. The group has been wonderful. I get calls from all kinds of groups all over. What I find is that we have become a clearinghouse for people who are interested in finding multi-cultural women artists. We have information on the 200 women we have exhibited all over the country. There was obviously a need for us to do this. The doors were cracked but not really open.

Do you find an internal conflict with the other organizations of just women artists?

No, not really. They understand that there is racism in their groups and the need to do something about it. The fact that our group exists has made it more of an issue for them to do something themselves about their power structure. It's time for them to stop writing about us without listening to us.

How would this show differ from other shows?

There are such a variety of approaches, not in the mainstream, such as new materials, inventive solutions to the book form, for example, in a show we did of artists' books. It also had to be autobiographical, to say something about who we were and what our interests are. There were not a lot of really slick things, but a broad range reflecting the cultural diversity of the backgrounds.

What most appeals to you and what most appalls you about the art that has been produced since 1945?

Since my work has really been traditional and figurative, I haven't really been touched until recently. But now I am interested in installations and the kinds of materials I use are very different. So I am very excited about moving from two to three dimensional forms.

But the sculpture you did is very traditional.

That piece you are looking at (*Baby Satchmo*) was done 15 years ago.

When did the change occur?

It came from some drawings I did, a series called *Rent*. They were about struggle, and to celebrate survival and self-preservation and determination. It was initially inspired by the shoe-boxes of rent receipts I found when my father passed on. He had saved them from the places we had lived. He worked so hard, and never really had anything. Several years later after seeing the receipts and thinking about him and his lifetime I started this series. There is generally a single figure and some cloth involved. It happened that the cloth was torn, the other meaning of the word "rent." I started the series in 1980 or 1981, and kept doing them over several years. Somehow they looked sculptural. Then I was invited to do something for a show called *Home* about three years ago. I saw it as an opportunity to do something on the homeless. I took one of my drawings and made a piece of sculpture of it. I knew I didn't want to carve, because I don't like hitting things. I like the rhythm and sound of carving, but not the physical strain. Making that sculptured head on the table cost me. I'd rather mold. I looked for materials that would suit me. I thought of the linen cloth I used to do the drawings on. I had some left over from a flood in my studio, that I had washed and saved. I used the cloth, and branches . . . I'm always collecting things wherever I go. When I went to Africa in 1971 I brought back dirt from Senegal, sand from the Sahara, stones I found from near the pyramids . . . I'm always collecting things from nature, like autumn leaves, in my studio. I decided to make the woman in my sculpture from branches. In Central Park looking for branches I found this huge clump of dirt with grass on it. That was the woman's head. And that's how I started putting these materials together. Now I have trees in my studio. I model the heads or figures. I have been taking the cloth and soaking it in a mixture of mud and acrylic media. Right now I have five pieces that I have to do, starting this afternoon. I felt that this was something I had wanted to do for a long time, but the way just never really came to me. Last year I did an outdoor piece, where I could excavate the ground and use whole trees instead of just branches. It has been exciting working this out; I didn't start out knowing exactly what I wanted to do. I would need a head, so I started finding natural clay in the Catskills or the Poconos. I would mix it with sand or acrylic liquid, to make the heads, and put them out in the sun to bake. That's about as high-tech as I get. My piece for the "War, peace and victory" show was about peace and the children who had suffered war. It was called "Lullaby for Soweto, El Salvador, Hiroshima . . .," all the places children have been victimized. Peace for me was the absence of fear, which is what a child knows until they learn to be afraid. So I used babies as symbolic of a time of peace. There are 60 of them floating in the room in various sleeping or playful positions. I had the room painted blue because I liked that idea with the clouds from a previous other piece. The babies were at different levels. You had to climb a lot of steps to get to the top where they were. Children loved it but the adults often found it painful.

More recently I've been working on a series called *Runaways*, about slavery, mothers and babies and what they have done to survive. It's the mud, acrylic and charcoal on the linen canvas.

For me, making art is a chance to say something about life, and the afterlife, and looking for something. Mortality is something out of our hands, we're all part of the earth, connected to all things.

—*October 1989*

Ten

Babette Cole

A Sampling of Works in Print

Babette Cole's Beastly Birthday Book
  Doubleday, 1990.
Cupid Putnam, 1990.
The Hairy Book Random, 1985.
King Change-A-Lot Putnam, 1989.
Prince Cinders Putnam, 1988.
Princess Smartypants Putnam, 1987.
The Silly Book Doubleday, 1990.
The Slimy Book Random, 1986.

The Smelly Book Simon and Schuster,
  1988.
Three Cheers for Errol! Putnam,
  1989.
The Trouble with Dad Putnam, 1986.
The Trouble with Gran Putnam, 1987.
The Trouble with Grandad Putnam,
  1988.
The Trouble with Mom Putnam, 1986.

A horde of tourists come off the train at Canterbury looking for the cathedral, but a taxi is easy to find. The driver seems to know the way, a good 10 minutes out into the rolling green hills of the Kent countryside, off the highway to a road by a pub, then a turn down a narrrow lane that appears to be a driveway, except it goes on for quite a way. Fortunately no cars are coming the other way. Finally the cab stops by a small cottage, enmeshed in greenery, that seems to come out of a fairy tale. Jolly young Babette Cole cheerily invites visitors into a low-ceilinged, lovingly cluttered living room where her pets can wander in and out. Through a window can be seen the meadow where her various horses graze. She talks to all her animals like friends, and they are obviously an important part of her life. The new colt comes over to say hello.

The house is 500 years old. The new office block under construction has to be in a similar style, and includes a new bedroom and bath as well as a new work room with built-in storage in all walls. It will take time for it to achieve the lived-in look.

Tell us about your childhood.

Babette Cole

My parents actually come from Kent (this area). My great-great-great-great-grandfather, a pirate, was hanged at Tyburn, and the other side of the family were gypsies and horse thieves, so I'm not very well bred, I'm afraid. My parents left Kent after the war to live in the Channel Islands. I was born in Jersey, and didn't come here until about 1970 to go to art school.

As a child, were you a picturebook fan?

My parents were not very literary people. I wasn't fed an enormous amount of books. I found some myself, and my sister found a few for me. I liked the usual things, particularly the very old ones, Edward Lear for instance. I used to read his nonsense poetry over and over again, and loved his illustrations. And Tenniel, Shepherd, Potter, Greenaway. They were just dusty old books that were found around the place. I didn't discover books like the Narnia books until I was about 30. A lot came from the things people would tell me. There were a lot of "old boys" on the island that would like to tell you about the days before the war and especially about the occupation of the island by the Germans. There were always a lot of stories. It was hot and sunny, so I spent a lot of time indoors. I had lots of little imaginary characters, imaginary animals that lived in the bushes. They had their own little homes, and I used to talk to them. Of course they didn't exist, and people thought I was quite mad. I had a sort of mid-summer ritual, of pudding-making from mud and bits of sticks. I used to make them up in flower pots and invite people around for tea, and try to make them eat slices of what I made in the garden.

Your sister was older?

Ten or eleven years older. She really didn't like me very much, I think. I can distinctly remember sitting under the tree in the stone seat at the bottom of the garden, and her reading me *Alice* and *Through the Looking Glass* and *Wind in the Willows.* I just couldn't get the pictures out of my head. I used to pick up books wherever I could get them and just go through them looking at the pictures. I'd read the story by the pictures, and if the pictures weren't any good I would redo them in my mind. Then of course there were ponies from a very early age. So I would read the books about ponies and think "I can draw ponies better than that." And I used to redraw them all. I'd take a piece of paper and stick them in.

In the art classes we had at school we were not allowed to copy anything. That was considered cheating. We could draw from life, a bowl of fruit or a crucifix, but copying was discouraged. I was mostly concerned when I was little with what I do now. I really haven't changed much. I've gotten older, but I'm still doing the same things. I just sort of played around with my horses and dogs and things, went to horse shows, showed ponies, went show jumping. I didn't even have a boyfriend until I was 18; I was too busy doing other things. Boys were frowned upon at school because they got in the way of your horsey activities.

Your pre-art school education was in Jersey?

I went to a convent school. It was the only school one could go to. You then had three career choices: 1) you became a nun; 2) you became a wife and mother; or 3) you went off the rails. I got derailed somewhere along the line.

And there are art classes there?

That's why I can't do sums and I can't spell: because I was taken away from the most important lessons to produce feast day cards for the nuns and various posters for fetes and religious festivals. I spent my time drawing because they needed me.

How did they discover your talent?

Oh, I could always do it. My father was a very good painter. I wanted to be a vet. But I didn't have the education. I did nine O levels and two A levels but that was only because I struggled to get free from the extracurricular activities of the convent art department requests. In Jersey you pay for your education. So if you're rich little boys and girls you can take the exams. Here they stream you because the state pays, and there's bias from the beginning. They couldn't really teach us science, and biology was out of the question, because we skipped the theory of evolution. We weren't even allowed to answer that question if it came up on the exam. As far as they were concerned a large finger came out of the sky. . . . I couldn't get the math, but I did the O levels in chemistry, biology (those were great because the diagrams were so good) and physics, got some A levels, and the art in about two weeks. I was told I couldn't go to university and be a vet with those qualifications; I had to do something else. I didn't really want to go to art school. I didn't know much about art schools, except they were frowned upon at the convent, because there were wild people there. So I got a job in an advertising agency, and found that was twice as wild as anything I'd seen ever — a terrible, crass organization. So I thought it was time I went to art school, to get back into a working environment. I wrote to the Royal College of Art to ask where I should go. They wrote back with a list of schools in London, some of which I got into. But then I suddenly realized I couldn't take my pony into London. There was no room for a pony. So I wrote again saying that I couldn't go to any of those schools because they don't have any fields or stables nearby. They suggested I apply to Canterbury, which was out in the country. I was accepted here, and pony and I arrived from the Channel Islands by plane. I found a friendly farmer not too far away from the school to put her up, and we were all right.

What courses did you take?

That was a problem from the beginning. There was a foundation course to take before we did our degree course [BA]. It was very good, and I was happy. But if you were an illustrator, which I basically was, you were frowned upon by the graphic design department as being not commercial enough, and you were frowned upon by the fine art department because you were too commercial. So you didn't really fit in anywhere. If you look at illustration courses around the country in those days, [1970] there were very few, so usually either you did graphics or you did painting. Because I'd been in advertising I could do their silly little projects in a couple of days and I got on with my own little books as long as I completed a quota. I was never a good graphic designer but as long as I completed enough work to get by that was all right. When it came to producing a show, which you do for your degree, I didn't have graphic designs, so I put up my little books and things. It didn't look like anyone else's and it didn't have anything to do with the course. They tried to throw me out quite a lot of time, when I came in in my Wellington boots with straw sticking out of me; they said I was unprofessional. When they saw my show they said I had to take it down because it wasn't representative of the course. But I had already infiltrated their inner sanctum because I found out that the external assessor whose word goes 90 percent of the time was an illustrator. So I left it up and got a first! They were as mad as herrings!

None of your tutors found your work refreshing?

Well, there was one, but he was in the etching department. I was really bad at print-making, and used to spend evenings working in the print department with him. Holidays I would just break in and use it when it was closed. I was nothing if not keen. Another old guy taught me how to make storyboards for cartoon films. I like to work with film. He liked what I did and taught me quite a bit. That was practically all I learned. I had to go to evening classes for the drawing.

You had already started to do books?

I was already going around to publishers in my second and third year. I thought I'd better get started and find out what it was all about. I did a lovely book, best book I've ever done, and started at the top. I said I was good and wanted them to publish my book. They said they'd never seen anything like it before. Since I hadn't published anything and they didn't know who I was, they said they would show it to some sister publishers to see if they were interested. They weren't, because they thought it was a little ahead of its time. We shoved it around a bit and eventually somebody else published it. Now they're standing in line for my books. British publishers were not noted for taking a chance. It's especially difficult now because of the great multimedia giants taking us over. They've taken over all my little publishers. It's not doing publishing any good. They have money for people like me, because I make money. They don't have money for the young talents that are coming along. They are run by businessmen and not necessarily people who are interested in writing as an art.

Can you relate your interest in cinema to the way you do your books?

Yes. I like to see my pictures "move." When I think of a book, the whole things comes to me together like a film that is running through my head. The words and the pictures come at the same time. Which is probably why I am a writer and an illustrator rather than one or the other. It's not just the words, and then the pictures come along later. With some people it's the pictures that come first, and the words will fit in around the pictures. But with me it's just like a film going through. I just sit down and I work it out like a storyboard. I know how many pages, 32 or whatever, and I go right through it from one end to the other. Then I'll modify this, and modify that, until I get what I want.

So you wouldn't illustrate other people's stories?

I used to a lot. But I don't do it any more, because I won't do it unless I get a royalty, and unless I get paid what I would get for one of my books, because it takes me half an hour to write a story, and it takes me three or four months to do the illustrations. Most of the work is in the illustrations. I can knock out one of my own in basically the same time it takes to do somebody else's. I'll do it for some people (Roald Dahl or Joan Aiken) if I'm allowed and get a small royalty that makes it worthwhile, instead of a flat fee.

You don't hang your own work on your walls?

I look at the bloody stuff all day. I'd rather look at someone else's.

You keep all the work you do?

Yes, it's all upstairs in files. It's going into the new office. Maybe then I can actually find it.

Do you work to size?

Yes, generally, unless they specifically want it bigger. But I like to work the same size. They might decide to pull out a bit and blow it up to use as a vignette. I do a bit of advertising now and then, because it's very well paid. My work looks better actually if it's blown up rather than reduced. It looks that little bit looser. And it tends to get better as it looks looser, I think. I think it's tight but most people think it's scribbly. Those (paperbacks) are reduced from the original art work, because those are a smaller format than the original hardbacks. You can't be that fussy with paperbacks. If people want to look at a nice pretty book with everything right then they can buy a hard back. If they can't afford that, they'll buy the paperback. Some people don't like to buy the hard backs because they don't think the children are worth it, but they last longer.

We noticed that you frame your pictures sometimes but not others.

You have to do that sometimes. I often put things in boxes, but my publishers don't like that. They all say, "We don't want boxes, thank you." When I'm changing violently from one page to another, and I'm changing the whole thing completely like that, I like to put it in a little box. You'll find the *Smelly Book* has boxes, but the next one won't have any at all, because they don't like them. I think it's a useful mechanism at times. But they don't even like me having boxes on the cover. It's probably out of fashion. It will come back into fashion again and they'll want it, like green covers. I work it out to keep everybody happy. I can put sloppy bits around the edges, or sitting in a cloud.

When you do pictures supposedly done by children, how do you know how they draw?

Well, I never grew up, did I?

Do you deal with an art director or designer?

No. They really say very little about my books at all; I just do them, and they accept them. They might correct the spelling, because I can't spell. The Americans didn't like my smelly cows [*Smelly Book*], so I took a page out for the Americans. It was quite a nice one: the cows were in the house. They had all their pearls and earrings on, and they were sitting down with their little fingers sticking out, daintily eating cow cakes and having tea, like a Ladies' Institute meeting. The text said, "Lots of cattle like to eat smelly cow cakes for a treat." They wouldn't have it because it looked too much like dung. They wanted me to do another page, but I said, "No, just take it out." So I think there's an extra title or something.

You use decorated endpapers sometimes?

We count it all in. Sometimes I paint them, sometimes I don't. It costs more to have colored ones.

Do you see other picturebook folk?

I see them at various events, at publishing "do's." There's very little of that here. Personally I see very few. I see BBC people I used to work with up the road. We all live all over the country. I generally play around with my horses.

Do you see other people's picturebooks?

I like to have a look at what the competition is doing. That's one of the reasons I go to Bologna. I do like to keep abreast of it; I think that's very important. You have to be very good in order to make any money; you've got to be very lucky, and pushy. It's tough out there. It's not the gentlemanly profession a lot of people think it is. "There you are, sitting in your country cottage writing little stories and drawing little pictures." It's tough at the top out there. Business women at the top are tougher than business men. They had to be to get there in the first place.

Is there a British approach to illustration?

There's so much background which develops people. Coming from a different country with a highly different atmosphere, they're going to produce art in their way. They're going to be a reflection of themselves as individuals. I do talk to a lot of foreign authors and illustrators at Bologna. What I have noticed about the Nordic countries, for example, is that they have a much less cutthroat approach than we do. "We do it because we like it. You have to be sensitive, environmentally sound. . . . We all get together and eat reindeer and drink Valhalla and have a wonderful time, no hurry to be published. . . ." The French say "We do the best. No one is as good as us. We only pick the very best illustrators to have on our list." The young Americans I've met seem to be very enthusiastic. They have a nice attitude as well. I haven't met that many established Americans.

We British have a whole building to ourselves in Bologna. I think that basically en masse we are the best. It's one of the only things in this country that we can export and make money at. It's a lucrative business here.

I think we're basically a bit scattier. It's that English eccentric scattiness that shows. That's the only thing I can put my finger on at all. If you look at all the old illustrators back to Caldecott, even Kate Greenaway was quite quirky; Grahame, Tenniel, they've all got a sort of English scattiness about them. Certainly the Victorian writers and illustrators were a bit scatty. I think that certainly comes out. German illustrations are not scatty, but very pretty, very frou-frou. The French are more literary, and "fine art."

Did comics play a part in your childhood?

I used to like stuff like *Dan Dare* and *The Eagle*, boys' comics. I didn't like the stuff the girls read in those days. I read *Horse and Hound* and pony magazines, all part of that tomboy stage. I didn't have that much time to read. And of course at school we didn't have comics.

Was the convent school an important influence?

We were very strictly brought up. You could never do anything wrong. Somebody was always watching. That's why you went off the rails afterward. I was a day student. But then I spent the time with the ponies, and that was very disciplined as well. The animals came first. I think in a way it wasn't a bad idea to be so disciplined. My publishers tell me I am one of the most businesslike and reliable professional people they work with. My work is always ready when they want it. I think I'm like that because I had a rather disciplined upbringing. If you have so much going on in your life, you have to organize it properly or you have ulcers and nervous breakdowns.

I have someone coming in every day to help with the animals. I don't do all the mucking out myself. My back's too bad after having done it all my life. And I have to get on with the work. I also have a lady who does letters for me, deals with publicity engagements, all those things. I can't cope with the mail. I get more than 60 letters a month from children all over the world. I won't just send a form letter or something. I think that's absolutely horrid. If I was a child and read books that I felt were special for me and wanted to write the authors, I would expect a letter back from them, answering my questions. So every single child has a letter from me. I think that's very important.

Do you go out to visit schools?

I do, but I don't like performing in public. It's wearing, and takes me away from my work. I could end up being a professional school and Women's Institute visitor and never do any work at all.

Is there any influence of Fungus the Bogeyman *on* Slimy Book?

I don't draw anything like Raymond Briggs. But basically children love things like that. I liked making all those slimy things and inviting people to eat them when I was a little girl. It's just another thing they like. They like tea parties, and painting, and hide-and-seek, and slimy things. Little girls may say "Ooo!" But it's a reaction at least. It's the shock of the new . . . . This is art!

Thinking about The Trouble with Dad, *how do you define art?*

That's a very difficult question. It has to be an expression of what you think about the world. I think that's what art is really, it has to be part of you. It's an arm or a leg or an eyelash that comes from you, it's part of you that you have to do; it's your statement you want to make. You can be a painter, or a gardener, a writer, anything you want to make statement about. That's like Dad's robots. They were works of art, and he loved them, although nobody else did. At last somebody else appreciated them, and they made lots of money.

Do you work from sketches, photographs?

I don't take photographs and I don't really work from a reference file. I look at things a lot. I used to keep a lot of sketchbooks but I don't have the time. I keep mental sketchbooks now. I wish I had more time to draw. The only time I have to draw now — what I call proper drawing, not making little sketches when I'm sitting in pubs — is when I'm on holiday. I have about a month off a year. The rest of the time I make mental sketches everywhere: people on buses. . . . It all goes into a mental filing cabinet like any artist.

For something like the motor bike in *Princess Smartypants* I might have a picture from somewhere and add bits to it. But it's not terribly technical. I used to have a motor bike so I know it's right. If I want to put in the workings of a specific motor bike, I will get a picture. But I may feel this knob will look better up here, or that will look a bit wiggly there. . . . If I want a certain kind of car I will go out and get a picture.

But I won't go out somewhere, and get a child, arrange him, photograph him and draw from the results the way some people do. There's nothing wrong in that, but I don't draw like that.

How about the castles?

They're just a castle. It just has the things necessary for that particular person's castle, like a line to hang out the washing, or rings to tie the dragons up to for grooming purposes. . . . *Princess Smartypants* is my own autobiography. The princes have all been turned into toads. The last one was turned into a toad as well, but he hasn't left. I get a lot of letters from boys as well about that book. And the boys get their own back in *Prince Cinders*.

Did The Trouble with . . . *start out as a series?*

No. I started with *The Trouble with Mom* only. But any of my books could be a series. I could do half a dozen adventures of Princess Smartypants. They asked could I do another as good as *Mom*, so I did *The Trouble with Dad*. I could do the trouble with anything you want. My publishers say, "The trouble with Babette Cole!"

Do you have any more fairy tales in mind?

I'm going to have a go at Tarzan. We're going to have Tarzana. I wanted to do another Princess Smartypants type, because I like her. I think she's really necessary these days. I get a lot of letters, especially from the States, about Princess Smartypants saying "This is what we want." So often the mother goes out to work and the father stays home to look after the children. This is what is happening, so we need these role reversals.

In Three Cheers for Errol! *how did you decide to get that real inner city feel?*

I thought we needed one of those, because I keep looking at these little books of animals running around in frilly frocks in the hedgerows. Beatrix Potter did that very well, perhaps uniquely. I thought what has this got to do with the kids in a tower block in London? We must have an inner city rat, rather than a frilly little mouse. So we have Errol, and why not? I'm fond of him. He's got a sister now, called Evelyn. It's now in dummy. She's the opposite of him, incredibly brainy. She gets a scholarship to go to a very posh school. The others discriminate against her, pull her whiskers, put ink in her knickers! A jolly schoolgirl tale. We were like that in my school, horrid to the scholarship girls. I got into trouble over *Errol*. I had a letter from a borough council labelling me racist because Errol is brown. What other color are rats? And Errol is a Scottish name! They couldn't see he was a hero. That was the only time anybody has had anything to say in 25 or so books. I was very angry at the time, but I can laugh about it now. You have to be careful. I have three African books that I've done published by McGraw-Hill. I had to be very careful that nobody was grinning too much. They were about a little African boy, because I used to live in Africa, in Botswana. But they do grin if they are happy. You can visit black people or even live with them, but you can never be one. Basically I believe in treating everyone the same. If I'm going to draw black or white people, I give them the same treatment!

— *Summer 1989*

Eleven

Peter Collington

A Sampling of Works in Print

The Angel and the Soldier Boy Knopf, 1987, 1988.

My Darling Kitten Knopf, 1988.
On Christmas Eve Knopf, 1990.

The train to Poole gives glimpses of the sea about an hour out of London. Travellers get on and off at the seaside town of Bournemouth, while some vacationers stay on to the last stop at Poole. Just before the station, a large meadow stretches down to the ocean. Many kites are being flown in the sea-breeze as parents and kids enjoy the sunshine. Collington has been kind enough to pick us up at the station in his classic "sardine can" Citroen. We spot him; somehow he resembles the visual qualities in his books.

The Collington home is a modest attached house on a short, narrow street. We are greeted by a pre-adolescent girl on roller skates with full protective gear and are introduced to Sasha, the daughter. Inside are stained glass picked up from demolition sites, stuffed dogs, and a large family portrait done by Sasha. None of her father's pictures hang on the walls because "he doesn't like to look at it once it's done."

What kind of a place is Poole?

It's an old trading post now in reduced circumstance. All along the south coast people come on holiday or to retire.

How did you happen to settle here?

My father worked here. He was born in Poole, as was my grandfather. I grew up in Mudeford, near Christchurch, along the coast a bit.

Do you remember picturebooks from your childhood?

There was one particular book I liked. . . . Every year at Christmas there was a *Rupert* annual. I used to love the pictures in there. All the stories are told in frames. After each frame there is a rhyming verse. Each page had four frames with rhyming captions. I never used to read the block story. I used to "read" the pictures. I was captivated by the pictures.

My father was a draftsman. When I was a child he used to bring home the drafting pencils, 2H and 3H, so I had a sort of drawing tradition at an early age. He also used to bring home patterns of aircraft and such that were blank on the other side so I had plenty of drawing paper.

So you were drawing from a very young age, and knew that was something you liked to do?

Yes. My brother also drew. He's a little older than I am, and used to draw a lot. This was a strong influence on me. He was very good at horses. The other thing he used to draw well was the Queen's Guards, the ones with the furry hats. I learned to do them from him. I never copied the *Rupert* ones. I never actually thought of them as being drawn by anyone. They were just there every Christmas and they were wonderful.

Did you have some art training in school?

Yes. It was the thing I did well. Because I have a stammer and found it hard to express myself in a verbal way, I suppose art was something I could excel in and get some sort of recognition.

When I was five or six, I made something out of plastic in the classroom, a duck or something. The teacher was very impressed with it, and she sent me to the headmistress with it. She had a special jar of sweets, and gave me some, but she kept the duck. I went back to the classroom feeling that it wasn't quite right that she kept it. It was, I suppose, my first "sale," but I felt uneasy about it. We did continue to do "arts and crafts" things through elementary (primary) school. Then I went to Secondary Modern School, where you learned a "practical" skill. Most students went out at 15 or 16 to be apprenticed in some trade.

Did you get to choose an arts course when you went to secondary school?

No. There was no choice there. Everyone just had "art" twice a week. A lot of kids thought it was a good time to relax. But I took it more seriously because it was something I could do. Every year we took exams in every subject. I began in the "D" class. The only way you could escape was through the exam. Obviously I felt a deep sense of humiliation being in the "D" class, and had to get out. I felt that I could do well in art.

After secondary school, what typically did one do?

Very few even of the A class took the A levels to go on to further education. Most students went out to work in shops or factories. It was important to get a good apprenticeship training. I thought about being a draftsman, with my father's influence. We did some of that kind of drawing training in school. We did plans and 3-D drawing. Girls did typing or cooking.

Self-portrait by Peter Collington

But when I was 14, I got a camera and began taking pictures. I was really hooked on photography. I began to print my photographs in the darkroom. At that point I began to lose interest in art, in drawing or painting. I had discovered this wonderful new thing. My art master said that all my work was "gray." I would overwork everything.

Photography was not part of the school curriculum, so I had to teach myself. I used to get *Amateur Photography* magazine with "helpful hints" on how to print, etc.

So at 15 I decided that this was for me, and applied at the art college to do the three-year course in photography. I needed four successful O-levels. I had worked my way up to the "B" group, but they wouldn't put me up any higher. So I really had to work just to get to take the exams. But I wanted to. I took some photographs to show as well.

What else did you study there besides photography?

Art history. I couldn't see why we had to do that. The classes were held at the end of the day just before we went home, so with the slides in the dark we'd be half-asleep. I didn't want to read or listen; I just wanted to take photographs. I never really read in school; only what I had to. But in a photography course we had to read, so I started to really read for the first time. There was one fellow in my class who read a lot. He used to say, "You ought to read this," so I started to read art history as well.

Did you do the history of photography too?

Yes. There was a very good library there where we went a lot. In the third year I couldn't decide whether to do the film course. I did half and half because I was still involved with still photography. So I saw a lot of films, and got very interested in them as well.

Did that influence the way you lay out and frame your work now?

Yes. I was intrigued by film then. But aside from a bit of graphic design, I did no drawing or painting.

What was it expected that you would do on graduation?

It was up to you. You went out with your portfolio to find a job. The idea was to work as an assistant to a photographer. But jobs were very scarce. And because I would have had to do secretarial chores such as telephone and reception skills for which I was not qualified, it was even harder for me. Although some people liked my work, they didn't really want me to take photographs. I got depressed and demoralized after 6 months or so. I couldn't see any way to break in. I had been doing a lot of reading. I began writing, poetry and other things. I wrote a children's book when I was 22, and decided to try doing the illustrations. I decided to do black-and-white pen and ink illustrations, about 12 of them. I was pleased at how well I could draw starting from scratch. I found that I still had the drawing skills that I had not used for so long. I sent the book to a publisher, who returned it. By this time my wife had gone ahead to New York. I had mixed feelings about joining her, but I thought I might try to get the book published there. The publishers liked some of the illustrations, but it was very iffy. So I did various jobs just to make a living. I was an elevator operator. I did some black and white illustrations for magazines, and was pleased to have something in print. But then I didn't get any work for a while. I did a portfolio and went around again. But there were so many other fine illustrators there. So I decided to do some of my own art work. I had gone around to a lot of the galleries and shows in New York. In the MOMA there were two pictures that particularly struck me. One was *The Eternal City* by Peter Blume. I thought it was brilliant. The other was *Hide and Seek* by Tchelichev. The precision . . . wonderful. I thought I might want to express myself with work like that.

Were there illustrators that impressed you as well?

While I was still in England I had seen Maurice Sendak's work and became interested. But I didn't really see many because I wasn't really involved. *Night Kitchen*, I think, I remember. When I got to New York City I was mainly interested in painting. I also became involved with psychotherapy, which had a big effect on me. I was always trying to find some kind of cure for my stammer. The conflict is between the attempt to express and the holding back. I began to do some line drawings concerned with my past, and my dreams. I started to ask other people about their dreams. I did primal therapy as well, took two or three weeks off from elevator-operating. How hard it was to go back to not expressing but concealing feelings!

Did anything visual come out of this experience?

Yes. I made a model out of papier-mâché; a surrealistic piece of head and throat and animals. . . . It was so big. My marriage had ended. The piece had to be destroyed because it was too big to move. I have only a photograph.

I was on my own. I decided to draw again. I had seen an exhibition of the work of Juan Gonzalez. He used colored pencils. They were so precise and meticulous, just brilliant. So I went to the supply shop to get hard lead color pencils and began to experiment. The drawings were still influenced by my experience in primal therapy, slighly surrealistic. In doing this, I felt I had discovered a style I was really happy with. I wanted to do a show. So it was back to the portfolio, this time going to the art galleries. I felt as if the art world was a closed door. The children's book world was closed as well. That's when I decided to come back to England, with my new wife, whom I had met in New York. My style was so laborious that it would take years to get enough for a show. I got quite depressed. I worked with my brother doing line drawings, black and white, for newspapers. Our daughter Sasha was born in 1981. When Bonnie was pregnant, I did some drawings of us for her to have after she was born. When Sasha was a year old, she could hold a pencil and put in the eyes if I did the circle. She picked it up quickly, so we did a lot of drawing together. I began to think about doing a book for children.

Did you start out to do it without words?

I think I began it as a sort of strip. Then I found that I didn't need words; they were superfluous.

Was it all laid out in advance?

I worked it all out roughly, then I did a lot of photographs. I had hardly taken any all the time I was in New York. In that way I could get the realism I wanted. It took me about nine months to do it. I used to have to get out and work in the shed, because otherwise Sasha would want to "help" me. I used to pretend I was going out to work, say goodbye, and go out to the shed. *Little Pickle* went through a lot of changes. I redid half the book. They felt it was too threatening for her to really be out on the sea, so I did the dream sequence. I had already done all the art work. I learned from that, so I did *Soldier* in black and white drawings first. I do a full-size dummy of the book in black and white, all the frames the way I want them in ink. That's how the art work is done, ink outline and then colored pencil. The style in the *Angel and the Soldier* isn't the same as that in *Little Pickle*. It's similar to the style I used in my earlier art work in the U.S. as a studio artist. I felt that was more my style. It's quite a precise technique using a small watercolor brush and doing it in small strokes building up the color bit by bit, so there's no wash. I use a very small fine sable brush. It takes a very long time. In a way it's going back to the time when I was doing photographs. The printing technique I liked because it was very precise, very sharp. The resolution of the print is like what I like in the art work, very clear.

Where did the idea for Angel and Soldier Boy *come from?*

I've always liked stories where little toys and animals, dolls come alive when the child is asleep, like a dream. When the child is awake, the toys are asleep, in the inanimate world. This always has intrigued me. There was a fair. Sasha was dressed as an angel, which was a sort of a joke because at that time we thought she was anything but. She had a white frock, and wings made from coat hangers, which accounts for their shape, with another coat hanger for the halo. When we went to the fair, she looked so sweet and lovely. There were some men dressed as pirates there. I think seeing them next to her gave me the idea. The use of the sea or ships in both books (*Little Pickle* as well) related to both my father and grandfather, the sea captain. I grew up close to the sea, and spent a lot of time on the beach at the harbor.

How about My Darling Little Kitten?

A very brief, simple book.

Do you feel the reproduction is OK?

Yes, I'm quite happy. But I've found it hard to sell books with no words.

Would you feel more self-fulfilled if your success in the picturebook world were in the "fine art" world?

Not now. Because I want to move on. I'm interested in film, in doing some animation in the future, to put the two together. I'd like to explore. Right now the *Angel and the Soldier* is being turned into a film to be shown at Christmas.

What role do you play in this?

I've come up with a few ideas. For it to last 25 minutes, they've had to expand it. I love Irish music and they're using haunting Irish music. There will be an album of music and a year later a videocassette.

What technique are they using?

All hand-drawn cells. Twenty-five to thirty people are working on it.

Are you happy with what they've done with it?

Yes. I think they're doing a very good job. Obviously it's their film. It's hard for them to match my style because of the technique involved, but they're getting the feeling. If I were doing it I'd do it in a different way. Animation is something I really want to explore. It's amazing. Those little drawings are really alive. But at this point I can't afford to. I have to keep doing books to pay the mortgage. When I can I want to get some animation equipment, take time off just to explore the medium, play around with it, make a short film, then a feature film. . . .

What are you working on now?

A Christmas book called *On Christmas Eve.*

Do you know some of the contemporary illustrators because of your daughter?

Yes. We have a good library here and we've gone through enormous numbers of books. I greatly admire Graham Oakley. I want to see the sequel to *Henry's Quest.* I hope he won't compromise. I also like Anthony Browne and Innocenti's *Pinocchio.*

We go up a narrow stairway to a gabled attic room crammed with photographs and props for the current Christmas book. The work table facing the only window holds the little brushes and hard color pencils that can hold a sharp point, and the illustration board he works on that can be put safely away after a day's drawing.

We like the small town. We can see the countryside, hills, tops of trees from the window. And here we have such good friends.

—*Summer 1989*

Twelve

Roy Gerrard

A Sampling of Works in Print

The Favershams Farrar, Straus, 1987.

A Pocket Full of Posies Farrar, Straus, 1991.

Rosy and the Rustlers Farrar, Straus, 1990.

Sir Cedric Farrar, Straus, 1986.

Sir Cedric Rides Again Farrar, Straus, 1986, 1989.

Sir Francis Drake: His Daring Deeds Farrar, Straus, 1988.

Up near Manchester, hills start to become steeper, almost mountains, and the road from the station must wind around them. From the car window a few sheep seem to be clinging to the hillsides. This is the countryside that Roy Gerrard loves, the roots from which he draws his inspiration and from which he departs only when there is no alternative. A bicycle ride in nearby flat Cheshire will refresh him more than a Mediterranean cruise. His house is tucked in a row of many on a village street. Its rooms are not large but are comfortably furnished, with a glassed-in porch overlooking the lush green garden and the steep hills beyond. On the walls are only one or two Gerrards, none from the books. Cigar smoke drifts above his head as he talks. Jean, his wife, makes a proper fourth for our conversation.

Did your family have interest or ability in art?

No. I come from a working class family, coal miners, very practical and sensible. Nobody in the family was particularly artistic. I'm the odd one out. I had some artistic ability in school, which was the only ability I had. I thought of myself as an artist as a kid. I just always enjoyed drawing. I was better at it than most of my schoolmates.

Did you copy from books?

96

Self-portrait by Roy Gerrard

Yes. I used to draw Walt Disney characters; I think everybody does. But I was particularly influenced by the British humorous illustrators, like Tenniel, and the Punch illustrators. Later when I became more sophisticated, there were people like the British watercolor artists that I admired from the golden age of English landscape painting before the Industrial Revolution decimated the countryside. I was very smitten by Paul Klee. There's a link between the humorous Punch illustrators and Klee. Not Turner or Constable. More designed. I hate the pre–Raphaelites. Samuel Palmer did very strange visionary landscapes, exultant things. But he went to Italy and when he came back he became a conventional landscape painter; he'd lost it all. One of my favorite painters was a destitute rag and bone merchant who didn't start painting until he was 68. He produced wonderful naive, primitive paintings. But they were sophisticated as well. Richard Dadd was a murderer, and did his best paintings while he was incarcerated. Lyrical but frightening paintings, eerie. There was a vogue of painting fairy scenes in Victorian times. I prefer the later Victorian: Rackham, Nielson, Dulac. Or Blake. I love Whistler. I'm not much of a theorist. I have a feeling that if you start theorizing something slips away. I've been painting so long, it's hard to get to the roots of what I'm doing. Someone showed me some old comic strips recently, and I was amazed to recognize a formative influence on my work that I had forgotten completely about.

That may be why I don't read poetry anymore. I'm committed now. . . .

I didn't really read the classic children's books until I was in my teens: Lear, Carroll, *Wind in the Willows*, Kipling. I suppose I was a bit retarded.

Jean: We never saw new books when we were children, because of the war. There was no paper available. We traded and passed along books after we read them.

Roy: We saw American comics occasionally, comics like *Dick Tracy* and the *Katzenjammer Kids*—very stylized.

Tell us about your education.

I transferred to a junior art school when I was 13, and spent 6 years there. I trained as an illustrator, but I drifted towards painting. I also trained as a textile designer for one year, before I dropped it, getting decoration and pattern. Solford School of Art on the fringe of Manchester.

At 19, you left school and drifted into teaching?

It's an honest living. We had all been in illustration and had drifted toward painting, but we were unemployable. I was a painter for years; great big horrible abstractions. But I threw them all away. I realized they weren't very good. I was keen on rock-climbing. I had a fall in 1972 which laid me up for a bit. That's when I started painting again. Then I switched to book illustration via *Matilda Jane*. And that was it; I gradually worked my way out of teaching.

How did you get involved with publishing?

I was painting at the time, and exhibiting in a gallery in London once a year. A London dealer suggested I try book illustrating; that I was probably more of an illustrator than a painter. So Jean wrote *Matilda Jane* and bullied me into doing it.

Jean: He didn't want to get started. I had to force him into doing it, so I scribbled what I knew he would paint well. It worked because I never had to push him again.

Roy: It was rather a timid book stylistically. The others are more weird. That's why I started writing myself. I wanted to write more quirky stuff to go with the quirky illustration.

Is that quirkiness a part of the Lancashire character?

I think so, a brisk, earthy folk humor that still exists to a certain extent. I'm trying to be colloquial so the Northern sort of speech patterns are going to come out. I don't want to be literary. I don't think children want me to be literary. I want it to be fun; I want to enjoy doing it. Then hopefully they'll enjoy reading it.

Your formal education ended at 19?

Yes, I'm largely uneducated, except for trips to the public library. . . . I managed to avoid anything academic that I didn't want to do. I had a very ramshackle education. I used to read poetry by the ton. I guess I've taken in enough. You may not be able to tell from the kind of verse I write but I've always enjoyed poetry. I liked E. E. Cummings very much. I love American jazz; I have it belting out all day [New Orleans through Brubeck] while I'm working, which doesn't make me very popular with the neighbors. It's a lifelong passion.

Did you ever try to put any of this into your picturebooks?

No, but I did a series of paintings: *Maisie Hoffmeyer and Her All-Girl Band* (a nude ladies' band) which I've not done for a few years because I've been working on books.

You don't keep your own art work from the books?

Most of it is sold to a dealer in the U.S. I wouldn't have any of my own work up. I don't like to see it once I've done it. I always think it could have been better. The next one is going to be a masterpiece although this one is a disaster. I don't like them around; they haunt me.

Do you do any non-book paintings now?

I've done a series of small paintings between books as a break. Jean's going to have them printed for greeting cards.

Is your "studio" life different from your book life?

The two overlap very much in me. But there's a subtle stylistic difference. I found my illustrations were affecting my paintings, devaluing them stylistically. In my training as an illustrator, I was quietly chipping away at the illustrative part of my work toward painting. Once I do a book I'm back to square one. There's that subtle line for me between illustration and painting. I can't maintain it if I stick to illustration for too long. I enjoy it and I put a lot into it.

Do you feel the reproduction of your work comes close to the original?

Yes. The books have been printed in Hong Kong recently. I leave it all to them. I suppose I ought to be interested in it but I'm not. Once a book is finished I don't want to know. I'm bored to death with it. I don't even bother with proof corrections, although they send them to me out of courtesy. It's always O.K.; it doesn't worry me. They do say a lot of artists are fussy about it. But what can the publishers do? It's in their interest to put out the best book they can. There is a technical chap who keeps them on keel. It takes me about a year to do a book, and I've had enough of it by then.

What is the impetus for other books besides Matilda Jane?

I suppose it's the way I was taught history as a child, with these larger-than-life heroes. It's the schoolboy's attitude toward history, not at all scholarly. It's regurgitating the views of the child. As the spur for the Favi-shams, I always like the Victorians, those crazy people. The books I read when I was a boy all seemed to be about Empire. We had an empire in those days, a white man's burden and all that. I was getting things out of my sys-tem. As for *Sir Cedric*, I was always keen on the *Book of Hours* of the Duc de Berry, and that led to him. *Rosie and the Rustlers* comes from the fact that I was a child of the cinema age brought up on cowboy films.

Why did you choose to do a book about Sir Francis Drake?

He was a suggestion from the publisher, because it was the 400th an-niversary of the Armada.

How long do you take for a book?

About 12 months.

How much research do you do?

As little as I can get away with. I have most of it already; but some I obviously had to look up. Some buildings are based on the Book of Hours. I played about with them and redeveloped them.

And the elephant?

I think I worked from a photograph there. I often work from photo-graphs when I tend to distort or alter things as I have always done. It's bor-ing otherwise. Plants from the local conservatory served as model for the jungle in *Sir Francis Drake*. The ship is a model in the public library.

The horses have those long legs. . . .

It satisfies me, contrasting long slender things with little squat figures; the tension between the two pleases me aesthetically.

In my first book I was stylistically timid; I thought I had to be very sen-sible and not have too much fun. That was silly really. By the end of the book I hated *Matilda Jane*. The publisher complained that she was getting uglier as the book went on. I was sure it was a psychological thing. I was writing, "Matilda Jane was astonished to see that a tram car had severed her legs at the knee." I hated her because I was containing myself. I was so bored with her, I thought I had to do something that I'm going to really enjoy.

You enjoy doing things like the walls, brick by brick?

Yes. A watercolor often looks a bit slight. I wanted to do something more intense. I wanted the page to have some impact. If you're working in watercolor I suppose you have to use a lot of detail to give it some strength. I work over several layers to give it more. Sometimes I'll draw with ink, and water it down to get a very fine line. Sometimes I'll draw with a fine brush line. I work to scale. I'm very short-sighted, which helps. My disabilities are paying off.

Did you have any censorship problem with the harem scene in Sir Cedric Rides Again?

No. Nudes make me laugh. I don't think they're going to corrupt anybody. They are certainly not erotic. I've never heard anything about it. Kids have mentioned it in letters, just saying, "It made me laugh."

You design the pages yourself, or do you need a designer for your books?

Yes and no. I like to fit the text fairly closely to the picture. I do a lot of measuring. I just make sure I'm leaving enough space for the text.

But do you spec your own type?

No. I always use the same size, so I just measure it from other books.

How do you maintain the rhythm of your layout?

I try to get a bit of variety.

Do you plan your books ahead?

I make a little dummy book, very rough, just to work out how the text is to appear. I write the words first. That's the hard part really. The pictures are a long, laborious process but they come once I have the words. I make sure the words are going to give me the sort of picture I'll enjoy doing. If they weren't fun I would go raving mad, I think.

Do you do preliminary sketches or do you go right to finished work?

I draw the main characters out, so I know what they are going to look like. Then I just start and draw from the beginning. Once you've established how they are supposed to look, you stick to that. I often refer to the pictures I've done before, of course, to get the color right. I don't mind doing the scribbly sort of roughs, but I leave something behind in the rough drawing. I like to get on with it as quickly as possible.

To what extent does Jean see the story before you do the pictures?

I often read the verse to her and ask her if it scans.

Ever think of doing a speaking tour?

It's something I've always avoided. I hate it. Life is mainly work and recuperation. I love working, but you have to get away from it occasionally. There has to be something coming in as well as going out. I was 45 when I gave up teaching to paint full time. By then I had a backlog of subjects to feed on for the rest of my life.

What is your work day like?

I'm usually at work by 7, I take time for lunch and I work into the evenings. It's a habit. If I have a couple of days off I start to twitch.

How long did the painting of the ships in Sir Francis Drake *take to do?*

A week easily. It's all drawn in line first, with a pen or brush. Then I start to fill in. The more crucial things are done with a brush, so I can wash out any mistakes. The easier things I draw with a pen, because you can't wash them out. I'm slowing down a bit; at one time I might have finished that in three or four days. I can't rush them working with details; the work suffers.

— Summer 1989

Thirteen

M.B. Goffstein

A Sampling of Works in Print

An Actor Harper, 1987.

An Artist Harper, 1980.

An Artist's Album Harper, 1985.

Artists' Helpers Enjoy the Evenings Harper, 1987.

Brookie and Her Lamb Farrar, Straus, 1981.

Fish for Supper Dial, 1986.

A House, A Home Harper, 1990.

Laughing Latkes Farrar, Straus, 1980.

My Editor Farrar, Straus, 1985.

Our Prairie Home Harper, 1988.

Our Snowman Harper, 1986.

The School of Names Harper, 1986.

A Writer Harper, 1984.

Your Lone Journey Harper, 1986.

"I always wanted to write books, ever since I found out that it was people who wrote them." M.B. Goffstein's books are generally small. Most of her illustrations are drawn simply with precise pen lines; others are filled in with ink or watercolor. Her new books are done in pastels. The prose is spare. Not surprisingly, Brooke Goffstein is small herself. It's hard to picture her in New York City. Yet she lives in an apartment house off Riverside Drive, with the wind blowing from the Hudson. A scaffolding covers the lower part of the building for some obscure purpose. "Makes it look like a ghost house," she says. The apartment, as might be expected, has a modern, uncluttered look, with the exception of a family heirloom, an upholstered chair with buffalo horn arms, completely incongruous but somehow fitting. There is also a curio cabinet filled with her treasures. The studio is almost Spartan, the desk clear. The pictures and words are honed here without distraction. Only some small samples of work in progress on the wall reveal the creation that takes place in this space. Although the city has not appeared in any of her books, its noises intrude constantly.*

Originally published in The Horn Book Magazine, November/December 1986.

102

Since I'm from Minnesota, I want to wake up in the morning and go outside in my nightgown and look at the squirrels. Otherwise, I'm grateful to New York. I also lived in Dayton, Ohio, and Arlington, Virginia, when I was a child. I set *Two Piano Tuners* in our house in Dayton; *Your Lone Journey* takes place in my bedroom at Lake Minnetonka. The outside scenes in *Two Piano Tuners* arc in St. Paul, where I used to walk home from grade school. It feels strange to live anywhere else, when it comes to art supplies or books. If there's anything you want to know about, you can get help fast from one place or another.

How do you work on your books?

I like a book to be like the sculpture and paintings I admire. I like things to be solid, whole, and round, so that nothing can break off. I take a long time writing. My stories may not be whole for many years. I don't think about them all the time, but I keep at them at intervals, until I'm sure they're what they should be. I recite them aloud, over and over. . . .

What happens in your head before you create the art on paper?

A lot of artists sketch and look at what their hand is doing. They're thinking on paper. I do most of my work in my head, and have very few, if any, sketches. In *Our Snowman* the father rolls a snowball. I thought of how, bent over in his business hat and coat, he would look like a rhino. So that's what I sat down to draw.

When I actually draw, I'm not really here. If I say, "No, I can't take this; I'm stopping for a minute," I'm sorry I did. I can make a wrong decision that way. Making the art is an amazing feeling. I finish something, look at it, and begin to see how the book will be.

For me, illustrating is completely different from writing. It has to be done without a break, because a whole world is being sustained. Still it takes three to four months.

Are the words and the art equally important to you?

I always write a book first. I also write it a long time before I do the illustrations. I would find it hard to write about anything, thinking that I had to illustrate it right away. The publisher accepts a book with the belief that I'll bring in the illustrations, even though at that point I have no idea how I'll do them. When I do the pictures, it's as if I got the story in the mail. I'm not concerned with the words then, except to interpret them. My work is always beyond me, but I like to stretch.

I think a text should be strong and able to stand alone. Illustrations should tell the story without words. Together they're stronger, just as in a marriage. You don't want to be half a person and lean on the other. But two whole people make something very strong.

What about the constraints of the story?

Artists truly love discipline. The picturebook is a most beautiful discipline. I love it the way the Elizabethans loved the sonnet.

M.B. Goffstein

Do you work to scale?

Yes, always. I dislike seeing my drawings blown up or reduced in size.

Why do you so often work in a small size?

It's my own autographic size and that of the mark my pen or brush or pastel makes.

You used to work mainly in black and white. Can you tell us why you have begun to work in color?

I always felt that black-and-white art belonged with type, and also, partly because of the expense, that a book shouldn't be in color unless it needed to be. I like things to be very plain and simple. I've been like that since I was a child. Still, I grew and changed. I got hungry for color.

Why are the watercolors outlined in An Artist *but not in* A Writer?

A Writer is the bridge between all my earlier books and *School of Names*. My first book in full color was *Natural History*. It needed to be in color, and so did *An Artist*. In those two books I added color to my pen-and-ink drawings. Then, working on *A Writer*, I lost interest in outlining.

A writer absorbs impressions, and they come out very quietly. But a painter works physically, slamming the paint on canvas.

Book artists are a combination of the two. They work for the printed page. There's a big difference between easel painting and book illustration. If you take a page out of a book to frame and hang on the wall, you must be disappointed. You can't see what you saw when you looked at the book, because all the pictures in a book add up to one picture that isn't even there.

How much research do you do for books like those about art and Schubert?

A lot, but I don't call it research. I read first, and the desire to write comes later.

Even fiction has to be well grounded in fact. The whole pleasure of reading comes when you put yourself in someone's hands and say, "I trust you." If that trust is betrayed, it's sad for the reader and for the writer. Anyway, I couldn't write those books if I didn't read, because that's how I learn.

For whom do you create your books?

I don't picture anyone in particular. A book is a communication. You have to want to touch someone on the arm and say, "Could I please tell you this?" It might just be entertainment, but you have to want to speak. When I was in college, I thought in terms of publishing something and having everyone say, "Oh, how beautiful." But I don't think anything can be good when you have that kind of ego. You have to be thinking of the work, and not about yourself at all. It's the books I give everything to. To me they are people.

My books are for whoever reads them. Everything people get builds an appetite for something good later. I feel lucky to have unending work that I love.

I've heard people say that children should be passionate about reading. But those same people might write or recommend books that couldn't be less passionate. Children are not a class or a group. They are individual people, more beautiful perhaps than we are, and more open and confiding. But they are interested in every single thing that we're interested in. I don't see any difference. We all need to be treated with respect.

But don't you feel that the level of experience of children is different from that of adults, so children might not understand?

Many of my books are invitations. I wrote *A Little Schubert*, for instance, to say, "This is yours. You can have it for life. And there's more." My books about artists are not only for people who have read about art. These books are for children.

I want to say to children, "This is beautiful and exciting and worth growing up for." I hope the words are engaging. They can read *An Artist's Album* now and not completely understand it, but later in life they can read or see something else, and say "Aha!" I've been doing that all my life. We all need things to grow on. We reread because we grow and understand more, so these things make a circle. I've often said I don't care if children remember my name or any of my books by name. But I like to think that they might grow up caring about something they read in one of my books.

My Editor, your first book for adults, seems different from your other books. Why did you do it?

I always wanted to illustrate a book with geometric figures. And, like my other books, it's something I very much wanted to express. If it didn't turn out to be a children's book, that was a publishing decision. I was bound to do it anyway.

Your Lone Journey was also published as an adult book. I would like children to see it, because it's about true love and marriage. It could be a companion to *My Noah's Ark*.

Are Fish for Supper *and* My Noah's Ark *true?*

The character in *Fish for Supper* was my Grandma Rosie. She looked just like that; in fact, she recognized herself in my book. She was about eighty then. She would have liked to have lived like that. But nobody ever carved me a Noah's ark. My books are true emotionally, about things that would have been good. The fun of writing is that you can take a persona. Once I told *My Noah's Ark* to a group of children, and a little girl asked, "Do you still have it?" I wondered: Do I look like I'm ninety-four? But it's true in its way.

For the art books Lives of the Artists *and* An Artist's Album, *why did you choose those particular illustrations?*

Mostly they are the same works of art that made me care so much for the artists. I'd like to give a prize to whoever invented art post cards. I see one I love, and I can buy it: a Cézanne, a Vermeer.

I used to read a lot about art intrigue and about fakes. At first I was almost in love with the forgers, because they were so good. But for me, art is only art when you're solving a problem. In the end, if you owned any forgery, you would start to lose interest in it, because the person wasn't solving a problem. . . . Nobody else cares, but he or she has to solve that problem. That struggle makes a work of art. There are so many people who draw well, for example, but there's no passion, no resolution in their work, so who cares?

Why did you come to teaching so late?

I had published 20 books almost in solitude. When James Marshall wanted me to take over his class at the Parsons School of Design, he gave me a great gift. It's such a pleasure for me to be there. I feel a freedom in myself I have never felt before. I love teaching that class.

I start each semester by saying that a children's book is a beautiful art form that is a combination of art and literature. I talk about how a book is meant to communicate the best that's in you, about how you have to be honest, be yourself, be unselfconscious, say what you want to say, and do it justice. There is no other reason to write or illustrate a book.

If you write from your heart, if your books have "an address," as I once heard I.B. Singer say, you can have a rich and harmonious career. You won't be writing off the top of your head, wondering where your next idea will come from. As you write, you will learn, so you will grow, and new books will well up in you.

My students do wonderful books.

What is the hardest thing to make them remember?

The format. I had to make it a class cheer: "Half-title. Blank. Title page. Copyright. Dedication. . . ." I still count on my fingers.

Have you been influenced by other children's book artists?

When I started, I studied children's books very carefully. I admire the work of other artists, but my art is in me. It's what I have to work with, what I want to work with.

Do reviews ever make you change your work?

I take reviews seriously. But I'm not going to do the same book over again, and I can't change the way I work. My books are born in me; they're things I want to solve. I look forward to seeing reviews of my new books, because it means they've landed.

Before leaving, we examined some treasures: the small collection of beautiful stones and shells, the art reproductions on post cards, the large and small volumes on art and artists. As we looked over it all, she quoted from Lives of the Artists: *""We seem to be miracles, yet we led simple lives," said the seashells.' My books are about kinds of life, ways to live, the quality of life, because that is what's important to me."*

—1986

Update

Having told you that I always write first, I started doing the opposite. For my photo books, *Our Prairie Home, A House, A Home,* and three as yet unpublished titles, *Pictures from Our New Prairie Home, Up at the Lake,* and *Tricks and Chips,* I explored with my camera first, then wrote captions.

When I spoke at the New York Storytelling Center last February, and I was asked what audience I have in mind when I work, I realized that the *book* is my audience, that as I find its voice and form, it rejoices with me.

This is exactly like teaching, helping my students find their own voices.

In addition to Parsons, I teach a one-week workshop most summers at Split Rock, the University of Minnesota, at Duluth.

As to the children's book field: If everyone read and absorbed the books of psychologist Alice Miller, then went on their way, "sorrowful, yet always rejoicing," to use a favorite phrase of Van Gogh, kind to animals and to each other, I think the children's book field would be great too!

—1990

Fourteen

Diane Goode

A Sampling of Works in Print

Cinderella Knopf, 1988.
*Diane Goode's Little Library of
  Christmas Classics* Random, 1989.
I Go with My Family to Grandma's
  by Riki Levinson. Dutton, 1986.
I Hear a Noise Dutton, 1988.
Random House Book of Fairy Tales
adapted by Amy Ehrlich. Random,
  1985.
Watch the Stars Come Out by Riki
  Levinson. Random, 1985.
When I Was Young in the Mountains
  by Cynthia Rylant. Dutton, 1982.
Where's Our Mama? Dutton, 1991.

---

*Diane Goode has just moved into the large, new but Victorian-style house.
She and her husband are still learning how to use all the buttons and switches
while worrying about the upkeep of the pale carpeting. They are only about an
hour from New York, but there is a small-town atmosphere to the nearby village,
and the house itself is set back among tall pine trees with a deer actually grazing
undisturbed on the lawn. Despite the recent move, the pictures are already on
the walls, the kitchen is complete with all utensils already involved in cooking,
and the studio is obviously being used to work on the newest book. Self-framed
and matted pictures cover the freshly painted walls: pages from old books on
birds, fine 16th century German engravings of social commentary, especially on
the handicapped.*

When you were a child, were you always drawing?

Yes, all the time. I was also sewing clothes for my dolls. I even taught
myself how to knit by close observation of the details while watching.

I always loved fairy tales. I had never had picturebooks. My mother had
an anthology she read to us. The pictures were all in my head. We were also

Self-portrait by Diane Goode

never allowed to watch TV in our house. My father was a great reader. In Italy my great-uncle presented me with two modern Italian picturebooks, but picturebooks weren't that big. Neither were toys. We had blocks.

Was your art encouraged at school?

Yes. They told me I was very good at it.

How about your family?

My mother painted, but she didn't consider herself to be a serious artist. I don't think there was any conscious effort to push me in that direction. But they took me traveling a lot. I was in Europe first when I was an infant. My mother is French, and would take me back with her to visit the family. Then my father would join us and we would "do" the museum and visit his family in Italy. So I had very early exposure.

Did you pick up your French there?

My mother always spoke French at home. My father did too. She would talk in French and we would respond in English.

When it was time to choose a college, how did you decide?

I wasn't thinking in advance about what I would be doing later. I just went to Queens College. I started out as an art history major. After a year or two I switched to the studio. They had a fabulous department. Evidently the college at that time had a lot of money, and attracted the best. In my last year I went to France, but I wondered, "What am I doing here?" We were so far ahead of them. I would be working in a studio there and the teacher would come up and say, "Could you show us what you are doing?" So I came back. I also had to think about what I was going to do to make a living after I graduated. So I stayed an extra year and earned a teaching degree, to teach art.

While I was at Queens, I studied with a color theorist, Herb Aach, who really turned me around. He had an intellectual approach to using color for problem solving. Before that I had only used brown tones. Also I had been taking all kinds of studio courses, and didn't know which way to go. He told me to choose one thing, it doesn't matter which, and concentrate on that. Another teacher of mine was *Rain Makes Applesauce* illustrator Marvin Belick. Because he was doing books I got the idea that this was a possibility. We bound our own books by hand, used a hand press. So when I graduated (1972), and they asked me what I was going to do, I thought I would teach. But someone said, "Why not go into publishing?" So while I was student teaching I took seriously what was probably just a flip remark, and I went to the publishing houses. They told me what to put in a portfolio. I took various drawings and prints, not particularly children's pictures. But then we moved to California, and my teaching license was not valid. So I flew to New York with my portfolio, going from publisher to publisher. Within a couple of months, I received my first manuscript from Bradbury Press. But I had no idea what I was doing, or what I was getting myself into.

From the beginning did you always do your illustrations on parchment?

Yes. I had learned how to work on parchment from Marvin Belick, who had used it for *Rain Makes Applesauce*. He introduced us to all kinds of papers. What attracted me to parchment was that he had shown us how easy it was to correct mistakes on it, by removing parts with a razor. But it is a terrible surface to work on. Once you learn how to work on it, it has this advantage, however. On normal paper you can't take anything out.

I came up with the brush technique because the book required color separations on acetate. I had no idea how I was going to apply the black color on this glossy surface. So I took the brush with China ink instead of pencil. I had never used a brush for line before. But after doing a whole book, I knew how to handle the brush. And the acetate is very similar to the parchment in its glossiness. It felt right. I could sculpt the line. I could do a lot of things I liked. If I had a different style, I couldn't use this paper. But I like it. They better not stop making it!

How do you feel about illustration and its relation to "real art"?

Illustration traditionally has had a very low position in the art world. I love illustrating. There has been a put-down of picturebook art as children's art, for women teachers and librarians. When very slick, sophisticated glossy books came out for a while, I felt their appeal was to adults rather than children. But personally I have chosen to do just book illustration, and I am "booked" years in advance.

How do you feel about the role of the authors you illustrate?

Before my father died, he used to count the words in the books I illustrated. He would say, "Eighty words. Why can't you do that?" The first book that I wrote myself, *I Hear a Noise*, was written to make him happy. He was dying of cancer, so though I'm not a writer, I decided to try. Ann Durell had been pushing me. After she came for lunch one day, I took out a pencil and drew this chicken dragon character. And the character dictated what the story would be. It took me an hour and a half to work the story out in a dummy. I sent it off, asking if I should throw it away. She said it was a book. When you illustrate somebody else's work, she reminded me, you are using that as a framework and telling the story visually, adding to it and enhancing it with characters added. My father was so pleased. It seems to me I keep getting sent the same kind of story. I've done *When I Was Young in the Mountains* once; I don't want to do it again.

Why did you use a toned paper to make the border in Watch the Stars Come Out, *and not in* Grandmother's House, *which is so similar?*

That was the designer's decision. Unless I specifically hand-do the color, I don't have control over that. Sometimes there's a committee that wants this or that. Even though I have a contract that says I have the last word, what does that mean? They are not going to redo the whole thing!

They tell me at Random House and Dutton that I can do what I want, pick stories, etc. And the book is generally the way I want it to look. But I don't go in and insist on a certain kind of paper, for example, because I know that the dollar is the bottom line. They have to make a profit. I don't make my books to cost so much that they are inaccessible, even if it would make my work look better.

Are you generally satisfied with the way your books are reproduced?

The color of some, like *Watch the Stars*, is spectacular. It's done in Hong Kong. They do a good job. Doing my own endpapers costs more. That is established ahead of time, and since they are choosing the cloth and color, they select the color of the endpapers to go with that. I've done my best, and then I have to trust them; there has to be an element of trust for people to work together.

I Was Young in the Mountains was a dead book; it didn't sell at all until it won the Caldecott. That's why the awards are so important.

Why is the style of the Little Library *different from other things you have done?*

It's done to scale, very small. For the mass market there was a lot of pressure, and not a lot of time.

When you collaborate with an author, are you free to choose what you want to illustrate?

You get the manuscript and you break it down. For *Tattercoats* I also chose to do the borders by hand.

You like borders. Why do you break them sometimes?

I break them because they contain what is going on and sometimes I want to go beyond that. I play with them. I like the border as a way of holding in and to create a more formal look. But sometimes you're too held in the frame.

What sort of research do you do?

It varies. For the *Random House Book of Fairy Tales* it was all out of my head. I had very little time to do it. For *The Good Hearted Youngest Brother* I went to the library stacks for books in Hungarian, with old photos, folk motifs, clothing, designs.

In that book, you have a gun breaking out of the frame.

I debated using a gun, even an ornamental one. I work very hard on my composition. Over the years I've concentrated more and more on that. I used to do a line drawing and work from that, developing as I went, without pre-thinking it out. But now I do. I sketch and sketch, and cut them out to recompose them. The last few years I have done an enormous amount of preliminary work.

The figures in The Good Hearted Youngest Brother *seem stiffer.*

When you are drawing a happy person, you tend to smile when you are doing it. But for various reasons, things were not progressing well with the book. Also in that book and *Tattercoats* my figures are very elongated. That's the way I used to draw. Then I decided to work on my characters more, and I shortened them.

You developed a softer style; your figures resemble cloth dolls, they have a tactile, comfortable quality.

People have compared them to dolls. I think that after I had my son, I had a different way of looking at children. In *Young in the Mountains* there are figures embracing children. That was my feeling looking at my son, those feelings I had as a new mother that I had never had before. Maybe that was an unconscious change in the way I looked at things.

Did you visit the mountain area where the story takes place?

I was living in Wilkes-Barre, PA, the old coal-mining town. I was working in a big house on the river, in an attic studio from which I could see the mountains I was drawing.

You have illustrated a series of classics. Did you read Peter Pan *or* Pinocchio *as a child?*

Yes, but I saw them differently then. When my son Peter was small, I saw the story of *Peter Pan* as a mother's anxiety about what happens when she's not attending to her children.

I didn't think of doing these myself; they were suggested to me. I loved the stories as a child, but when you take on the giants you are very inhibited by what came before you. You try not to look at them.

When you did Watch the Stars Come Out *that was very different?*

I had never done anything like it before. My publishers went to the archives and museums to get me photos. I had a stack of material to work from. I used the red hair so the children would stand out in a crowd, but it turned out that Riki (Levinson) had red hair as a child.

Do you have any specific models for any of the people in the story?

No. I don't use models for the physical look. I draw on feelings that I had for my family when I was a child. For *Grandma's House*, my grandparents and several generations lived in the same small place. Everyone came from everywhere on Sunday to Grandma and Grandpa's. The feelings are those we had for one another being all together there. There was a little garden in the back and we used to fight over who was going to water the tomatoes.

Who had the idea to color-coordinate the families?

I did. I had to keep a list, so I could tell who belonged to what family, and make sure I didn't lose a baby somewhere. I did it so you could remember who was in which family. I didn't have as much time to do that book, so it isn't as fully developed as I would have liked.

For your black and white pictures in the Random House Book of Fairy Tales *you still used the vellum?*

Yes, but I used a pencil. I never use a black outline. I can't get the soft feeling.

What can you tell us about the art in Dream-Eater?

It's one continuous scroll if you take it apart back to back. See how the characters are awkward; I hadn't developed my characters yet. From my research I discovered that the Japanese don't believe dreams come from the brain, but from the stomach. So there they are, like indigestion.

What did you think about the paperback edition? It was reduced from the hard back and chopped.

How can they do that! Sometimes it is upsetting to see this. It looks like muck. They don't go back to the original; I don't know what they print from.

Perhaps I'm not paying enough attention to the finished book. For me the most important part is the process of doing it; that's what I'm interested in. Once I'm finished, I don't even remember the book. I'm already doing something else. I was upset when I saw my first book and it didn't look like my originals. It was explained to me that it wasn't going to. "You work in paint, they work in ink. There's no way that ink is going to look like paint." So I started to change my thinking as to how the finished product is going to look. It may not be exactly like my originals look, but it looks good.

I learned from sad experience how the gutter works. I learned to leave a little extra space. I had to redo a book because they do a different kind of binding in England. It changes the whole composition.

Are you always working ahead?

Yes. I'm doing a Christmas book, a companion to *American Folk Tales* called *American Christmas*. At this point I hate the illustrations. I wish I could do the whole thing over. After spending so much time on a work, you almost get to hate it and never want to see it again. I decided to try painting on regular paper, because it goes so much faster. I liked the way it looked. But when I tried it on something big, it didn't work. But the stories are good, old and new, and there are songs and poems.

For Random House I am doing Noel Streatfield's *Ballet Shoes,* in black and white, as a gift book.

It took me a long time to learn that you have to be very careful of the projects that you choose. I took *When I Was Young in the Mountains* because I had been reading Walker Evans and James Agee's *Let Us Now Praise Famous Men* and I loved that, and thought the Rylant story was beautiful. Because it was so esoteric I didn't think there would be a wide audience at that time.

Watch the Stars Come Out was a hundred times more difficult, the research, the composition, telling it in the pictures. I had a very strong personal feeling about the book. I had to do it.

How do you feel about the usual practice of not having the author and illustrator meet?

I think they may be right, because the author has a vision of what the story should look like, and it may not be our vision. Cynthia Rylant and I never met. It may sound weird, but I feel that when I get that manuscript, that it is mine, that it is my story.

When the author was also my art director (Levinson) somehow she managed not to be the writer any more. She even offered to change if I needed it.

How do you feel about reviews?

One review of my first book called my characters idiosyncratic. Well, they were right. That was my first book, and I'd never known how to illustrate a book; I was just learning. I just did it. I knew at that point that I had to change the way I drew characters who were children. Maybe they are still sort of idiosyncratic . . . they kind of look like me, and what does that mean?

Were you involved with color separations?

My first book was my only one. Some people like it. But I hate that mess. It started out as a three-color separation, but then they said, "This is so good, let's do four." I thought the color was hideous.

I find it interesting that in reproduction the camera may lose some of the texture, but it sometimes picks up what you don't see, things that the eye compensates for.

Do you go out to talk to groups of kids?

I used to but I really don't have the time now. I find it very hard to explain the process to very young children. They think I make each individual book. And I draw so slowly and so small that I can't really draw for them and be entertaining. I like to talk to people in the field.

Then how do you determine how a child will perceive your work?

I think you always have to look for the childlike feelings within yourself. Having children and being around kids helps you to see this as well. I often read to children and talk to them about books.

Do you have a particular child in mind when you do your pictures? Are they different because you have a child of your own?

I know they are different. I am very conscious of the fact that a child is going to look at them, and how they are going to see them. I know my son loved slapstick humor. And I noticed, for example, that kids are interested in other kids, and the details about them. You have to separate yourself from your own personal taste. To be an illustrator you have to let go of what you want to do, to express what the manuscript is telling you and do it to please the child rather than to show what a great artist you are.

I think humor is very important. I do elegant things sometimes too. But I really feel that I am a slave to the manuscript. You can only go beyond that to a certain degree. If there's a lot of text and the parent is going to be reading for a long time, I have to put enough in the illustration to keep the child occupied. What I try to do is get the basic visual image. Then if you have time you can explore for other things. But there has to be one immediate image. The same way you time the text of the story from page to page, you have to time it visually too.

It is like doing a film; you're composing visually what has to happen. You have the characters, the costumes, the sets, the look . . . .

How do you do the costumes for the period pieces like Cinderella?

I look at a lot of pictures. For *Cinderella* I love the palace of Versailles, so I used the staircase and some costumes I had seen in the museum and a combination of a lot of things, photos, drawings . . . I love elaborate costumes.

How do you lay it out? Do you storyboard?

I do a dummy. But the dummy is very crude. It just lays out visually how I want it to look. The sequencing is internal. It's very hard for me to plan. If you plan too much, there's nothing left to do, no spontaneity.

—*October 1990*

Fifteen

Shirley Hughes

A Sampling of Works in Print

Alfie Gets in First Lothrop, 1982.
Alfie Gives a Hand Lothrop/Morrow, 1984, 1986.
Alfie's Feet Lothrop/Morrow, 1983, 1988.
Angel Mae: A Tale of Trotter St. Lothrop, 1989.
Another Helping of Chips Lothrop, 1987.
Bathwater's Hot Lothrop, 1985.
Big Alfie and Annie Rose Story Book Lothrop, 1989.

The Big Concrete Lorry: A Tale of Trotter St. Lothrop, 1990.
Dogger Lothrop, 1988.
An Evening at Alfie's Lothrop, 1985.
Moving Molly Lothrop, 1988.
Noisy Lothrop, 1985.
Out and About Lothrop, 1988.
The Snow Lady: A Tale of Trotter Street Lothrop, 1990.
Wheels: A Tale of Trotter Street Lothrop, 1991.

In a neighborhood of large, well-aged houses on the opposite side of the green heath from John Burningham and Helen Oxenbury, Shirley Hughes and her retired architect husband live a busy London life, with time off for sketching trips to the Continent. The furnishings have a somewhat crowded, just shy of disarranged, lived-in look. The art on the walls is an eclectic assortment, but each piece is worth a second look for the obvious care in the choice. On the next floor Hughes's studio, looking out over the garden, is full of work in progress along with reproductions of fine art. Late afternoon is time for tea, the necessary social pause before the work later. The tea-time talk included the two couples and an architect colleague, and it ranged from Ted Turner's colorization of old films to British politics and the new look of the Victoria and Albert Museum. Although we had just met, we felt part of a friendly circle of folks with common values.

Self-portrait by Shirley Hughes

What books do you remember from your childhood?

We didn't have many American books as children, but we did have one or two French. I saw comics. In fact the very first impact was very old comics, which came somehow in the aftermath of the American GIs, I think. We lived near Liverpool, where there were a lot of GIs. I thought the American comics were eye-opening, fascinating: L'il Abner, Nemo, Mutt and Jeff. I don't know where we got them. English comics weren't like that. These were very New World and exotic. For a child the war was very dull. You couldn't go anywhere. The only excitement was the cinema. The comic books were American, and America represented that wonderful exciting place that you saw in the movies. And I liked the line, the way it was drawn.

Did you try to emulate them?

Oh yes. You try to emulate everything as a child. I drew and drew. But I don't think I ever copied them.

Did you make your own comics?

We wrote our own stories and illustrated them; we did endless magazines.

Paper was scarce than, so you had trouble finding any?

Yes, but we managed. There really wasn't anything else to do. That's what it was about: make your own things, your own plays for any luckless person who was about. We had a lot of books that were my mother's books from way back. We had a lot of Victorian books as well, that were left over with gravure illustrations. We also had the classic books: Rackham, Heath Robinson, who is my absolute favorite I think — all those marvelous books with the black and white illustrations in the letter-press, and then you got to the wonderful tipped-in color plate. Dulac, Nielson, all those, sometimes a bit doggy and old, but we had them. We didn't have Crane or Greenaway; but there were a tremendous number of black and white artists at that time, unsung now, but brilliant artists who could really draw. And sometimes we got the color plates. Then we had the annuals. At that time our comics were less sophisticated than the American ones, and we had strips in the newspaper that were really for children, not adults. At Christmastime they would make these into a book, and you would have the thrill of getting these characters appearing in annual form with some color plates, with stories. You got strip cartoons and stories mixed in. I learned to read by knowing the strip characters and looking at the little stories that were interposed in the annual, usually on very big, sort of soft poor paper, set generously, with big type. I can't say it was great literature, but it was nice. You knew the characters, you felt reassured. You weren't worried trying to figure out who were these characters in this story.

Picturebooks didn't really exist at that time. We didn't have the experience that your grandson had with Alfie; he knew who he was and where he lived having "read" the book, because it's all in the pictures. I think if you start reading and you haven't got that. . . . It's easy to underrate how hard it is for a child to sort it out: who is this person?

Your two sons and daughter are grown. Do you draw the children in your books from memory, other children you sketch?

I didn't draw my own children very much, and none of the children in my books are my children. Neither are they anybody else's children. In other words I don't use models. They are always out of my head. But having said that, I suppose the stories are inspired by real children, by a mixture of my own and other children; by making very close observation from life. I do draw children a lot, and always have but I don't put those drawings into the books. When you come to imagine a child, you are drawing on a memory bank, which is what sketchbooks are. If you've an eye for movement and an eye for a gesture, that develops from drawing from life. And that is the mark from which your imaginative drawing grows. But I don't think you can actually draw from models when you're doing a children's book because it isn't just a question of anatomical accuracy and reality. They are sort of actors on a stage and you are producing the play, showing the drama. So you do sometimes fudge it all up. You couldn't just set up models and say, "Hold that pose, I'll put you into my book." Have you met any illustrators who say they do that? For a detail? Yes, you might use your own hand for that. But if you look at people all the time you do remember it. I also have a huge collection of references cut out of newspapers. I can't remember what cars look like or bicycles; objects don't interest me as much as people, so I have to have help to remember. My latest book is about a concrete lorry [truck]. My husband went to get references for me. Of course it's not about the concrete lorry, even if it's called *The Big Concrete Lorry;* it's about a family. But

I couldn't possibly have drawn this lorry otherwise. The family is squashed, and Dad is building an extension himself. There's a terrible moment when the big concrete lorry arrives. I also have a grandson who would be terribly cross if he didn't see this lorry looking accurate. That of course comes from many, many photographs and observations of the real vehicle. I couldn't do that from memory. This is really a book about neighborly solidarity. We call these people "cowboys," builders who work on their own and are a bit dodgy. They slurp the cement on the pavement, and it's quick-setting. It has to be moved very fast through the house, because it's a row house with no space between. What's left at the end is a wonderful rock-hard thing, and the children like it better than anything else.

How do you convey the sense of movement in your books?

You do pace a book. Doing a picturebook is more like shooting a film than writing a book and then illustrating it.

Do you storyboard it?

No, I make a rough. [Showing original art work for the *Alfie* and *Annie Rose Story Book*.] This is what it looks like when I show it to my editor. It's fairly well thought out. Every bit of it is written by this time. Then I just draw very very quickly with a felt pen. Then this is really one of the tests of professionalism. When you're drawing like this you're very unselfcon-scious, you're very free, you're very excited about your characters. You draw very fast and you don't have to worry about decisions on color or tone. Getting this vitality into the finished work is one of the great tests, because you have all sorts of other things to worry about when you're doing the art. I just deploy it like that, I make the jigsaw puzzle with the shape. You ac-tually decide you're going to have the running band or whatever. Then I draw around the shapes the story makes. I wanted it to be a proper story-book. I may change the odd word, but it's pretty much there.

Were you always able to do the book out of your head like that?

No, but I'm a pretty old hand at this now.

When Grandma is telling the story, we got the marvelous idea of hav-ing a photograph album, which is wonderful for children to look back to what Granny looked like when she got married. But of course in the finished spread I suddenly realized that this was a book and I'd made the gutter and got Granny's hands and Alfie's hand pointing at himself. But when you're holding it and your real hand is there, there is another pair of hands in the picture. You can do all sorts of things which perhaps don't occur to you until you're doing the finished art work. So you add to what you've done. Often it's suggested by the color. I decided that as we were talking about the past I'd drain all of the color out of it there and go into sepia, which is an old filming trick. . . . But Will as he now is, a middle-aged gent, is back in full color. So you do all kinds of things. But the expression, the feel of the child and the way the child is moving is all in the dummy for me.

Have you ever felt the first black and white drawings could stand on their own and color isn't needed?

That would be nice, but you know we're stuck with the fact that color is what people expect, they see color television. But I'm very committed to black and white. I was trained as a black and white illustrator. I'm so old I was trained for hot metal. That means every line you draw is incised into the metal, so all the tones have to be done with lines. I feel that in a way I'm rather under-used. Apart from *The Secret Garden*, which I did last year and loved doing, I don't get much of a chance to do either black and white drawings or interpretive illustration of other people's texts, which I was also trained to do. I'd love to have a go at some more classics.

Ardizzone drawings are inspiring. He was a friend. Also early pencil drawings by Shepherd. All of those chaps who worked for *Punch* were brilliant black and white artists. I fear that now as we approach this enormous industry we are no longer the quiet backwater we used to be. I love doing these, black and white or color; it's my joy. It doesn't worry me that it has to be in color; it's an attractive idea. Were there the time, I would like to do more black and white. But I think the pressure on the young people now is enormous to produce the sort of winning picturebook preferably set somewhere in the mid–Atlantic that will sell everywhere, to deliver books that will sell abroad. They all have to now; they don't see the light of day if we don't sell them abroad. There's no such thing as a book that would be published for an English market now. When you think that as short a time ago as Ardizzone or Shepherd it was the English child they were addressing.... We got into the international market back in the '60s, when there was that great explosion of picturebooks. Now it's exploding again because it's going to be books in supermarkets, all over the place. I don't know if they'll get cheaper; they may. For the new generation, I think there will always be good artists who survive and do their own thing. It's amazing now how they are maximizing on their backlists. They are looking at old stories, reviving stuff....

I think when people say a certain picturebook is not a child's book, I don't think that matters. I think it's an enormous range we're talking about. There is such a thing as a picturebook for adults, and that's fine with me; but there are some books that are completely child-centered, and some of the best people do everything, like Ardizzone. He could illustrate a wide variety of texts, and yet he had this wonderful style, like a suit of old clothes he was so at home in; it suited him, it was totally recognizable and totally his own, and yet it was immensely adaptable. In a film recently Maurice Sendak said about him, "He is such a modest illustrator." There is no pretentiousness; there is sheer skill, and yet the simplicity and accessibility is what you see, and what the child sees too. The child is not going to be stunned by your brilliant color technique. He had this without you necessarily being aware of it. It has all those levels. Those are the best people in any field, who succeed universally, on every level. But that modesty is something I think you have to have when you're working with children.

We have this immense responsibility, I think, because we are working for a generation of children who have been, in a sense, visually overstimulated in a way that is unique to this century. They see vast amounts; their visual circuits are heated up from a very early age. To slow them down, to get them to look at a still picture, is terribly important. It's more important than it ever was, because at least in England I think we are esthetically a very backward society. We aren't taught to look. It's not a thing you are taught in school. The only time we get it is in this picturebook experience. When you walk into a school you can find enthusiasts who are having this vital experience with the children, getting them to look. You get very young children who can readily recognize very sophisticated styles. They may not know the name . . . I go into schools, where sometimes an older one will be lurking about looking bored while the little ones are having books signed. They'll suddenly recognize a black and white drawing and say, "I remember that. I read a book like that." He remembered my drawing style. It's wonderful when they do that; it's a very sophisticated idea. I don't mean that in an artificial sense; it's something he has learned to do through books. He won't learn it from anything else. Learning to look at a picture and make your own visual explorations is crucial. When I'm sitting here drawing I don't think I'm doing something very important here; I'm absorbed, I'm enjoying myself. But sometimes I'm brought up short by the importance of the pictures they do see when they're little, because the skill of looking is something that has to be brought on in people. You don't pass examinations with it. You might go all through school and nobody could ever find out you have a perfect visual memory. They'll know about your other memories, your verbal expertise, your numeracy. . . . But visual memory is not in our academic system: "If you've got two eyes, you can see, so what?" You may be going around half blind but nobody will notice. Many highly educated adults whose esthetic responses are very poor cover it up, but they don't know very much about looking.

It's a field I'm being drawn into because I talk to teachers a lot in teacher training colleges and library schools.

I think that the art work that children do is important. But I go into schools where that's the only thing that's hanging on the walls, that's all they ever see. For the children, the doing is what's important, not looking at their own efforts. When we were in school, reproductions of Victorian paintings and the old masters adorned the walls. Then when we went into the National Gallery and saw a picture that was totally familiar from childhood, it was marvelous to say, "There it is!" They don't introduce art to children in a way that is relevant to them, such as showing them a lot of faces, self-portraits from different ages. . . . Art is packed with mythical beasts, for example, but I never see them on the walls of schools to help them draw their own from their heads. It's a kind of mulch to draw upon.

Narrative content is what switches children on to looking at art. . . . When I was a child, the galleries in Liverpool were full of Victorian paintings packed with narrative content. I adored it. When I started introducing my own children to paintings, we started with the pre–Raphaelites of course. It's odd that we have divorced looking and narrative and art.

I think that learning to draw underpins whatever you do afterwards. . . .

I got into art schools to teach illustration students. There it's the other way. There's a reliance on photography; they get all their data from photographs to do their illustrations. They do a certain amount of drawing from life, but you have to be able to dramatize from photos. I had a very traditional academic training and I'm very glad I did. One has to know where the joints are. But that's not it. As an illustrator you have to take all that into your head and then start drawing out of your head.

I think there's a return to figurative art in England, and in the Glasgow school of young painters. I couldn't believe my eyes; it's staggering work. They've gone right back. In Scotland they never did dismantle their life classes so they have a very strong base. In illustration it's a question of them just bringing a pencil and a piece of paper, and saying now draw out of your head. But they can't if they haven't a reference photograph; they can't remember. They don't have the connection between the fact that drawing is me drawing you sitting there from life and also me drawing a lady sitting in a chair or something more complicated like pushing a pram; they can't remember what they look like although they've seen it hundreds of times. This is what the Victorians and the Edwardians right up to the magazine illustrators of the '30s and '40s could do so well. They were all trained to do that.

Photography is a wonderful aid, but it's not a crutch.

Is there a difference in British illustration?

One of the two talks I give (the first is about my work, for children, teachers and librarians) is about the history of illustration, and the influence on us. I think there is an English line. It gets thrown out in these different forms. And it does feed back to Gilray and Rowlandson, and a long way before. In the children's book field it is a very direct line that comes out in young English artists like Charlotte Voake and Patrick Benson. It's in the British tradition, and you can see it coming out in them although they all draw in a very different way, just as their handwriting is different. It's very difficult to pinpoint what it is. And one wouldn't want to, because it's awful to feel self-conscious when you're drawing. In writing too, I think there's a British quality.

Is there a narrative versus decorative tradition?

We of course also had our great "clear-out" in the '60s when you were a laughingstock as a student if you went to the life drawing room. I have a feeling that there never was a time when the technique of doing things was as good as in the Victorian tradition. The sheer skill in all the applied arts was phenomenal. Perhaps in a way this became such a heavy burden that we had to cast it off. A lot of narrative painting had become mawkish and oversentimental. We probably needed to clear it out a bit. But it would be nice if we could go back to using all the best of that tradition in a fresher, newer way. I see signs of this happening. It's a good time. We have some good filmmakers. The narrative is coming back, in painting too.

Unfortunately the teachers are fighting this, being defensive; they can't deliver, because they weren't trained that way. But the kids will prevail, they always do. They can see a lot around.

I think the problem is there's going to be a lot of books, but there aren't going to be enough really good stories. We'll get more and more ephemera, and more and more dross.

Writing a picturebook text is sort of like a sonnet; it has to fit into the form, it has to be 32 pages with endpapers. That's the commercial stricture, which is actually good in a way, because you have to really discipline and hone yourself into that shape. . . . That's fine with me. I find it interesting; I wouldn't want to have all the pages I wanted. But fitting it in and getting it absolutely right, getting a text that reads well aloud and can be read more than once. . . .

Your balance between text and pictures. . . .

Very often you find you're saying something you didn't need to say because you're going to draw it in the pictures. Of course all the characterization, the details of the place you're in showing the story is all there to be discovered in the pictures, with an accent on *discover.* You want to look more than once to see exactly what's happening. You are actually trying to make people look, not just skim. I was very tentative about writing, because I was trained as an illustrator. But I did have a very good start, because I did read masses of books that I had to illustrate. I read an enormous number of chlidren's books very carefully because I was going to illustrate them. I learned a lot from that, how the good ones were constructed. And of course when you have children of your own you read them until they are coming out of your ears. . . . You get to know where the slack is; you cut and cut ruthlessly. Writing a good text takes ages; it really does.

How long do you work on a book?

It takes three to six months on the drawing table while the actual story takes less time. But it is in my case an iceberg that has been around a very long time, largely submerged. I do think it's rather like producing a play. A picturebook is a proscenium arch in a way. It's lit, and with all the gestures, the drama, the grouping, the way people run through, it's a mixture of film and theater.

Why are there two versions of Up and Up *with different cover and background color?*

Things went a bit wrong with the Prentice-Hall edition. The Lothrop edition is the right one. They have also republished *Dogger*, my very best seller on this side of the Atlantic. It's gone to China and everywhere. It was rechristened for some reason *David and the Dog* but it is now *Dogger* again.

A very cinematic book?

I'd like to think so. It is very filmic. I like the whole idea of shifting your viewpoint. The whole of *Up and Up* is very like the '50s movies, where you fly in over a town, go to a window and look in, and there they all are doing whatever they are going to do.

In the Alfie book when Alfie slams the door, solving these problems is always filmic. I wanted to show him inside and them outside struggling to get him out. You could tell that story, but to put it into pictures you could show it like a doll house with the front off; but then the people on the front steps have their backs to you and you need to see their faces. In the end it was like a split screen. All the kids understand that. They've all seen that in old films on television. You can explain the idea of the gutter, the sewing, the actual form of the book that you're always trying to pretend isn't there. I suddenly realized that I could make the form of the book tell the story. All I had to do is draw a line, and that was the door. I could make my beholder see the door even though it wasn't there. It's one of the oldest silent movie tricks in the book.

In the *Lorry* book I have them tearing through the gutter with the fresh cement. I didn't have to draw the house they are rushing through at all. There are a lot of things that you can solve in cinematic (cinemagraphic?) ways. Obvious things like close-ups, long shots, view from above, varying your eye level. . . .

For Another Helping of Chips *were you told to make it multiracial and non-sexist for American audience?*

The higher you go in age level the more you get the pressure to be that way, even in England, as soon as school is a factor. School is a bit different here. I thought they would change a lot of the words for the Americans. But there was no pressure to change anything in those books.

It was all your idea?

Absolutely. It's in all the books. It's a pressure one would put on oneself anyway. Because when you go into schools and talk to classes, there they all are. And it's important that they see themselves in the books. As a writer I think it's possible to inhabit anybody, male, female, anything, if you have an imaginative range. But I would find it hard to write a book about a West Indian family in London because I haven't lived it. I don't actually live in that flat with those people, although they live here and there near me. But I haven't lived it, and it's really the details that floor me. For instance a family from Bangladesh will live very differently at home from a family from Pakistan. I think when you come to write a book you need to know everything. For a children's picturebook you have to know instinctively what kind of a set-up it is. I don't feel confident enough yet to write as a person from Bangladesh, even London-born. But I need them in, because they are there.

They are not in suburban U.S.

Actually not in some suburban areas here either. But the children are in school, and one reflects what one sees. If it looks artificial, it feels artificial and it's wrong. But if you don't, it's also wrong. So it can be very difficult. You can't propagandize in a story; propaganda is always boring (for example, Daddy in apron while Mom does brain surgery).

In those books (*Chips*) I was trying to explode the page. They were for older children, and I was trying to make a book that was not a strip cartoon, and not a story in a pattern, but that lapsed in and out. I wrote it much longer, and I wrote all the conversation the way we would write it, with inverted commas. Then I realized that if you put the conversations into speech balloons, you got a whole new graphic thing on the page, with two people shouting at each across it. I wanted to mix it up; I'm not through with this yet. I really want to make the page do all sorts of things. I don't want to put in flaps. I don't want it to be three-dimensional, or jump out at you, or smell, or feel. But we're not through with the form yet. It's a fantastic form. A book is amazing. And just by doing things like that, by realizing that you don't have to have conversation like that. Or the idea of a domestic animal commenting on the vagaries of human behavior in a thought balloon is actually very ordinary in a comic. But if you're writing it as a writer, you've got another sort of novel. In this country you can do it graphically without any strain at all. You can also have your hero, Chips, step directly down to the footlights, like Hamlet, and comment on the action to the audience, which is also not that easy to do in a novel. All kinds of things are possible. I think we should really be addressing the older age group in ways that are thought to be common to picturebooks. We should be breaking up novels in this way. We could do all sorts of things if we were allowed to. There ought to be a very close relationship between author and artist. It's just beginning to happen (Walker is like an atelier). Publishers are word people. They have very skilled people who do the design and graphics. But the idea that an artist and a writer could get together and make a book for older kids by actually drawing and writing together throws everybody. You write the words and then you get an illustrator to draw the pictures. For the picturebook, you're doing these jig-saws of word and image anyhow. . . .

The Chips *books are untraditional. How successful have they been?*

In America I suspect they don't know quite what to do with them. Is there a wariness about the idea of strip-cartoons; that they are down-market trashy stuff? In England there has been a colossal response from the academics, the people who teach teachers. And *Up and Up*. They are using it for projects with reluctant readers, getting kids to write about them. In the shops, for black and white they are doing well enough. But the real sellers are the full-color picturebooks. People like to go out and buy a nice color picturebook for a present for children or grandchildren. *Chips and Jessie* has been bought widely by libraries, and is in paperback. But I sort of wonder whether if one were to kick over all the traces and start doing more of this, people would feel rather uneasy about it. It might take years. . . .

With your own calligraphy?

I'd love to.

Paperbacks don't do your books justice?

Walker's do. He uses the same paper, the child's experience is virtually the same. We agreed to change the cover slightly to differentiate it. He doesn't crop, he doesn't reduce. He can afford to by enormous selling and co-publishing.

They're never exactly the same, but I'm satisfied. There's none of that where everyone is either looking jaundiced or has bright red faces . . . a pretty good rendering. They make it easy for you. If you say you want to do a book of 64 pages, full color, they say "Right." He's the boss and can make these decisions. Their fine designers mix word and image at a very early stage in the editorial process. He came in at the right time with the baby books.

For your Secret Garden, *how did you choose the scenes?*

Almost every paragraph has a wonderful picture. The problem is to decide which one. I wanted the story to be accessible to as many children as possible, to have a drawing on nearly every page, an enormous number of drawings. To keep the price down and still have color in every section, rather than all together, I took upon myself the challenge, because I can't stand it when the color plate says "See page 146," of doing a color plate for that page of the story. If you can have the color plates wrapped around each section, it saves a lot of money. I fiddled around until I got most of the color plates where I wanted them to be. That's the kind of challenge I like.

Is this a story you remember from childhood?

Oh yes. As a child I had the Charles Robinson edition. I accepted them absolutely as a child. They are extraordinarily art nouveau-ish. And my daughter read another one. They do have immense atmosphere. But when I came to look at it again . . . it's not a baroque mansion, it's an old gray stone Tudor house in Yorkshire with a really tough landscape. She was an admirer of the Brontes. I wanted mine to be firmly set in Yorkshire, with the wind whistling through every page. I wanted a Tudor paneled house, not a baroque Georgian mansion. I have gone for the Briar Rose theme, because in a way it's a Sleeping Beauty story, about two children who don't know how to love and respect other people because they haven't been taught how. They've been indulged, but they've never been loved. I wanted the tangle of briars to make this analogy with the theme. I would love to be doing the Cinderella story, which is *The Little Princess*. I would like to do the two with the two themes. She's a marvelous writer. She is in a way the beginning of the modern children's novelist. They're not good little children, they're very real.

I'd love to do *The Railway Children*. The film has refreshed memories. Nesbit is another very tough writer. Many ideas are on the loose at the moment. I have another Alfie book up my sleeve, and there are going to be four of the Trotter Street books.

What do you think is the role of endpapers in the totality of a book?

The question is what are you going to get? Sometimes you get color, sometimes you get two colors. (*Secret Garden* mystical, slightly mysterious.) I love them. You feel very free with them, because the jacket is an advertisement; it has to sell the book, it has to make people want to pick it up in a shop. It also has to have a lot of lettering on it. But with the endpaper you can really let go. It's a whole empty spot. And it's also a preliminary, the overture. You don't want it to do anything too specific, just generalize in a rather nice sort of way. You feel very free to mess about with it. For a young child, they like to see something related to the story to introduce your characters; they're all on stage to set the tone, to respond to the story.

What is your option on the endpapers?

You are told the number of pages and the endpapers come out of that. You've lost pages, but they're worth having. You just have to fit the rest of your story in. You get 64 pages if they are sure they are going to sell a lot, like the *Alfie Story Book*.

I'd like to do a picturebook for adults. I've got one going. But people won't know what to do with it, will they?

Children take such obvious enjoyment from your books. . . .

For years publishers have said that no American child could understand my books. "Very nice, but we can't buy these for American children. . . ." Of course there are fortunately other publishers, like Dorothy Briley, at Lothrop. She took them and we never looked back. She thought the story was the thing, that once you had a story that people could identify with, there is some interest in seeing things like a red letter-box, for instance. I always knew Babar was a French elephant.

—*Summer 1989*

Sixteen

Pat Hutchins

A Sampling of Works in Print

Don't Forget the Bacon Morrow, 1989.
The Doorbell Rang Greenwillow, 1986, 1989.
Follow That Bus! Knopf, 1988.
Good-Night Owl Macmillan, 1972, 1990.
Happy Birthday, Sam Greenwillow/ Penguin, 1978, 1985.
One Hunter Greenwillow, 1982.
Rosie's Walk Macmillan, 1968, 1971.
Tidy Titch Greenwillow, 1991.
Titch Macmillan, 1971.

The Very Worst Monster Greenwillow/Morrow, 1985, 1988.
What Game Shall We Play? Greenwillow, 1990.
Where's the Baby? Greenwillow, 1988.
Which Witch Is Which Greenwillow, 1989.
The Wind Blew Macmillan/Penguin, 1974, 1986.
You'll Soon Grow into Them, Titch Greenwillow/Penguin, 1983, 1985.

At the tube exit near Hampstead is a group of small community stores. But there is also a new bookstore, several art galleries and enough ethnic restaurants to show that this is not an average neighborhood even in London. Many houses on the nearby streets are large and well cared for, while the road and several other houses are undergoing repair and what appears to be extensive renovation. Pat Hutchins's gate opens into a front yard full of the typical English profusion of growing things. The house itself is large and high-ceilinged, with garden extending out in back. The furniture is casual and comfortable, the shelves and surfaces scattered with books and mementos, the walls crowded with artwork of many styles and media.

Have you lived here long?
This is a house we've always loved. We used to live in a house down

Pat Hutchins (courtesy Laurence Hutchins)

the road, and we couldn't believe our luck when this came up for sale. We think it's wonderfully quiet for being so close to everything. The house is Georgian, and Alfred Lord Tennyson's sister lived here. Their mum lived in a little cottage next door, and a door was knocked through so that Mum could come visit. We like to think that Tennyson must have visited here. We keep hoping he won't "come into the garden Maude."

Your art education was at the Darlington School of Art?

I took a general art course there, a two-year foundation course. During that period you do everything: pottery, drawing, painting. Then after two years you decide in which direction you want to specialize. I decided I wanted to do illustration, so I then went to Leeds to specialize.

Were you planning to go into advertising? That was your first job.

I really wanted to illustrate children's books. I knew what I wanted to do from the beginning. In fact, when I first came to London with my drawings, I took them straight to a couple of publishers. They said, "They're very nice, but come back when you have something published." By this time I was desperate, and needed money, so I took a job in advertising. I took all my drawings, which were nearly all of the countryside, put acetate over the top and wrote on them to make them look commercial, and got the job. In fact, the three years I spent in advertising I found of enormous help to me, because you are given a problem, and you have a set amount of time to deal with it. You try to cut it to the core. It helped in presenting the idea, obviously not in the idea itself.

What kind of advertising work did you do?

Some newspaper, some television. I had an account that made children's clothes. The man who owns the company used to do his own drawings. I was asked to do the cover of the autumn catalog. I did children playing in the leaves. He sent it back and said the children looked too industrious to be playing. But the discipline was good.

You were drawing all the time when you were young. Were there books that influenced you then?

I always loved books. We didn't have a lot of books but I read anything I could lay my hands on from the library: *Wind in the Willows,* most of the classics. I found Shepherd's drawings exquisite. I could never hope to draw like that.

It wasn't until you went to New York that you were able to get a book published?

Yes. That was *Rosie's Walk.* It started off as a very long, boring book about animal life. I had brought some of my drawings to Susan Hirschman (Greenwillow) hoping she would give me something to illustrate. I didn't think I could write a story for children. She said, "Why not try to write your own?" So I did a story about animal noises on the farm. It went on and on about each animal. When it came to fox it said: "This is fox. He doesn't make any noise at all." Susan went through all the other miles of writing and said she liked that line. She said I should take it back and think along that line.

That night I thought I would make it into a sort of silent film. It's much more fun for the child to know what's going on, but the hen doesn't. The reader is actually one jump ahead of everyone else. But it took Susan pointing that line out to me to start me thinking.

Is there an analogy to film in the picturebook?

I feel that. But for very small children it's not fair to jump too far, for a scene to shift too quickly. It's easier for older children and grown-ups. For three- or four-year-olds to have a close-up on one page and a distance shot on the next, they don't read the gutters the way we do. They see a shrunken person and the same person as a giant. I would sacrifice the look of a book if I thought it would make it difficult for a small child to follow.

Did you get that from watching your own children?

I think it's just common sense. I discovered this when I put my portfolio on the top rack of a train. When it was time to get off, it had slid down to the other end of the car, and I couldn't find it. When some people pointed it out down there, I said, "No, mine is much bigger than that." If I wasn't using perspective to see, think how much harder it is for a small child to assume that something big has "shrunk." So I would try not to confuse them. It does depend on the story, of course. In *Happy Birthday, Sam* I deliberately kept the text on one side and the pictures on the other and kept the drawings in proportion throughout, because small children are struggling to "read" the pictures and I don't think it's fair to throw in other problems at that age. It's different when they're five or six.

In Henry's Palace *you are varied the layout more.*

To be totally honest, I don't like drawing. I find it the most difficult thing in the world. Painful. I think as most trained illustrators do, because no matter what you do, you're never satisfied. If I spent a year redoing a drawing, I would never be happy with it. Having been trained in art college, I'm very conscious of the mistakes in my drawings, what I think is wrong with them, so I find it very hard. I like having the ideas, I love writing, and I enjoy doing the mock-ups, but when it comes to actually doing the drawings, I'm really scared. I have to force myself to sit down and do them. I'd much rather be cleaning the oven. I find it so frustrating because I can never achieve what I have in mind.

How do you do a book? Are some connected with your children?

I would never sketch it out first. My stories usually start from ideas. For example, I had an idea for a story that didn't work as a picturebook. It was about a tree growing in the forest. There's a little sapling growing alongside it. As the first tree fills up with animals and birds, the other grows bigger. When it's full, some woodsmen come and chop it down. But by this time, the tree on the facing page is fully grown, so they transfer to that tree. On the last page there's another sapling growing, so you can feel the continuity. But it didn't work at all, because there was no reason for them to chop the tree down. I think now I could have made it work if I had in the background someone building a log cabin, then there would have been a reason to use the wood, not just a brutal act of destruction. But from that story, I got the idea for *Good-Night Owl*, and indirectly for *Titch*. So it's the idea that's important, and it's almost incidental how I present it. I just try to find the best way.

Do you have in mind from the beginning how large the book will be?

I do play around a lot, to decide. It's very frustrating to have an idea in my mind how the book will look, and then physically to do it. So often I can spend three months. With *One Hunter* I started off doing four-color painting, but it didn't work, because it was too painterly, not patterned enough to go "1, 2, 3." I tried cut-out shapes, but I'm very clumsy at that, and useless with glue, so there were little pieces of animals stuck all over. It was a nightmare. So then I realized I had to do it with a black outline and very simple colors. That way I could get the shapes so it made a pattern you could count. A counting book is so basic. You can't abstract the animals too much or a two-year-old couldn't recognize them. One could have made a beautiful counting book that would have meant nothing to a two-year-old. It would have become a coffee-table book.

What is the role of editor with pictures?

We all (including art director Ava Weiss at Greenwillow) look at the pictures. They might have some small suggestions about moving this or that. But after doing so many books, I think we almost read each other's minds. Initially, when I started out, I needed a lot of help with details—things like not sticking the main character in the gutters to get sawed in half.

You have always published first in the U.S.?

Yes, because I began when we were living there. And I can't imagine working the first few books without Susan's help.

What do you think of the current publishing scene in U.K.?

I'm ignorant of what's happening here, because I work directly with Susan. Occasionally the British publishers may ask me to lunch when they're printing one of my books here. I know times are particularly bad here now. The signs are that it will be sales only that are important. I believe that's happening in America too. I don't think it will affect those of us who are well-established in the field, because they know they can sell our books. It's with the new people trying to break in that the tragedy lies. They'll probably go for something that looks like an instant seller, rather than something a bit more subtle or clever.

Where did you dream up that strange style of drawing Rosie?

It was sort of forced on me. I was allowed to use three colors, and I had to pre-separate my own art work. I had no idea what pre-separation was. I came home with tears of frustration, saying, "Finally they want to do my book. But I have to pre-separate, and I don't know how!" Fortunately we had a friend in New York who was an illustrator. He sat down and showed me how. It was purely financial. But having done *Rosie's Walk,* I realized that certain books worked better using just a few colors and strong outline.

Are your animals abstracted?

I haven't abstracted; I've stylized.

But your other stories with children are in a different style?

They all need a different approach. The story is all-important. The pictures should reflect the story. I think that there are good picturebooks with awful pictures and good stories; but there are no good picturebooks with awful stories and beautiful pictures. When I say awful pictures, I mean pictures that may have been drawn by the writer with no formal art training, so technically the drawings are bad, but they can be charming. But I don't think you can have a good book with beautiful four-color pictures and a pathetic story. It never works. I don't like coffee-table children's books. I think they're an insult to children's integrity.

Would you keep these books from children? Comics are OK but not these?

No. I would never ban any of my kids from having them. But if you want to give them beautiful pictures, you might as well give them the gallery guide to some museum.

You believe in a balanced diet?

Absolutely. I just don't want to see those coffee-table children's books forced down their throat by doting grandmothers.

Where did you get the idea for Doorbell Rang? *Does Grandma really make the best . . . ?*

No. Actually my mother is a terrible cook. What happened was this. One year I got really cross with my husband at Christmas. Every year at Boxing Day (the day after Christmas) we have our next-door neighbor's mum, who lives with them, over for lunch, along with our friend and his mum, and usually ours as well. So it became the mums' lunch. The year I wrote the book, my husband had been going to lots of Christmas parties. For some reason, he decided that anyone who had a mum living with them should be invited to that lunch.

Meanwhile I had already ordered the meat, for the traditional roast beef, bubble and squeak, etc. But then Lawrence would come home every day with someone else he'd invited. We ended up with 30 people for lunch on Boxing Day. I had to keep going to the butcher and asking him for a bigger piece of beef. That gave me the idea for the story: of sharing. I was cursing him because I had to make mince pies for 30, but it did give me the idea for the story.

Where did the idea for Where's the Baby *come from? Was it done just as a sequel to the* Monster?

I actually wrote the story 14 years ago, when Sam, my 16-year-old, was 2. I wrote it with a real baby, but it didn't work. But I always liked the story, and I never throw anything away because there's always some way to use an idea. So when I had invented the monster baby, I thought it might actually work with him, since monsters are supposed to be terrible, and he was established that way. But otherwise it's word for word the book I did when Sam was a baby.

You have been quoted as saying, "I don't believe in talking down to children."

I think you can't cheat with kids. They are incredibly logical.

Do you have any particular kids in mind in your books, American or British?

No, I don't. I think kids are kids. But if I do have a child in mind, it's probably a slightly insecure child that needs reassurance. I like to think that my books are reassuring.

Do you go out to talk to groups of kids, librarians, whatever?

I go out about once a month. I also get a lot of lovely letters. We've always been surrounded by kids. I come from a big family. I always think that it's more how you remember yourself and what it was like to be a child, the insecurity. . . . People often ask if I try my books out on children. I think that's ridiculous; you can't do that. Having two children I know. If I showed Sam a book he'd say, "That's nice, but why isn't the stuffed animal the main character?" because he was so fond of his, while Morgan might have said, "It's great, but why isn't there a space ship?" You've really just got to please yourself and hope that the children enjoy what you've done.

Do you storyboard your books?

It depends on the book. I always think you should work with a mock-up, because part of the book is the turning of the page. So I always work immediately with a dummy even if it's just a few scraps of paper stuck together. Because turning the page makes something happen. But having done that, with the book I'm working on at the moment, I do have to storyboard it, because it's one pan across the landscape. I have to work on two drawings at once, because I have a bit of something happening on one page and when you turn over there's an extension of it. So I've done my dummy and still on this particular book have to do the storyboard so there's no cheating; so it's accurate. Also at the end I've got the vista.

Does the loss of endpapers in the paperback of One Hunter *bother you, since the story really starts there?*

The story doesn't really start there. It's nice to think that it does. But that was just an extra treat. It's unfortunate to lose in paperback, but it also costs much less. I'm all for paperbacks, for kids whose parents couldn't possibly afford books for them otherwise.

You don't hang your own art work on your walls?

No. I don't like my art work. I prefer other people's. I don't give it away because I think it's nice to keep together as a complete book. Also you never know when you might need it again if the book is going to be reprinted. I think that so much sweat has gone into a book that you feel it's a complete thing.

Your husband does illustration too?

He illustrates my longer books. He did an illustration course at art college as well. He's a film director and makes television commercials.

Where do you get your images; from photos, sketch books?

I don't use photographs. I don't carry a sketch book. I do quite often ask people to pose, especially for hands. I can't get hands right. The kids hate it when I'm working on a book because I'll ask them to please stand and hold something.

Were the kids in the books found here?

The original Titch was Morgan, our older son. But in *You'll Soon Grow into Them,* Titch is Sam, who looked just like Morgan when he was young. I don't really like sequences or sequels. But when I had the idea for *You'll Soon Grow . . .* I realized that Titch was the perfect character to use to tell that story. It could have been any child, but Titch had the right sort of personality for that story. It would have been easier for me to create another character because "Titch" was already 12 years old by then and I found it very difficult to draw in the same style, which it had to be if it was going to be him.

Do you still have to do color separation?

I still use color separation out of choice. I chose to do *One Hunter* that way. I didn't have to. I could have done it full color. I felt I needed the line and that wonderful flat color, and that's the only way I know to get that. I tried doing it in full color and it didn't work.

Is your studio in the house? Does the family respect your privacy?

It is, but they don't. When Morgan went to art school, drawing paper and pencils all ended up in his room, pinched from mine.

Who are the artists on the walls?

The art is by friends. But quite a few of our friends are picturebook artists. Ron Maris's work there, and Jacob Lawrence's from a book. We meet at the publisher's parties a few times a year and might have dinner together. . . . Mostly we just sit at home and do our work.

How much time do you need for story versus time for illustration?

It takes me between three and six months. It depends. But then I often become dissatisfied after a month of working on a book and will start all over again. If the drawings go well, then closer to three months.

Do you send your editor the whole book?

No. I'll send the mock-up with perhaps one finished drawing. Then I'll finish it. I go through too much agony to change it.

Do you do any "studio" drawing or painting?

I'm quite sure that I would enjoy drawing and painting if I knew it wasn't going to be in print looking at me. If I were doing it for pleasure, that's the pleasure. But I haven't got the time. I have to do the other. When you draw professionally it's not relaxing. It's just hard work. I'd rather relax by gardening, or scrubbing the kitchen floor.

—*Summer 1989*

Seventeen

Ann Jonas

A Sampling of Works in Print

Aardvarks, Disembark! Greenwillow, 1990.

Color Dance Greenwillow, 1989.

Holes and Peeks Greenwillow, 1984.

Now We Can Go Greenwillow, 1986.

The Quilt Greenwillow, 1984.

Reflections Greenwillow, 1987.

Round Trip Greenwillow/Scholastic, 1983, 1987.

The Trek Greenwillow, 1985.

Where Can It Be? Greenwillow, 1986.

In 1982 when Ann Jonas's first books appeared, When You Were a Baby *and* Two Bear Cubs *seemed so perfect for the preschooler that we assumed Jonas must be a writer-illustrator who had children that age. Then the ingenuity and sophisticated design of* Round Trip *took us by surprise. But when we found out that she was married to Donald Crews and was working in the graphic design field, we simply settled back in delighted anticipation, waiting for the rewards of each new book. When Ann Jonas was in Columbus for the 1986 Children's Literature Conference, we were able to interview her about her work.**

Could you tell us about where you live and work?

We moved to a brownstone in Brooklyn seven years ago. We used to live in an apartment in Manhattan and then in a sublet loft. When the sublet ended, we bought a house in Park Slope, a pretty neighborhood of uninterrupted brownstones.

Do you and your husband ever work together?

No, not on children's books. We have had our own graphic design office

**Originally published in* the Horn Book Magazine, *May/June 1987.*

Ann Jonas

for over 20 years, and on those projects we work together, each doing the part of the job we do best.

How did you start doing books?

Don had started doing children's books, which took more and more of his time, and I found myself at loose ends. Susan Hirschman, Don's editor at Greenwillow, and Don encouraged me to do a picturebook, and I finally decided to try.

Do you and your husband consult each other about your picturebooks?

We always ask each other for an opinion early on. But lately we wait until the thumbnail sketch is the way we want it to be before showing it to the other. If one of us gets stuck, the other will jump in and help.

How do you explain the differences in the styles of illustration in your books?

They probably stem from my days as a graphic designer when I was given something to illustrate that was written by someone else. I had to suit the mood and the style of the design to what the author had written. This continues to seem like a valid approach. Certainly a book for the very young needs clear drawings lacking any ambiguities. Books such as *Round Trip*, in which there are double readings in the illustrations, need styles that will intensify whatever illusion I am trying to create.

Are there books that you remember from your childhood?

I remember the cloth baby books very clearly. I tried to get a bit of their feeling by using big, simple pictures and a similar palette in *When You Were a Baby*.

Are there artists that you admire or who may have influenced you?

There are many. Over the years I have grown to prefer most artists' drawings and graphics to their paintings. I enjoy the work of graphic designers and illustrators such as Milton Glaser, Paul Rand, Seymour Chwast and Leo Lionni. I am also a fan of 19th-century architectural renderings.

Can you tell us someting about how you work?

Two walls of my studio are covered with bulletin board. As I start to work on a book, I pin up assorted clippings, photos, scraps of fabric, anything that seems to be relevant. My finished drawings will gradually replace them. First I make tissues from the rough sketch, refining them until I'm satisfied. I transfer the tissue to watercolor paper and start building up the color. When I'm working with watercolor, the strongest colors must be saved until last, since they tend to run. So I start gradually with the lightest shades and work up to the reds, which are the trickiest of all. I usually complete each illustration before moving on to the next, so I mix large quantities of the colors I'm using and save every intermediate color I've mixed until I'm finished. This allows me to go back and make adjustments later on.

Do you find that current technology in book printing makes your work easier or different?

It makes it much easier since laser separations have made full-color art no longer a luxury. The present technology certainly produces reproductions that are faithful to the original. Some of my first books were done as preseparated art. You get crisper color by preseparating, but it is a lot of work. Essentially, you have to do each piece of art four times, once for each color. The hardest part is trying to hold dozens of colors in your mind as you represent them with grays on the art. But I do like the result; I just wish it was easier to achieve.

Many of your books have very special endpapers. Why is that?

Because picturebooks are short, I want to make the endpapers an integral part of the book and in that way extend the experience.

Why do you seem to prefer one typeface?

I believe that the function of the typeface is to be as readable as possible and suit the style of the artwork. So far, Helvetica in its various weights meets my needs.

Do you use actual children as models now?

I don't. Don took thousands of photographs of our children. So when

I need a model, I go through the contact sheets and enlarge the pictures to get a pose or to remember proportions or movement.

Your children are grown up, yet you seem to know so well what will appeal to little ones. How do you manage that?

I use things I remember from when they were little. My daughter Amy reminded me of how afraid of holes she had been when she was little. I remembered that she had coined the word *peek* for a "good hole." That gave me the idea for *Holes and Peeks*. *The Quilt* is my daughter Nina's book. I made her a quilt using scraps from other things I had made for her, and she used to have very vivid dreams about it. Sally, the dog, really exists, although she's quite tattered by now.

Are you influenced by children's reactions to your work?

It is wonderful to get feedback from children. Every once in a while you meet a child who has a really well-thought-out question, his or her own particular concern. I don't really get book ideas from children, just a sense of what they like best.

Would you ever want to illustrate a book by another author?

If I were ever really stuck for an idea, I think I would. But it's a lot of fun to both write and illustrate a book because you have total control. You can change the words to accommodate the pictures in a way you can't in a book by someone else.

Let's talk about some specific books. How did you happen to do Round Trip?

I had been thinking that it would be wonderful to do a book that went from beginning to end and then back to the beginning again, if I could find the way to do it. I finally realized that if I created pictures that formed a different image when turned upside down, there would then be a reason for the return trip. I drew on my graphic design experience to stylize the images sufficiently to make this reversal possible. For instance, I had always noticed that the shapes between skyscrapers mimicked the shapes of the buildings themselves. I took some pictures of the Manhatttan skyline from the Brooklyn Bridge. The drawing that resulted had possibilities. I looked at a lot of landscape books, too, even upside down, to try to get my mind to see things fresh enough to find related forms. I did many thumbnail sketches. Many of them I had to discard because when I enlarged them, they didn't have enough content. I made a lot of mistakes, too. I was so convinced that I could do telephone poles and have them turn into a bridge that I just worked away at it without checking on the progress of the upside-down bridge I was creating. Then when I turned the drawing over, I was shocked at what I'd done. I had to make many changes before it worked.

How did you choose the style for The Quilt?

My other books had used simple, flat color or had been done in black and white. This book was clearly going to need a more realistic approach.

I experimented with many techniques: collage, watercolor paintings, and a combination of both. It was only after having collected many patterned papers and assembling them into quilts that I came to the decision to do the art as paintings. It was the only way I could get a satisfactory transition from the patterns in the quilt to their transformation in the dream sequence.

What gave you the idea for The Trek?

I used to love the pictures in children's magazines that contained hidden animals. It seemed possible to combine that idea with the game that we have all played, that of seeing animals or objects in other objects. To make it work as the book I envisioned, I would have to hide animals among things that resembled them in form or color or pattern. I looked through many nature books, took photos at the zoo, and built up a collection of sketches from which to develop a story line. I think the hardest part of the book was to judge how difficult it would be for others to see the animals. In retrospect, I think I could have made them somewhat more difficult to find.

The Trek *has more text than most of your other books do. Is there a special reason?*

I wanted to play the girl's fantasy against the world around her. I thought that by showing every other person in the book, except her friend, oblivious to the animals, I could set the tone I wanted. I also wanted to reinforce the fact that it wasn't a fearful journey, but clearly a game in which she was in control.

What do you feel is most important in your work?

The books that are the most satisfying for me are the ones in which I can help a child to use his or her own imagination or the ones in which I can get in some reassurance about a problem or concern children have. But I don't want the message to get the upper hand. I want to entertain, not preach. When I have been able to combine both those aims, that is when the book is the most satisfying.

—1987

Update

Are picturebooks dominating your working hours or are you still heavily involved with graphic design commissions?

Picturebooks still dominate. It takes me six to eight months to complete a book. I also do a fair amount of traveling to schools and conventions and work on some children-book related projects. This spring I did several posters for library summer reading programs in other parts of the country. Working in a larger format, on a single piece, was a pleasant change.

Are there pressures from your publishers to modify your ideas in ways to enhance their sales or do you still enjoy artistic freedom?

Greenwillow Books makes no demands other than that the idea be valid and that my approach to the writing and illustration doesn't befuddle the original concept. They have never tried to steer me to a "commercially successful" formula.

Have you ever been tempted to co-create a book with your husband?

At present Don and I are quite content doing our own books, but the possibility of doing a book together is always there. The question is: Who would do the illustrations?

Did Where Can It Be *produce any particular headaches because of the page folds? Was this device of your conception from the start?*

From the first thumbnail sketches, I planned *Where Can It Be* with alternate short pages to enhance the sense of opening doors and cabinets, throwing back bed covers and tablecloths, etc. Ava Weiss, Greenwillow's art director, thought the pages should vary more in width to minimize the lump that is apt to form in that kind of book. The book was printed and bound in Japan, by a printer who has the special equipment necessary to handle the trimming and binding problems.

Where did the concept of Color Dance *come from?*

Most color books that I've seen fall short of giving kids any real sense of how to mix colors. I thought that if they could see colors overlap, and see the components of the mixes, it would become clearer to them. The device of the three girls, representing the primary colors and carrying scarves that are tints of the colors, allowed me to demonstrate and explain the mixes. Finding a red, yellow and blue that would give me true secondary colors took a lot of testing. Not surprisingly, the final colors are very similar to red, yellow and blue printing inks. Usually I paint a book page by page. In this case, I worked on all the pages at once, going through and painting all the large areas of each color before the watercolor could evaporate or change in any way.

What was the concept for Now We Can Go? *What special problems did you have to solve for this and* Color Dance? *Are you pleased with the final books and of the press work?*

Now We Can Go, like several of my books, is based on my children. They always took an inordinate number of toys with them on even the shortest excursions. A book about that seemed a good way to name objects and to also illustrate "empty-full." This was an easy book to draw because of all the repetition. For the same reason that it was easy to paint, it was somewhat difficult to print. Matching a color from page to page is a more demanding printing job than a book that has more varied pages. *Color Dance* had similar printing problems. I think that in both cases, the printer solved them very well.

Reflections *can be compared with* Round Trip. *But you've added in-finitely more problems when you chose full color. Would you tell us something of the way you went about designing it? Once the theme was set did you have to change it because there were visual hurdles too difficult to overcome? Given the chance today, would you change any of it?*

Yes, *Reflections* did have infinitely more problems than *Round Trip.* But I was able to use much that I had learned in doing the first book. The biggest problem was the specificity that color brings. Setting most of the book at the edge of the water helped. At least I had blue at the top and the bottom of the page and could contain the activity in the center. Even so, much of what I wanted to illustrate seemed to need a more realistic ap-proach. For instance, clouds that when turned over become a group of chil-dren probably couldn't be done in the same style as *Round Trip.* It would be interesting to try to do a turnabout book in color that was as stylized as it. Maybe some day I'll figure out how to do it.

And what's on the drawing board now? Do you illustrate anyone else's stories but your own? Would you?

What is on the drawing board now is still too unformed to be discussed, but there is a new book, *Aardvarks, Disembark!* It's a story about the animals whose names Noah didn't know and takes place as the animals leave the ark. What started as an alphabetical listing of unfamiliar animals with unusual names changed its focus as I researched each of them. Originally I had hoped to simply amuse children with odd names in the same way that dinosaur names amuse. But I found that many of the animals I had picked were endangered and some even extinct. So, the focus shifted, for me at least, to what Noah saved and what we have lost or are in danger of losing. This isn't mentioned in the body of the book, but in a listing at the end.

I still haven't illustrated anyone else's stories. I enjoy the freedom that both writing and illustrating a book gives me. But if the question ever comes up, I will consider it.

—1990

Eighteen

Errol Lloyd

A Sampling of Works in Print

Nandy's Bedtime Salem, 1982.
Nini at Carnival Crowell, 1978.
Sasha and the Bicycle Thieves Barron,
1989.
Shawn Goes to School by Petronella
Breinburg. Crowell, 1973.

Errol Lloyd was waiting outside a Northern tube stop to drive us the 15 or so minutes through streets of modest two- and three-story homes to the house he shares with his wife, school-age daughter and brand-new baby girl. The eclectic furnishings include many shelves of books, recordings of music of all sorts, artifacts of several cultures and Lloyd's large oil paintings on the walls. The Jamaican lilt to his voice brings a vision of the island to anyone who has been there.

Do you think you bring a Jamaican cultural background to your work?
In my illustrations the influences are very strong, particularly in the use of color, as well as in imparting a certain Caribbean spontaneity to my characters. In my storytelling it's not always obvious. The storytelling skills you find in Jamaica are tremendous. Though none of my published stories to date are in a Jamaican idiom, I think I have absorbed some of the fascination with storytelling, along with some of the skills but translated into standard English. As my initial involvement with children's books has been as an illustrator it took me a little while to realize that I had absorbed some of these storytelling skills—not until after I started to write longer stories and plays and more recently adult short stories.
As a child were you part of an extended family with grandparents and

Self-portrait by Errol Lloyd

uncles or elders who told stories about either the early days of Jamaica or even before? Was there an oral tradition you grew up with?

We never had relatives living with us but we children often spent time with our grandparents on both sides of the family, but more often than not with my mother's side of the family. My maternal grandfather was a farmer and I remember in those early years they had no electricity and they relied on kerosene and Tilly lamps. After dinner there wasn't really anything to do except sit down on the veranda and listen to stories. In fact I have recently begun to rework some of these stories I heard from my grandparents into short stories for adults. I think I have a store of ideas for children's stories as well. Since I do mainly picturebooks and spend a lot of time on the illustrations, my storywriting side isn't quite as prolific as I would like.

What were those stories they told you about?

Quite often family anecdotes. My grandfather told me the story of how the first time he saw a plane it broke his leg — well, in an indirect sort of way;

he was riding his horse when the airplane flew overhead and his horse reared, throwing him to the ground and thereby breaking his leg. That would have been in the early part of the century. My grandmother told me about the time she went to a fortune teller who told her that if she slept with her ring tied up in a handkerchief under her pillow, the first man she saw the next morning was the man she would marry. And that's exactly what happened! She saw my grandfather first thing in the morning and they were married for over 60 years. I have recently written a fictional account of this story in the form of an adult short story which starts at the funeral of the husband after 60 years of marriage. During the service the widow remembers the time she went to the fortune teller and had her fortune told. The hymns, prayers and oration, etc., constantly jolt her back to the reality of the funeral; so the story slowly unfolds moving backwards and forwards in time. I got a picture of the past as well as a sense of family history from all that. Ghost stories and Anansi stories, folk tales, etc., I would have gotten from other sources. I remember as a young child hearing these kinds of stories, stories from servants before going to bed and these would in fact spring from the rich oral tradition.

These were your oral influences. Visually did you see any kind of picturebooks as you grew up?

We had a modest collection of books at home and my nursery school and junior school had a fairly standard selection. So I grew up being exposed to the standard European classical fairy tales — *Sleeping Beauty, Jack and the Beanstalk, Beauty and the Beast, Cinderella, Hansel and Gretel*, etc., as well as the usual Anansi story books. But I have no abiding memory of affection for the books as such. Children's books in those days (1940s and 1950s) didn't have many pictures in them and when they did they tended to be black and white line drawings. So I never took any note of the names of the illustrators. I have a vague recollection of reading *Seven at One Blow* as a young child and being puzzled at the pictures, trying to visualize the society that the stories came from. I remember a feeling of being alienated and puzzled by it. It seemed so far away especially those with castles with lofty spires, etc.

Assuming you were middle class there, were the schools you attended segregated or mixed?

Schools were not segregated in Jamaica [or the rest of the West Indies] in any formal sense and tended to be open to anyone who could afford the fees — admittedly more often than not whites and light-skinned Jamaicans in the early days. There is quite a complex class structure in Jamaica which was shaped by a plantation society with the white plantocracy at the top and the black slave at the bottom. There has been a good deal of mixing of the races in Jamaica as in the rest of the New World, but in Jamaica there emerged from the early 19th century a relatively well-off brown-skinned middle class. For reasons of their own, the British encouraged this, and an education system evolved to accommodate this new class. The school I attended was established in 1855 and is one of many such schools of that age.

My father was fair-skinned and my mother brown-skinned like myself. My father would have benefited from certain social and other advantages and for whatever reason we grew up with the usual trappings of affluence — big house, car, servants, etc. I guess that part of my being an artist implies a rejection of those values. Mind you, in those days you didn't have to earn a fantastic salary to enjoy that lifestyle for there was always a source of cheap labor to support it. It's curious. When I was in Zimbabwe, I could see that that the lifestyle enjoyed by white Zimbabweans was not that different from that of the brown-skinned middle class Jamaicans. It has the same potential for conflict as well. The difference is that in Jamaica the brown-skinned middle class has been supplemented by black-skinned people, thus reducing the racial or "shade" element. There has also never been the sort of racism you find in Southern Africa, which is racism on the statute books. It has been much more fluid and flexible, much more tolerant.

You have what might be termed a proper British education.

The school system was colonial in those days and modelled on British public school notions of education. At my school a good number of the teachers came from Oxford or Cambridge — though there was already a strong Jamaican element by the time I started school, which has steadily grown since independence.

Where did your art education come from?

My interest really started when our new English teacher, an eccentric Yorkshireman, arrived at our school (a boy's boarding school) with virtually all his possessions, which included some terra cotta busts. I showed an interest in them, and when he started a portrait of one of the boys he allowed me to join in. I discovered that I had some talent in that direction and showed more interest in art thereafter.

You hadn't done anything before?

Just the routine art lessons at school. But when I was seven or eight I found some clay in the back yard at home and made little heads of all the members of my family. I remember they were displayed on top of the radio and when visitors came they served as quite a conversation piece. Later at school when I was about ten, I made a head of Abraham Lincoln out of plasticine and the art teacher made quite a fuss of it and had it on display. But my earliest memory is of drawing a bus when I was about five. It was a drawing of the bus that often stopped near our house and to this day I remember the realization I had of the curious process of storing up an image in my head and then transferring it on to the paper. A kind of magic.

By the time I got around to A level art I had an excellent teacher who was very serious about art. She was a young Israeli called Ruth Cohn who had studied with Kokoshka. She made me realize that art was more serious than putting down pleasing images on paper or canvas. I did very well at A level exams and got A's in drawing, painting, sculpture and the history of art. If I had grown up in a society in which art was considered a viable career I guess I would have gone to art school.

You came to England to become a barrister? What happened?

I became a law student at the Middle Temple Inns of Court. But I discovered that there was a lot happening in the black community and the services of artists were needed for posters, book covers, illustrations, etc. and there weren't many around. I remember being commissioned to do a bust of C.L.R. James, the noted West Indian historian and man of letters. I remember him speaking to me at length about Michelangelo whom he admired greatly. Later I received other commissions to do busts of prominent West Indians including Sir Alexander Bustamante (then prime minister of Jamaica) and Garfield Sobers the cricketer. These commissions helped me start as a professional artist.

How did you decide to stay in the U.K.?

My plans were to return home, but I got married to a Guyanese whose immediate family was in Britain. It is also more difficult to make a living as a writer or painter in the Caribbean. Many artists have to introduce a commercial element in their work in order to sell to well-off local people or tourists. Because of my experience in Britain, I have a more radical approach to art and politics which would make it difficult for me to introduce that commercial element. It is still tempting to go back. The middle classes have a more laid-back lifestyle but that is partly possible because of the exploitation of others. I was also surprised by the extent to which tourism has become a central part of the economy.

You started in England as a sculptor?

Yes. But then I joined a group of mainly painters called the Caribbean Artists Movement and we organized exhibitions. It was through my activities with this group that I did a painting of a group of children which was eventually reproduced as a greeting card. This came to the notice of a publishing house who was looking for a black illustrator for a story called *My Brother Shawn* by Petronella Breinburg. In that way I got involved with children's books. All this happened during the time I was studying law and disrupted my studies. I'm afraid that I was more interested in art than law and my passage through law school was not smooth. I completed the preliminaries, then got carried away. It wasn't till a few years later that I returned and finished my final exams.

Then you decided to keep doing children's books?

Yes, for though I was introduced to children's books by chance, the Shawn series went well. I received a Kate Greenway commendation for *My*

Brother Shawn and this encouraged me. Then I started to illustrate my own stories as this gave me more freedom to choose my own subjects, those that complement my style of picture-making.

How do you develop a book idea?

Initially I used to think in terms of the visual aspect of the book; i.e., what sort of pictures I wanted to draw. I would then think of a story that would allow me the opportunity to create those pictures. For instance in *Nini at Carnival* I wanted to draw colorful pictures of children enjoying themselves in glittering costumes and came up with the idea of a girl who has no costume on carnival day. Similarly, *Nini on Time* was inspired by a desire to paint street scenes. After that, as I became more confident as a storyteller, the story ideas came quite independent of pictures. The current picturebook I'm working on is a reversion to my earlier approach. It's about an East Indian boy and his grandmother at a funfair. He's always getting lost at the funfair till he goes off on his own to the Ghost Train and learns his lesson. It really is based on photographs I took by chance at a funfair.

Do you have a specific boy in mind?

At the moment the concept of Ravi has not yet crystalized fully in my mind, so I have started on those illustrations which have him being virtually lost amongst the crowd and where the reader sees him from a distance. I have a good idea of what he looks like in my mind, but I don't want to commit myself in case better ideas come to the fore.

The rides and fair in the book are the kind kids would see around here?

Yes, in fact the book is based on photographs I took by chance at a funfair I took my daughter to, held in the local park a hundred yards down the road from here.

Do you work with pencil?

Yes. I first outline the figures, etc. in pencil and all the hard craft is done at this stage when I'm never without an eraser. I then decide what medium I'm going to use to color in the pictures with. I often use color pencils to color the pictures in as I find this quite a clean, efficient medium which allows me to put in a lot of detail. After that I then outline the figures with a superfine pen as it helps define the figures. I guess however I'm best known for the textured illustrations I often do. Most people think I use pastel crayons, but in fact I utilize an unusual technique of applying a thin layer of glue to my painting (done in water resistant acrylics) and before it's dry I sprinkle a fine layer of sand (I've been known to use sugar which brings the ants out) and when it's set I add another layer of color. It then has a highly textured appearance.

Where did you get the idea of sanding?

Out of desperation I guess. I found it difficult to do small detailed illustrations at first as I was accustomed to work on large paintings. Just before I took in the pictures I had done for *My Brother Shawn,* I thought

I had better texture them to disguise my lack of craftsmanship. The sand gave an overall fuzziness to the pictures and I think made a virtue of what was a shortcoming.

Have you used the sand technique in recent books?

No, I haven't used this technique for my last three books, but I think I'll revive it as I am beginning to realize that though it's time-consuming, it is what people really like about my illustrations.

Your new Playground *book was done in watercolor?*

Yes. It's quite unusual for me to use traditional watercolor, as I'm not very good at giving my work in this medium that delicate wash-like quality often associated with watercolors. I end up using watercolor as if it were oil paint. I chose watercolor in an attempt to keep the paintings of this particular book fresh and light-hearted and not too detailed. This was to make the book fit in with the particular series that the publisher had in mind.

You were given the format and the number of pages?

Yes. I was asked to do two books, which were for very young children, of 32 pages. They needed really simple pictures and I had to really restrain myself from not overworking the illustrations and burdening them with too much detail. For that reason I made sure I didn't work from photographs as I would run the risk of getting carried away with details.

You don't do sketches?

Some artists do endless sketches before they start on the finished work, but I don't. I find I get bored if I do, so I go straight into the finished work. I however do very rough thumb sketches by way of a mock book just to give the publishers some idea of the contours of the story. They tolerate my doodles as they have some idea, from past experience, of what the finished work will be like. With the *Playground* book I did go along to the playground in the local park and made some quick sketches which I used as a reference. Some of the background figures I lifted from the photographs of the funfair, but kept very simple. I also had to make sure that there was not too much depth to the pictures as with the use of perspective, you can find yourself putting in more and more background details.

Do you work here in the living and dining room area?

I do now. My studio was converted to a nursery for the baby and I am now in the middle of clearing a spare room for studio space.

Have British picturebooks influenced you since your daughter was born here?

Not really. When I had my first commission, I went to a library to look at picturebooks, but it depressed me. I thought they were all so good and slick and professional. My first attempt at *My Brother Shawn* was way off the mark. I realized that I had to be myself and so I did some research to find out what the interior of a nursery school was like and what sort of clothes children were wearing, etc. A friend of mine ran a nursery school and I went there one day with a camera and took some pictures. In fact that started me out working with photographs; not simply copying them but using them to establish some sort of social reality if the story demanded it. The story of a child going to school for the first time is so universal and I thought the story demanded some fidelity to everyday reality, so that children in a similar situation would be able to see their experience reflected in the book. That book helped me to establish my own style. I noticed that a lot of picturebook illustrators tended to present an idealized and somewhat nostalgic view of life and I felt that my contribution could be to focus on modern urban reality which children could recognize and relate to. Shirley Hughes does something like that too.

My Brother Shawn shows the influence of the artist Munch?

No. When Shawn screams on his first day at school he is expressing something which is quite normal, even healthy. As a West Indian I find it difficult to comprehend the kind of despair that Munch expressed in his work. I suppose it's down to having a different history. So the psychological base is very different. The emotions in that story are intensified because everything is seen in close-up. This came from an inability at the time to do small detailed work. I compensated by making everything big so that when, for instance, Shawn is shown being taken to school by his mother and sister, only the figure of Shawn is shown as I literally couldn't fit them all in the one page.

Are you required to work to size? They won't reduce it for you?

I think they would have reduced it if I asked, but at that time I got the impression that there were technical complications involved. The large paintings on the wall are mine and that is roughly the size I was accustomed to work in. Working on illustrations to size has forced me to work on a scale I wouldn't have thought I was capable of before. I have nearly ruined my eyes working on the crowd scenes in *Ravi at the Funfair* with the aid of a magnifying glass. It's useful, mind you, using a magnifying glass as you can give even small figures expression.

Most of the books of yours we have seen are more conventional. They don't have that edge you could bring to them.

In the past I have, to a certain extent, relied on the visual element to bring that edge. *My Brother Shawn* was the first picturebook published in Britain to feature a black child as the main character when it came out in 1973. So merely to feature a self-confident black child at the center of a story was a potent statement in itself. The more I have developed as a storyteller rather than just an illustrator, the more I am aware of the potential there is for introducing issues of race, class and sex into stories. I don't think picturebooks aimed at young children are necessarily the best vehicle for this, but I am now beginning to write longer stories and I am already exploring social and environmental issues in plays I write for older children.

At the moment I am writing a teenage novel for Methuen Children's Books which deals with issues arising from the movement of families from the West Indies to Britain through the eyes of a young girl, particularly the fragmentation of the family with all the heartache involved. Most of the families didn't come in a straightforward way as a family; they didn't all jump on a plane. First the father comes to find work and accommodation; saves money; the wife comes often leaving the children with the grand-mother. There is a relationship developed between the grandmother and the children, but the children are invariably wrenched away one by one. So even in a single family you have a series of relationships being established and broken, creating a tremendous amount of heartbreak. This has not really been fully explored in children's literature. That's the experience of my wife's family and there are a lot of people who would benefit from knowing what it was like in those days, the physical conditions they had to face and the problems they encountered in trying to fit into British society.

An immigrant experience?

Indeed, but I have never seen a television or stage play about it, that explores all these emotions and issues.

Painter to storyteller, do you see your emerging future becoming less visual, less the illustrator?

I have become very interested in literature over the years and I am more excited by writing than illustrating picturebooks at the moment. It really excited me to have a short story published in a literary journal a few years ago. Unfortunately it does not produce income, as you have to pro-duce a collection of stories and then find a publisher to market them as serious literature. This is difficult as it's a kind of departure for me. Anyway I've spent the last two years devouring short stories and working on the craft of writing. Mind you, I've always liked short stories, but now I'm more aware of the field and my own shortcomings.

Is there time for large paintings as well?

I'm working on that one at the moment, a sort of composite carnival scene, consisting of 24 separate scenes.

How do you feel about your Nini at Carnival?

I can't really understand why it is so popular with children. There are so many superbly illustrated books around that I can't help but be aware of its limitations. However it's popular with all children including white children. When it was first published I think that the assumption was that it would be meeting the needs of black children primarily, but there has been a much broader response than anticipated. Because of the general popularity of my books I am reluctant to be categorized as a black or West Indian author as my experience is that children themselves do not cate-gorize the books by reference to race. It's when they outgrow the picture-book stage and are 13 or 14 that racism raises its ugly head. I sometimes feel

that I should be attempting picturebooks that explore the relationship between black and white children in a sensitive way which reflects the everyday give and take of multiracial Britain. It's not at all easy to tackle issues
of race, sex, class, etc. for young children and I've come across some pretty
clumsy attempts. Curiously enough, it could be that someone like myself
reflecting a multicultural Britain in my work could be nearer being the
future mainstream rather than those white illustrators who stick a few token
black faces in their illustrations.

You are in a unique position to report on different cultures?

In some respects yes. My activities as an author/illustrator bring me
into regular contact with children up and down the country through visits
to schools and libraries, and I have a pretty good idea of the wide range of
children that make up the school population, particularly in inner-city
areas. This is a pointer to the shape of British society in the future. I also
think that my Caribbean background of racial tolerance helps to give me
the right outlook and necessary optimism. I plan to do books with Indian,
Chinese and African main characters to reflect the diversity of British society.
Perhaps even a white main character. Why not? The idea I have in mind
is for my books to be a mirror of society so that all children can have a sense
of belonging. Picturebooks have a role to play as they help to shape the
outlook of young children.

When I look at the body of work I have done over the years I can't help
but feel that there is a whole part of my consciousness that has not found
expression. That there are so many issues—environmental issues for instance—that I have not addressed and I feel that in the coming years I
would like to develop my writing skills so that I can learn the tricky art of
translating these concerns into sensitive literature for children that will
help them develop.

It could well be that this is nothing but a misguided desire to create
the kind of books that may end up being stilted, or it may also spring from
a devaluation of the stories that exist simply as stories with no other desire
than to entertain or enchant. Having recently read *The Wizard of Earth Sea*,
however, I can't help wishing that I could someday write someting that had
even a fraction of the deep wisdom and insights of such a story. However
I am convinced that I can't really know my limitation without at least trying
to extend myself.

—*Summer 1989*

Nineteen

Deborah Niland

A Sampling of Works in Print

There's a Hippopotamus on Our Roof Eating Cake by Hazel Edwards. Holiday, 1986.

When the Wind Changed by Ruth Park. Coward, 1980.

After the disorienting hours cramped on airplanes and camped in airports, enduring endless day followed by an eternal night, we had moved from steamy summer to crisp midwinter. But as if anticipating our arrival it is Children's Book Week in Australia when we arrive. Sydney's imposing Victorian Town Hall basement is teeming with uniformed schoolchildren, all talking at once in an oddly accented but comprehensible English. And what they are discussing with the same enthusiasm as the boys and girls in the U.S. are books and authors we recognize. Along with American and British favorites, like Arnold Lobel and Anthony Browne, are local stars. Pamela Allen is talking to a group of excited youngsters in an impromptu tent in a corner. She lives in Sydney. Julie Vivas and MemFox live here, as does Deborah Niland. Can we meet with any of them? Niland is our preference; we have seen more of her work, and the variety of styles particularly intrigues us. But we are told that she does not do many interviews or lectures; she has two small children and is expecting another shortly.

We spend two hours touring the publishers' booths, examining the books that, increasingly, demonstrate the native Australian writing and illustrating talents and their new pride in their local flora, fauna and heritage. Some of the best of these, we hope, will appear in the U.S.

A few days later on an excursion from Sydney to Adelaide we have the opportunity to meet with students who are aspiring illustrators. We enjoy examples of their fine work and the chance to answer their questions concerning what we

---

*Originally published in Magpies, *July 1988.*

Self-portrait with children by Deborah Niland

know about the business of children's picturebooks. It is obvious that here in Adelaide the climate is right for the development of picturebook artists.

Meanwhile, friends have been busy on their telephone in Sydney, and a final call brings an invitation. We can interview Deborah Niland at home. Detailed instructions are noted, train schedules consulted, the efficiency of Australian trains jealously compared to our American railways, and we are on our way to Chatswood. Going over the famous coat-hanger bridge with the Opera House in view, we observe that Sydney appears to be an amalgam of the harbor of San Francisco and the sprawling character of Los Angeles. We exit the train into a building full of shops, and go out into the street bustling with activity.

Following directions we come to the humming Pacific Highway which takes us five minutes to get across, and we are grateful to have done it safely. How can Niland possibly live here? But then we go over a small rise and suddenly we are in a different world. Small houses are nestled behind fences and surrounded by greenery even in winter. The noises of the highway are unheard; it is unbelievably quiet and peaceful. It is so quiet at the Nilands' that we are sure we have mistaken the date; they are away for the weekend, and we will leave Australia never having seen the elusive artist. But then the door opens, and we are greeted by her and her family. Her dark-haired, neatly bearded husband shakes our hands politely and then deftly steers young Katie and Alex out of our way. They play a little peek-a-boo with us, and we overhear a minor altercation, but he seems to have them well-amused for the hours of the interview. He even manages tea and cookies for us, with their help, in the comfortably furnished living room. The other member of the family, a handsome large Dalmatian, wasn't sure we were trustworthy, but finally settled down to watch us warily. Niland herself, blonde, attractive, and quite pregnant, seems almost too young to have produced such a body of work and be managing, even with her husband's co-operation, this obviously well-functioning household. How could she do it?*

How do you have time to do the work with two small children?

I have always worked at home. But now, with the competition from the children, I have cut down a bit.

How did you become interested in doing picturebooks?

I think it comes from growing up with creative parents. I always saw books and pictures around the house. It seems like a nice way to make a living. Mother (Ruth Park) writes children's books. I saw that books were a way. I saw things done in a creative way. There are other art forms, of course, like music, that would be quite different, but this was the form I saw it take.

You and your sister, Kilmeny?

Yes. So we decided to go to a general art school called the Julian Ashton Art School here in Sydney. We took courses such as drawing and painting since they didn't have a course called illustration. We were sure that this was what we wanted to do, so we went there early, at 15. Our parents didn't worry about it because we were pretty keen on what we wanted and weren't likely to drop it or change our minds.

So at 15, when you entered art school, you already had in mind a career that involved illustration rather than "gallery art"?

No. I wanted both. I have had several gallery shows and work in exhibitions as well. There are people who know my gallery work and have no idea that I do book illustration.

How do you feel about the division that is generally made between book illustration and "fine art"?

I wouldn't think there was such a dividing line. I've thought that you'd get good drawing or good art in any sphere. It's just academic snobbishness. The things I do for the art gallery are still "illustrative." And I might use oils for my book illustrations someday. Now I get my effect with acrylics.

Do you sell your original art work for your illustrations?

Yes. The local dealer who does this started with me. That started a chain of others. But I like to keep a few just to remind me that I did them better than the book. There seems to be a loss of intensity or of subtlety; sometimes a real change of quality.

To go back to your training, what happened after art school?

We were at art school for years. At 17 we went to England, to London, and freelanced from there. We worked in an animation studio for a while, just painting cells and tracing. My sister stayed on and she became an assistant animator. But then she left, too. I tried some greeting cards back here. I've even painted "pet rocks."

To go back earlier, do you remember any children's picturebooks that were a particular influence or inspiration?

There weren't very many picturebooks around then. They were quite limited in those days. I remember *Little Black Sambo*.

Are you aware that that is considered racist in the U.S. these days?

But they are such good little stories, and the illustrator is super. And there are a whole series of them.

Any others?

There really was not that much available in Australia then. *Peter Rabbit* must have been, but I wasn't aware of it. I am now, of course. There were books all over the house from my parents and my older brothers and sister, of course, so I didn't go to the library to choose my own. We had lots of books in the house.

Have you discovered other illustrators you like since you have had your children?

We've enjoyed Raymond Briggs's books about Santa Claus and the snowman. I like the work of John Burningham and Helen Oxenbury, for example, because they keep developing. They aren't frozen in time like some others. I have particularly enjoyed the work of the Ahlbergs, and Shirley Hughes. She really lives in that child's world.

How do you work? Do you do a series of stages that evolve into the book?

No. I work with tiny little pictures first, just a draft in pencil spread out on one big page. I know the number of pages so I can see them comic strip fashion. I can compose the picture quite well in a tiny space. If it looks good I can just bring it up to full page size.

How do you choose the medium for a particular story?

It's just there. It's what's right for the effect, to bring the effect I want.

Do you key your art to a particular audience in a particular book?

I try to relate the style to the style of writing: a simpler text for a young child, my own three-year-old, for example. *There's a Hippopotamus on Our Roof Eating Cake* is for them.

Have your own children influenced your work?

Yes. I used to go by what I thought I would have liked as a child. But now I've become more distracted by it. I've become more aware of specific children rather than children in general. If I had done *When the Wind Changed* when I had children I might have wanted to hold back.

Are there any of your books that did not give you a sense of satisfaction, or came really hard to you?

Not really. I don't accept or plan to do a book that I don't feel comfortable with. I have trouble when I have too much to do or if I am too tired at the end of the day. Then I am not thinking creatively. But I have always enjoyed what I have done.

So when you accept a commission or decide to do your own story, you have a good sense of what you want to do. Do you find you make many changes from your original idea as you go?

I usually spend quite a bit of time thinking about the format before I touch the art. I scribble out some ideas so that before I put it into the right format I know what I'm going to do. Then I usually don't change much from the original layout.

Is the typeface chosen for you?

Yes. The page number and the size are also given. But I cut the text and place it where I want to see it as part of the total design. I'd rather do that myself, because when someone else, like the editor, has done it I haven't been entirely satisfied.

How have you felt about the finished books as compared to the original art?

I do get to see the proofs and ask for changes; I insist on that. But I do that without having the original art there. Then when I have accepted the proofs and get the original artwork back, it looks so much finer. It's hard to be completely satisfied.

Your books have very different styles. Why?

I consider both the story itself and the children for whom it is intended. Then I choose the style because I feel the book will be most effective that way. I usually spend quite a bit of time thinking about the form before I even touch it. I scribble out some ideas. So that before I put it into the right format, I know what I am going to do. I usually don't change from my original layout.

Have you ever been tempted to try something in a really outlandish or different style?

Not really. I've just always seen whatever the text dictated; nothing I'd like to impose. It's just important to relate the two.

So you really haven't established a single style?

I like to think that I haven't.

You have worked for many different publishers, not a single one?

Yes. If a publisher comes to me with a story and it appeals to me, I'll consider it.

How many books offered by publishers do you turn down?

Quite a lot lately, perhaps three out of four. I like original things. When something really appealing comes along, I make time. But it's been hard lately. I can't work at the speed I used to. But I'm still always practicing in my mind.

Would the publishers hold something for you if you couldn't do it right now?

They have, but sometimes they can't.

Do you see a relationship between film animation and your picturebooks?

Mulga Bill's Bicycle was influenced by animation. The different angles of view, for example.

Have you ever thought about picturebooks as analogous to films?

No. I haven't really thought of it that way.

How do you set up the pacing from page to page?

It's just instinct. I'm not that conscious of working it out to a design. It has to be there, something I've thought about before. I don't exactly plan it much that way, but you know when it works; you feel it. And you know when it doesn't work.

Do you like to use decorated endpapers?

Sometimes. It's not necessary, but it can help start the story and make it flow through.

What was it like doing a book with your mother? (When the Wind Changed, The Gigantic Balloon—*also with Kilmeny.*)

I don't know what it would be like if we lived in the same house, but living separately it isn't much different from working with someone else. If they leave it up to you, it works quite well. My mother gives me the story and I show her the finished artwork later.

Isn't there any marked difference between working with a relative and working with a stranger? How did it work?

There has to be trust on both sides. If they know your style and work, they'll know what you can do. We do meet with the author.

In the U.S. that is not the pattern. They frequently try to keep them apart.

I quite like to meet them, to see if they have any ideas of what they'd like to see.

Do you work with art directors here?

Not really. I wouldn't want to lose track of what I want to see. I'm open to discussion of changes with the editors, but I like to keep the power. I like to see if they have ideas of changes to a degree. But they might put in the impression of what they'd like to do, and I'd lose track of what I'd like to see.

When the Wind Changed is a real favorite. Did your husband pose for the man's faces?

No, I wasn't married then. I did it myself, me in my mirror. I thoroughly enjoyed it; it was very involving.

You own a dog, but have done the Jean Chapman book, Velvet Paws and Whiskers.

I should really do a dog book.

How did you and Kilmeny divide up the work for your joint ventures?

Usually I did the drawing and Kilmeny did the textures and patterns.

How do you decide what particular scene to illustrate in the fairy tale collections?

You are more limited in this kind of a collection because you have to have a certain large block of text and the picture has to be above or close by it.

Financially are you successful enough to live on your income from your picturebooks?

Without children, yes. But not as a mother.

How do you feel about paperback editions?

I'm in favor of anything that can get more books to children. But any books I really like, I buy hardbound. My older sister is a librarian, so I am sensitive to the problems of bindings as well.

Have you ever had any interest in teaching?

No. I don't think I have any talent in that direction. But I've certainly introduced books early to my children. They're very keen on them.

Do you ever go to talk to groups of children or adults about your work?

During Children's Book Week I get a lot of invitations to speak at schools. I go if it is close by.

Do you enjoy this?

If they're really interested. Sometimes I get groups of letters from children that I know teachers have put them up to writing, but I do answer.

Is it difficult to remain a private person as you get more and more well known? Or would lack of public response bother you?

It shows they know you're still alive. And sometimes feedback helps.

Do you ever get a chance to socialize with other illustrators?

Only at the art gallery functions.

You have done a Monster ABC. *Have you thought about doing another?*

Yes. That one was done before I had children, and it's not for teaching. The children love it for the monsters, and not for the ABC.

What else would you like to do?

I'd like to paint on wood, wood cut-outs. I'd like to develop that. I like that style in American folk art. That's the only historic style or art that really appeals to me. Anything I do in the future is going to involve that.

Do you ever fear that your inspiration will run out?

I always fear that; but it doesn't happen. There are always new directions to take and new influences. I think that picturebooks have improved to a real art form.

Always pumped up after such pleasant and insightful conversations, we fair flew up the street and over the highway to the train station where friends picked us up. Ms. Niland's comments about "new directions" and the picturebook as "a real art form" sat comfortably in our memories. And we began at once to plan a return tour of Australia, this time to meet with the many other artists who have struck out in their own new directions.

—*Summer 1986*

Update

My family now consists of Alex, 8½, Katie, 6½, and James, my youngest, 3½ years old. Jackson, the Dalmatian, is still with us. All the children are showing artistic tendencies and have a great love of books. I have been encouraging this. I feel one of the best things I have done as a mother is to teach my children to read as early as possible. The older two read well before school, and James at three is reading at kindergarten level. They love reading!

In picturebooks, the illustration only needs to enhance the text. I don't feel it should be there to explain it.

I have illustrated several more books since our last meeting: *There's a Hippopotamus on Our Caravan Roof Getting Sunburnt, The Sniffy Dog, All-Australian Funny and Frightful Verse,* and *Families Are Funny.*

Later this year another book will be published, written by my mother, Ruth Park. I illustrated it in an American Folk Art style.

At the moment I am giving illustration a long rest. I have returned to painting and am preparing works for an exhibition coming up shortly. I am better able to work around the children's lives with painting rather than the stress of the deadlines of book illustrating.

—*June 1990*

Twenty

Graham Oakley

Graham Oakley wanted to retire to an old mill. He didn't care where it was; obviously it would be near water, and that was all he required. He found the mill, a short drive from a small town, a station on the train to Bath. Horses are stabled nearby. He has completely gutted the inside, put in new floors and walls, and lovingly restored it to airy, light modern livability, hand finishing the wooden banisters. Although he is still working on the interior, much of his time has been occupied with landscaping the grounds. It is hard to imagine them as he describes them when he started, because the shrubs, trees and plants look as if they have always grown where they are, on hillocks and banks of a pond that Oakley has created. A dam has helped sculpt the waterway to his taste as well. There is even an enclosed garden with old-fashioned rose bushes.

Inside the kitchen is modern and eating a country lunch here we found it very functional. The two-story living room looks out over fields and river; the fireplace must be cozy in winter. A studio in a gallery above also has a view, along with the artist's tools in an efficiently designed drawing area.

How did you land here?

I spent most of my working life in television. When I was coming to the

Graham Oakley

end of my contract, I thought it would be nice to live in the country by a river, preferably in a water mill. So it was wherever I could find a derelict water mill that needed to be "done up," because I couldn't possibly afford one already "done." I bought this as a ruin. It took a good many years of my life to make it habitable. Chippenham itself is just one street. It was once upon a time a nice Georgian street. But that was just an invitation to knock it down. Bath was saved. . . . I was born in Shrewsbury which has been much altered and spoiled like many other "black and white" towns. They must be regretting it now that tourism is booming.

　　As a child were you always drawing?

　　I certainly liked drawing. At grammar school that was about the only thing I could do; that and biology, really anything that did not require a great deal of discipline. Science, mathematics and French were completely beyond me.

　　Drawing came very naturally and did not require a great deal of effort. I regret not having paid more attention to mathematics. . . . All the conflict in my life has been between representational art and non-representational art. My instincts have always been for representational. I love the pre–Raphaelites.

When did they come into your life?

Right from the days when I first became aware of pictures. I remember getting a book in my library called *Narrative Pictures* by Sacheverel Sitwell, full of pictures like *The Blind Girl.* I decided that was the kind of drawing I wanted to do and was further influenced by seeing books by other turn-of-the-century illustrators like C.E. and H.M. Brock.

How about Beardsley?

He was more in the other school then. I very much like him now, but I preferred the more naturalistic. And American illustrators, like Norman Rockwell. The whole school of American illustrators, Howard Pyle, etc.

How about the traditional British Golden Age illustrators?

Oh yes. And now that's all coming back. So many illustrators and designers go for impact now. That's great for billboard-type advertising, where impact is what you want when you see it from your car window. But it doesn't seem to have a place, to my way of thinking, in book illustration, where you get an impact when you turn the page. But you are going to turn the page dozens of times and the impact becomes less and less until it just becomes boring; there's nothing to look into. I've always thought of pictures as being something which you have to look into and see new things. You look under a leaf in a Pre-Raphaelite and you see ladybugs there. Or apart from the main story of the painting in the background there's another story going on.

The perfect books are the medieval Books of Hours. One can't claim to be anything like their standard, but that's the kind of book illustration I like.

There are a lot of book illustrators whose details are not that excessive and obviously go for effect but at the same time they are pictures you can look at over and over again. One American I am thinking of is N.C. Wyeth. The compositions are so striking but they are still pictures you can keep on looking at.

Any current picturebook people?

Yes. Juan Wijngaard, Maurice Sendak, Nicola Bayley, Helen Oxenbury.

Where did you get your art training?

At a tiny art school, Warrington in Lancashire, now Cheshire due to political meddling with boundaries. I only stayed there a couple of years, one year before and one year after my army service.

How did you become an illustrator and set designer?

The set designer bit was from all those articles in magazines when I was a kid on how glamorous it was to work in films. It was an ambition I suppose I could have fulfilled, but it died after 15 years of television. I

wanted to work in films as a set designer. That was in the days of the Errol
Flynn films; Robin Hood, etc., when film sets were film sets; huge castles or
palaces and things. But now it's mainly squalid bedrooms and kitchens.

When I went to art school I became interested in illustration because
I always drew realistically. When the pressure was on you to do abstracts,
I clung to doing representational things. So the only outlet was as a set
designer doing realistic sets or an illustrator. The first job I did was in reper-
tory, which you call "stock." For years I painted sets for all the usual plays.
I went into advertising. I did a stint at the Royal Opera, not as a designer,
but as a production assistant. Then I went into television.

*From the collaborative world of television, how did you come to the iso-
lated world of picturebooks?*

I've always been an illustrator. I trained as an illustrator, and illustrated
dozens of books by other people. I was still illustrating free-lance while I
was working in television and continued to do so all through my television
career. The editor I worked for occasionally said it was much better to do
your own books, so eventually I thought I'd try one. *Magical Changes* was,
oddly enough, the first one I did. But no one would publish it. So I invented
the church mice.

I started doing the church mice, one a year, while I was still in television. When you work all day at one thing it's good to go home and work at
something entirely different. Television is far from being the glamorous
world some people outside think it is. It was very much a grind. In those
days we did one show after another. Then it was nice to be able to go home
and do your own thing. In television there were so many other people to
please: directors, producers . . . .

Do you still do any work for television?

No. I finished 10 years ago. My last BBC film was *Treasure Island.*

Where did the idea for Magical Changes *come from?*

It's really the old party game of heads and tails, that comes in many
forms, the one you play with paper and pencil, fold the paper and pass it
on.

But the sorts of pictures you put together are far from common. . . .

I just thought it would be nice to try to actually make pictures, rather
than just single objects, which is all the game does. I wondered if it was
possible to make complete pictures. It was much more ambitious when I
first started. It started life as an alphabet book. That was going to be the
justification, the "handle." You would have the right picture when the letter
fitted together. But when the book was finished, my publishers didn't want
it. It was only after the moderate success of two or three of the Church
Mouse books that they agreed to do it. Then the editor and I agreed that
the alphabet wasn't necessary, so it came out with just the split pictures.

How did you go about sequencing, since there is no obvious narrative?

It was guided, as you probably noticed, by the thick uprights on one side and the four or five thin uprights on the other. It was really finding things, subjects that had the right number of uprights: towers, and legs, and ducks' necks. . . . You can make an illusion of it being a complete picture by having nothing in the middle. The horizon line is just under the cut of the page. The sky is so pale as to be white on the upper part. So it gives the illusion that there is a complete picture, when in reality if you look there is nothing in the middle but sky and horizon. The sequence was random. It doesn't really matter. Not many people ever go through it seeing the pictures as they should be. They mostly just flip through. It was possible to work out some satirical kinds of things. I was conscious of that: all the soldiers saluting flagstaffs and then underwear, for example. There's a compositional relationship, because they all have these repeated uprights. Lots of people have made their own stories. I'm told, in letters I get from teachers, that they get kids doing exercises with some of the surreal combinations you get, trying to write some sort of explanation. Which is a curious thing to do since surrealism is noted for having absolutely no meaning whatever.

I got so desperate in the end finding things with uprights. . . . At one point I had a very ambitious idea, which was a non-starter. I was going to put some text in it. It was going to be verses. The forlorn hope was that no matter what combination of verses came up it would still make some kind of funny sense, but I abandoned that. To start with, I can't write verse. So to give myself the additional difficulty of having universal meaning. . . .

Where did you get the idea for Hetty and Harriet*?*

I was trying to find something to do instead of another church mouse story. I thought I could make a story out of this idea of the grass always being greener on the other side. I got all my references from the chickens next door. But then the fox finished all of them off. This is hunting country. So I had the combination of the chickens and the grass being greener on the other side, and things never being exactly what you want when you get there. And I like the idea of circle stories, where you end up where you started.

It wouldn't stand a sequel. Chickens are somehow not sufficiently interesting. The great thing about mice is that anthropomorphism is very easy with mice, because they're so human in a way. They even have hands. The hands are the biggest problem when you are trying to be anthropomorphic. With chickens they're out, claws are a bit off-putting.

Is or was there a real model for Samson (the cat)?

Not really. But I certainly like cats. There was a cat next door who spent most of his life here. Oddly enough, in the church mice books, I now find Samson a bit of a problem. Because you could almost dispense with Samson and just have mice, I find it hard to invent a plot and fit him in.

There is one page in Church Mice Afloat *reminiscent of Japanese wood-cuts (simultaneous action). Are they an influence?*

I've used that once or twice. I got it mainly from animated films. In fact, the structure of my stories is really television situation comedy. I've been criticized for that, but I don't see anything wrong with it. Situation comedies are very concisely and carefully plotted, as these books have to be. In the 32-page format you have to work out the story carefully. But I think working in television is really what brought about my particular kind of picture and word story. I regard a picturebook as a film that doesn't move. That's why I resort to these action pictures with the same characters run over and over again in a spread. It's just like a strip of film where you develop all the pictures and put them in one page.

Do you use storyboards?

I certainly do. First I do a book on one big sheet, in just squares. Then I do a dummy. I do the text and the pictures at the same time. Because I have to consider not so much the book; the page is what I'm working on. So I have to consider how much of the story I'm going to tell on that page in words, and the exact words, and where I can use pictures instead of words. I'm a great believer in never using words and pictures to do the same thing. The problem in illustrating other people's stories is that you are in fact doing in pictures what they have done in words. Somehow what I, and a lot of other people, need is a word for what we are. We're not artists, and we're not writers. I suppose we're picturebook makers.

These are not really like the 19th century books with pictures. A lot of those didn't really tell stories. They were a series of incidents. Even when they told stories, they were just illustrated stories.

What typifies my approach to this, and others like it, is that if you say, "And then a strange thing happened," you don't have to say what happened, you can draw it. Before the invention of the cinema, people didn't have cause to tell stories with pictures. People say, "What about stained glass windows?" But they were telling stories to people who knew them already. It was really just isolated incidents.

It really happened in cinema for the first time, and even they couldn't manage it for a long time. When I see one of the silent classics for the first time, I'm always slightly dismayed at the amount of captions used.

How much visual research do you do?

I don't do a great deal. I have a pretty good library of costumes and such. Oddly enough the hardest things to do are everyday things like bicycles. I keep a file of cuttings of bicycles, sewing machines, etc.; that's the hardest reference to find. If you want to know about something in the 18th century, there are stacks of books on that, but if you want to know what a modern sewing machine looks like, it's very hard to find that kind of material. So that's mainly the kind of research I do.

Are you disappointed in the production and printing of your books?
Usually.

Is your original work larger than the finished book?
No. I'm not really happy working larger than the finished picture. I use a magnifying glass. I get worried as my eyes get less good. Large magnifying glasses have short focal length, and I can't get my brush under them.

Do you choose your own type?
What I usually do is try to work out exactly what's going on each page, so I can work out the type. I'm not that particular about the face itself, because most of these Roman faces are much the same. I tend to work it out on the type that was used in my last book, and I say "use that." They don't really take any notice of the face I suggest; they say, "This will fit in that space, we'll use it." I don't like sans serif; it's very hard to read. It's very tiring on the eyes.

What are your thoughts on the current picturebook business?
I've been feeling a bit remote from the business of late. I've been doing not that much work on books. I've been tired of it all. [And of course very busy with the house and grounds.] It seems that the realistic work is coming back with a vengeance; it's become ultra-realistic, more realistic than the old realism. In fact I think that now it's probably gone a bit too far. It's going to the air-brush school, where the older illustrators would have done a nice free wash and conveyed every bit as much. . . .

There is quite a boom in children's books, isn't there? When I go into the shops and see the lines of them I wonder how can anyone possibly make a living at it?

How about you?
I make a reasonable living at it. I'm fortunate, because my books are old, but they're still in print and they still sell reasonably well! You only make a steady living by having a lot of books in print. The paperbacks are really the main source of my income. There are few hardbacks sold. I suppose a few are, as presents.

Are you satisfied with the visual quality of the paperback editions?
Not really. But all of mine are going to be reoriginated. The plates are all being remade. They were actually pretty worn out. Most are going back to the original art work. One or two have gotten lost. Some of the late printings are pretty poor. The reissue should give them a boost.

Will we see any more books about the church mice?
I'm trying a new book on the mice, but it seems to be a laborious plot. . . .

Because of the limitations you have set?
I've done nine mice stories. What I always look for is a nice bold theme. I did the advertising world in *Abroad*. When the moon craze was on I did the *Moon*. But there's no big theme now. I've gone back to complicated

comings and goings. Immigration was an alternative; some white mice from a pet shop as intruders trying to get accepted. The problems would arise because they're white. But there was no mileage in it.

My attempts to break away from the church mice have never been too successful. I feel that I should have a new series, but none of the books I've done would warrant it. I'd like to do another *Magical Changes*, but I don't think the sales warrant it. I would have liked to do a sequel to *Henry's Quest*, but I won't get the chance. It wasn't popular enough. The problem may be that it's aimed at an older age group; a group that doesn't go for picture-books. It may be bought by adults, but they think it's a bit beneath them, so nobody buys it. My American publishers have refused my latest book because of the failure of *Henry*. The last church mice *Diary* also didn't do well. I don't like doing books that are not going to sell well.

I'm not really a painter. I would never want to do pictures just for the sake of doing pictures. I would always want to know that somebody would buy it.

Do you ever do anything just for itself, not to sell?

I expect if I did one I could do the blackmail bit and get it published. But I don't like doing that.

What about the new book you're working on? Is it one that is likely to make it?

It's about a modern character who gets entangled in the motorway and ends up in storyland . . . marries Beauty and brings her back, to exit through the London Underground.

—*Summer 1989*

Twenty-One

Jan Ormerod

A Sampling of Works in Print

Bend and Stretch Lothrop, 1987.
The Frog Prince Lothrop, 1990.
Just Like Me Lothrop, 1986.
Kitten Day Lothrop, 1989.
Making Friends Lothrop, 1987.
Mom's Home Lothrop, 1987.
Moonlight Lothrop, 1982, 1984.
One Hundred Things to Do with a Baby Lothrop/Penguin, 1984, 1986.
The Saucepan Game Lothrop, 1989.
The Story of Chicken Licken Lothrop, 1986.
Sunshine Lothrop/Penguin, 1981, 1984.
This Little Nose Lothrop, 1987.
When We Went to the Zoo Lothrop, 1990, 1991.

Bicycles are parked in rows and heaps by the train station in Cambridge because it is a distance from there to the peaceful river and venerable old buildings of the university. Off in a slightly different direction, past some residential streets, lies a small bustling shopping area, with butcher shop and bakery. Small and larger inner city Victorian terrace houses front the same street. We are warned to check the number carefully before we ring, so we don't disturb a touchy neighbor. The mother and younger child at the door are recognizable immediately from the pictures in the Ormerod books. So are the Burmese cats who glide by. The tall, slim and lovely pre-teen who blows in from dancing and out to referee is no longer the little girl who inspired Sunshine. *But Sophie will appear in her own way in the new book we see later, a version of* The Frog Prince.*

Young Laura, who is sure she is *the girl in* Sunshine *and* Moonlight, *is already busy drawing and making books when not skipping rope. She draws as we begin to chat in the living room, decorated with drawings on the wall and collections of shells and gourds.*

You were born on the more remote west coast of Australia?

Yes. It's the most isolated capital city in the world. Singapore is closer than Sydney. It's very beautiful. The people who started *Magpies* magazine and run the bookshop called The Singing Tree are very vigorous people who are doing a lot in the community getting things happening in children's books. They are finally getting visiting authors and artists to go to Perth. As young art students we did feel isolated. We had the panicky feeling it was all happening somewhere else.

Was your schooling pretty much the same as anywhere in Australia?

Yes. What was very different was this feeling and reality of being so isolated. And therefore it was like a big village, in that to a large extent everyone in a particular field knew everyone else in that field, what they were doing and who they were doing it with. It had all the positive and negative aspects of village life; it was safe but it was stifling.

Did you have art training in school?

Yes. Then I went to art school, and did an Associateship in Graphic Design at the Western Australian Institute of Technology, which is now Curtin University of Technology. Then I did an art teaching qualification and spent several years as an art teacher in secondary schools, and working in a school that offered enrichment to secondary school students who wanted to do extra work in art. They had to give up lots of their free time because all their Saturdays were spent in classes where artists would be brought in as teachers. Quite soon I moved into Teachers College, teaching art educa-tion and creative growth and development.

Back when you were young, were you drawing all the time?

I think that's probably true. I find it very difficult to remember any-thing at all about my childhood, but I do know that I drew a great deal.

Do you remember any picturebooks from childhood?

I didn't come from a bookish house at all. There were annuals which came from England at Christmas time, and I can remember poring over them. At that time there were very few Australian picturebooks, unlike now. There wasn't a sense of value in anything Australian. We were soaking up British culture as fast as we could, and American culture didn't really take hold until television arrived, when I was about ten.

What was not satisfying enough about teaching as a career?

I had decided not to have any children, so when Sophie arrived it made a change in my life necessary. I decided to resign rather than take leave. I felt that I was 30 and hadn't left school yet. Caring for her and slowing down to her pace gave me a chance to reorganize priorities. Before long I would have been out of teaching and into administration, where I would have spent all my time at meetings talking numbers. I loved teaching, but I didn't really want to do it for another 35 years. Meanwhile I was looking at children's picturebooks for the first time, because my husband was a

Jan Ormerod

children's librarian bringing books home for Sophie. I was taking her into
bookshops where she was choosing books and devouring them. We were
discovering them at the same time, and I thought it was a magical world.
I decided I wanted to see if I could be part of it, so by the time she was four
I had a folio together. It was clear I couldn't work from Perth. We could
have moved to Sydney, but that was a huge move anyway, so we let the
house, left our jobs, and left Australia. We had a preschooler, so that move
was possible. We lived in Ireland for a while, and then Holland. Eventually
I took my folio around to publishers in London and my career in children's
books was off.

Was there a teacher who motivated or encouraged you?

There were a group of friends, in retrospect, who were really responsible for that. Certainly the fact that my husband was very supportive was an
enormous help. He was quite happy to resign his job and come to England
and see how it went. After Laura was born he was "houseperson." If he
hadn't been prepared to do that it obviously would have made it all a great
deal harder. There were several friends who were determined that I had

to at least find out if I could do these things. Probably the man who was responsible more than anyone else for making sure it did happen has just died. He was like a catalyst. Every time we met, something important would happen. I am full of doubt about my own ability still. Whenever I meet other illustrators at publishing parties I find that none of us are very different in that respect. I don't find many chirpy confident people.

Initially I worked to understand being a parent, because I hadn't intended to have children. But I loved it, and it's been a wonderful experience. The first books were just about the experience of being a parent. The real joy of having a baby was something I didn't know about, since I had never been the kind of girl who peeks into prams and coos at babies. Because I'm not that sort of person, I came to it fresh. As an artist I am an observer rather than one who gets inside an experience and draws from the inside out. I feel separate and record as the observer.

Do you draw from mental images, or sketches?

Each book evolves in a different way. Very often the focal point will be one very strong image, either a person I want to draw very much, or just one image that will occur to me and I will work around that. The Dad and baby series are based on Laura when she was crawling, and her constant companion, the black and white cat called Jack. They went everywhere together. They were exploring things in the same way, smelling them, touching them. It was going to be a series of books about the child and the cat exploring things together, going through a house. I was interested in drawing them both, because I found them fascinating, and they were around. Later, when I'd already done dummy books, a father appeared in one of the dummies, which was logical, because my husband Paul was caring for her at that stage. The format was almost square, a compact little rectangle. It was intriguing to fit a tall adult male into that format for eight spreads, in four books, and that became what interested me. I need to be very interested in doing the drawings or it doesn't work; it shows. As a designer, I need a problem-solving aspect to really keep me interested in a book. I work to size. So much changes in the printing process anyway, and in the fact that it becomes a book, where you turn the pages. There's so much to keep control of that an added complication like drawing larger and anticipating how it will look when reduced I don't need. Certainly from a production point of view there doesn't seem to be any advantage.

Do you do your own design and type selection?

I work with the designers and production people at Walker Books from the first drawing. I'm not instinctively a fine typographer; I prefer to have someone who has a good feeling for type work on that, and I work closely with them. Walker is very concerned to produce a fine book. I cringe when I see the books, but not because they haven't been produced carefully. It's seeing that my draftsmanship hasn't been what I hoped.

Sometimes you break the frame. Why?

I think it's fun. It strikes me as funny to put the edge of the mattress there and poke the pillow out and put the head there. I like to use it as part of the story-telling. I don't have any deep meaningful thing to say about it; I just enjoy doing it.

Do you think in cinema terms?

My books are very much like storyboards for a very short film. I do think of them in terms of continuous action, then decide what is the absolute moment to freeze the frame so you can see what has just happened and is about to happen. I'm thinking of the undressing and dressing sequence in *Sunshine*. It's terribly important to stop it at the right moment. If I stopped it a second later, I wouldn't have seen that little hand. I'm not using words here. I don't feel comfortable writing; I'm not happy about my use of words, but I feel confident that I can tell a story in pictures. When I do use words, they come later. I first of all complete the drawings. I'm jotting words down all the time as I'm drawing, but they very much come after the drawings. In fact my latest book, *Kitten Day*, I designed as a wordless book, and bowed to pressure in the end that words should be added. When I was in America and Canada recently everyone kept saying, "Why does this have words? We want more wordless books." But it was the American publishers who insisted on the words. I get very conflicting messages. Teachers and librarians want wordless books, and publishers are terrified of them.

You have chosen to do continuous stop action in boxes and not just in space like Oakley or Zwerger?

That's a very strange thing. Before I became an illustrator I got hold of Turkle's *Deep in the Forest*. I adored that book, and pored over it minutely, and then forgot about it, I thought. When I first took the idea for *Sunshine* in to the publisher, it was in a different format. This format was their decision, and it happened, when I looked back, to be the same format as Brinton Turkle's book. The strip-style device is exactly the same. He does the same thing, taking his drawings slightly out of the frame. I think that his influence in *Sunshine* is terribly strong, not in subject matter but certainly using child's eye-level rather than adult eye-level and drawing along a base line rather than using more sophisticated perspective. I think that was the strongest influence, even though when I was doing *Sunshine* I was not aware of that.

[We move from living room to studio, where there are a large drawing table and many piles of work around.]

I have a photocopier for enlarging, or reversing. I do drawings on layout paper and can photocopy onto art paper, so I don't panic when the cat knocks over water on top of the art work.

From beginning to proof, how long can a book take?

It depends on which book. This one, about the zoo, a couple of years, because I haven't been working constantly on it as I work on several books at the same time. If I had been sitting at my desk working steadily on it, *The Frog Prince* would have taken six to nine months. The finishing of the art work is not the longest part of the process; I spend a long time on roughs and dummies, and rework and rework. Often the finished art is redone over and over too, but I suppose three months would be the least time I would spend. . . .

Are the Gemma *books about a family you know?*

They had a very different beginning. I had been talking to Jan Pienkowski and he had been bemoaning the fact that there were very few books for black British children showing them involved in day-to-day activities. You have some in the U.S.A., but we didn't. Then I was offered *Happy Christmas Gemma* to do for a Christmas book. I just asked what they would feel about my doing it about a black family. The author was very enthusiastic about it, but it took quite a bit of rewriting. I have a West Indian friend who is a teacher-librarian working in a multicultural resource center, and was familiar with the problems I was going to face. Plus she had a family of stunningly beautiful children and a drawer full of family photos which she let me work with to evolve the characters.

Do you try your books on your children?

No, because the difference between the book you can hold in your hand and look at and the book as a concept or the dummy book is so vast that I wouldn't expect Laura at her age to be able to respond appropriately. Certainly I use Sophie now, but as another adult rather than as a child. And I don't go out into schools at all. I don't have any excuse; I just don't want to. I talk to art students, students of children's literature, parents, teachers, librarians, but I don't talk to kids. Most of my books are for *very* young children, and there's not much I can talk to them about, and I'm not an entertainer. I don't have an act that would be appropriate.

How did you come to do Frog Prince?

I've always wanted to do *Frog Prince*. It's *my* fairy tale. I think also possibly because Sophie's just reaching adolescence. Essentially to me it's all about a young girl's emerging sexuality. I can't see whatever else it can possibly be about. I've done years and years of books about babies and small children, factual and earth-bound, that I felt I needed a little bit of fantasy and elaboration, having a bit more fun.

Trina Hyman's early book *Quitting Deal* was a very strong influence. She had men, women, and children in loving poses without any sentimentality, so well-drawn.

Are the costumes in Chicken Licken *based on real ones in a real play?*

No. Two or three ideas coincided in that book. I had an idea of a crawling baby disrupting a performance of some kind, but I imagined it would be a home performance. I love to see children dressing up and putting on plays, which happens such a lot on long summer evenings. I've watched a lot of that and I thought it would be fruitful material. Then it occurred to me that I could combine those two ideas. Sophie happened to bring home the story of Chicken Licken as a reading book at that point, and I thought "Aha! This might be it." It was clear that it had so many characters it had to be a school play rather than a home one.

How hard is it to be simple, as in Messy Baby, *etc.?*

I love that simplicity. It intrigues me as a designer. I'm interested in cutting back and cutting back to absolute fundamentals. I'm very pleased with those little books because I think they've got to the point where I couldn't have cut anything else out and still have made sense. People often say of my books that they are crammed with details, when in fact they're not. There's nothing in them that is extra. I think that what people are saying is that they were able to talk with their child about the pictures, and there was a lot to talk about. They confuse that with me putting a lot in. I don't actually talk to the child, because I don't remember being a child, and I'm not a very child-centered person. I'm talking to other adults who have a child on their lap. What I think about when I'm doing the work is that sort of conversation they'll be having, so I like to leave space for the child and the adult to bring their own experience to it and talk about it and enrich it in that way. Which is another reason I like to cut back and back. If I put too much in it limits that process.

One kind of book is no harder than another. I keep using this word "urgency." That's what I call it for myself if I'm intrigued by a problem or a concept. It just becomes terribly important to work on it and the adrenaline starts to flow. If in one case it means a lot of elaborate visual material and in another case it means cutting back, it doesn't mean that one is harder than the other.

What's your idea of what a book should be?

I can't presume to answer a question like that. I'm not an academic. It's communicating visually using that particular format that's been laid down in history. I suppose it's closely related to narrative painting of another time, but it's not what I would do if I called myself an artist and produced work to hang in galleries.

Would you say the picturebook is less valuable than fine art?

No. I keep on doing these despite all my doubts because (this sounds horribly pompous) I do get feedback when I go to talk to people. It seems that, although it is not in any major way, I am enriching some people's lives by producing books. I enrich mine by making them and then I enrich other people's because they share them. That just seems a fairly complete cycle and it's as close to making sense of life as an artist as I can get to at this stage.

— Summer 1989

Twenty-Two

Ken Robbins

A Sampling of Works in Print

At the Ballpark Viking, 1988.
Beach Days Viking, 1987.
Boats Scholastic, 1989.
Bridges Dial, 1991.
Building a House Macmillan, 1983.

City-Country; A Car Trip in Photographs Viking, 1985.
A Flower Grows Dutton, 1990.
Tools Four Winds, 1983.
Trucks of Every Sort Crown, 1988.

The Hamptons lie on the lower of the two thin arms of Long Island that stretch out into the Atlantic Ocean. Well off the highway and down a thin gravel drive, Ken Robbins and his wife, Maria Polushkin, have built their refuge from New York City. Their modern house with high ceilings and exposed beams is home to a dog, two cats, a wide range of books and a darkroom, designed by Robbins, where he converts his film into unique illustrations. A genial, bearded philosophy major who enjoys his wife's excellent cooking, Robbins reflects before answering questions, but the photographs on the wall clearly demonstrate the qualities he aims for in his work. The pictures he creates are spare in detail, stage sets composed from ordinary life experiences that challenge the viewer's imagination.*

My mother was the owner of a suburban art gallery when I was growing up, but my interest in art didn't emerge until after my schooling. I also had many friends at Cornell who were architects, because the architecture school had more spirit and brio than any other department. But I studied English and philosophy. I was very word oriented, and after college it

---

*Originally published in The Horn Book Magazine, *November/December 1988.*

Self-portrait by Ken Robbins

seemed quite natural to work in book publishing. Of course, every editor has to find a niche, and I subsequently signed on quite a number of books of photography—as many, I'd guess, as anyone in mainstream publishing at the time. So I called John Szarkowski at the Museum of Modern Art, and he said that if I were willing to give up my precious publisher's lunches, I could come up to the photography department every noon, and he'd have one of their interns pull out portfolios and lecture to me. It was a truly fabulous offer, so for weeks I had my own private tutorial at the Museum of Modern Art. Later I had a similar tutorial at the Eastman House in Rochester, New York. Then shortly after, in 1972, I was fired. But I was already a photography enthusiast. Of course, I wanted to make images myself. Although I wouldn't yet be making a living at photography for several years, I was taking pictures and learning to print. By 1975 I was already coloring some of my photographs artificially—making positive black-and-white transparencies, mounting pieces of torn colored paper behind them, and using one or more layers of tissue paper to soften the effect. I made many pictures that I still love, and they sold well in galleries. But by that time I was trying to get commercial work as a photographer, and art directors had trouble with my work. There was just no way to reproduce the three-dimensional effect of those pieces. So I started experimenting with ways of getting a similar effect out of flat art. Then, of course, I had to find art directors who were willing to take a chance on an unknown photographer. For people who supposedly earn a living from their aesthetic judgment, a surprising number are quite timid about their own taste. They may like your work; they may even love it; but they are reluctant to take a chance on you unless someone else has already done so.

Did old tinted photographs suggest the effect that you wanted to achieve?

I'm sure they did, but I don't know how conscious the whole process was. Since I'm not formally educated in art, I have a tendency to react on an emotional level. But if I like something—if I do have an emotional reaction—then I try to use my intelligence to parse it, to analyze it, and to understand my response to it. That process is how I create my own work as well. In the darkroom I'll make six or eight prints on an intuitive, speculative basis. I'll go on and color them only if I think I have something I like. Then I'll work one print up into a colored piece, but the trick, of course, is not to work the photograph to death and destroy whatever it was that I responded to in the darkroom. If I still like it after all that, then it goes into the portfolio. If not, I throw it away. Of course, if the image is for a commercial job, I cannot throw it away. Generally, there is a particular problem posed by the art director, or intrinsic to the job itself, and that problem, whether it is aesthetic or purely practical, has to be solved. But the stretch involved in solving commercial problems does wonders for my personal work.

I think the artist's job is to make people see things in a new way—because often that is the only way people will see things at all. I make images that are now considered very romantic and old-fashioned, but I do it not just to make them look nostalgic but to make the images new and fresh for me. I also think a certain amount of holding back, visually and verbally, is terribly important in art. To be moved deeply by a work, people have to be able to project themselves into it. Highly detailed art does not interest me as much as art that in some way invites the beholder to complete it.

What picturebooks do you remember from your childhood?

The first that really excited me was the Tenniel edition of *Alice in Wonderland*, and I still love it. I have a strong feeling for etchings, which goes straight back to Tenniel and Doré—who conveyed so much with less.

I do not see too many contemporary books that I really love but when I do see one, it makes me jealous. I wish I'd created *The Wreck of the Zephyr* or *The Polar Express*. I like Van Allsburg's color and especially the amount of information he conveys. There is just enough information in his textures to fuel your imagination—to create mood and feeling, but he lets you put yourself into the rest. People's faces are not so specific that they couldn't be everyman, yet they are not just cartoons.

How did you get to do your first children's book?

Maria was a children's book editor, and I was editing adult books. When we left New York, she began writing children's books and doing some translating. Her editor, Norma Jean Sawicki, came to visit around 1979 when I was first trying to make a living purely as a photographer. It was she who suggested that I might create a book about something that children were interested in—like trucks. We did two books of black-and-white photographs—*Trucks of Every Sort* and *Building a House*. They were full of information but not very esthetic. Eventually I persuaded Norma Jean that I could do a book of mostly esthetic value like *Tools*.

How do you work with the art director on your books?

I had absolutely no input on the first two books. I gave them the pictures, and they said, "Thank you very much; now go away." For *Tools* I produced a dummy, which meant I had to make all the pictures twice in order to paste them up and see what they looked like. It was more work, but I had more control that way. Art directors do like to have their own input, but I like to be consulted on all aspects of the book design, especially the cover. That privilege is one you don't get without a struggle.

How did you decide on the sequence in Tools?

The first problem was selecting the tools. I wanted ones that could be found in Daddy's tool chest but were still somewhat surprising. I also chose them for their sculptural qualities. I took all of the pictures first, and then we sequenced them in Norma Jean's office, laying out two at a time to see the spreads. We played with them visually to make the colors and shapes work. I think my pictures tend to need space around them, so I did not want them to bleed off the page. I think of pictures as windows through which you see something, and bleeding diminishes the window effect. The art director did a wonderful design, based on what I had originally shown her and improving on it as well.

Are the scenes in your books set up?

A few in *Beach Days* were. Most of *A Horse Named Paris* was staged. In fact, for one shot in a corn field, I was lying on my back on the ground while a very young rider did her best to keep a charging horse from running over me. In my mind's eye I kept seeing a newspaper headline: "Stupid photographer trampled by horse."

How do you perceive the relationship between words and pictures?

For me, the pictures deliver the emotions. Words are capable of that too, of course, but pictures really bear the weight. The words are the connective tissue; they give a sense of identity to a collection of pictures and take the reader from one picture to the next. For *At the Ballpark* I thought of dispensing with words altogether, but it didn't quite work. Especially in children's books, people are not prepared to expose children to an experience that presents itself as being purely esthetic. I think children's book people are delighted when a book is beautiful, but the worst thing you can say to an editor is that you want to do an art book.

Your recent prints have the quality of an earlier century.

I've consciously attempted to make them look like old photographs. Originally I just wanted to make my hand-colored images look like full-color photographs, and when they were successful, they did look remarkably like the real thing—albeit with some subtle differences and a lot more control on my part. But now I'm much less interested in trying to make my work look realistic. I'm not so much involved with documenting the hard-edged reality of things as I am in creating a mood around them.

What cameras do you use?

I have a Hasselblad and a couple of Nikons. But my equipment is only a tool for making images, and a few basic tools are all I need. High-tech photography can be diverting or amusing or even astounding, but I am not interested in it. The darkroom is my favorite part of the process. I've got about seven versions of everything I've done—from straightforward, Kodacolor-like versions to versions that are bleached, distorted, done in new techniques, cropped differently, with soft or hard edges. Photography for me is all a matter of intonation.

Do you apply color to each photograph individually?

Yes. It sometimes creates a problem when two people want prints of the same image, because they never are exactly the same from print to print. As I have developed a more painterly technique, the differences from print to print have gotten even greater.

Where do you get the ideas for a book?

I get them from an image. Sometimes I will walk by a scene 50 times and just not see the potential. But a very exciting moment occurs when a series suddenly opens up and I see it. That's how *At the Ballpark* happened, but other books were more calculated.

When you photograph, are you thinking about what a five-year-old or a ten-year-old would want to see?

No. When I take on a book project, I have in mind what a child might or might not be interested in, but I don't concern myself with that problem when I make pictures. To me, a photo is a photo, and anyone can relate to it.

More so than for other kinds of illustration?

I think so. Some illustrators draw for children exactly as they would for anyone else, but most do not. Maybe they feel that since the story goes beyond the child's personal experience, they have to stylize the accompanying art—simplify it in some way—in order to compensate. But I try to take photographs that I would be proud to have on the walls of a gallery. Adults may be more impressed with my photographs because they understand the technique, but children experience them on a very direct, esthetic level. They don't think about how the photograph was done or the time required to produce it.

What about style?

I keep trying to find new techniques—new ways of expressing things that I couldn't express before—like a vocabulary I keep trying to add to. I don't abandon old styles when I come up with new ones; I just add to them. That way for any particular photograph I can use the most appropriate style—the most expressive. I want to be more articulate with my photographs. That is my style.

—1988

Update

When I mentioned a "very different" sort of book last time we spoke, I was referring to a technique I've been employing lately that produces a softer, even more romantic image than I've employed in the past. It was my feeling (and still is) that this new technique would be highly appropriate for illustrating a book of children's fiction. Well, that ambition is still there, and still unrealized. I did take a stab at it, but some very astute criticism from an editor/friend convinced me that the story wasn't quite there yet. The technique is alive and well, however. I used it to pretty good effect, I hope, in a book Dial recently published called *A Flower Grows*. It documents the life cycle of an Amaryllis bulb, and as such it is, like all my others, essentially non-fiction. But in this case the subject is so beautiful that the enterprise of the book became in effect more esthetic and, perhaps, rather less informative. So in a way you might say the book did have some fictional pretensions. Anyway, I'm still looking for the right story to illustrate.

To that end, yes, I would certainly consider tackling someone else's story—at least in theory I would. It would have to be just precisely the right story, of course. Setting and action would have to fall within the realm of what can be captured photographically, either by staging a shot or by creating illusion through manipulation of one sort or another. And with photography there is always potentially an additional problem: It boils down to the fact that the very wealth of information which the medium is so well equipped to convey, the explicitness of photography, so to speak, can work against the power of fiction, which to my mind is largely implicit. Let me say it another way: The power of a story is in what it does not tell, and it seems to me that in order to effectively illustrate a story, a photographer has to somehow learn to suggest rather than show. On the other hand, a photograph that does succeed in suggesting more than it shows can be as powerful as any painting.

But, back to the question of illustrating someone else's work. I have often thought of trying to illustrate fairy tales. That would be a real challenge. Of course, there could be no give and take with the author, but that's rare in this business anyway, even when the author is alive. Somehow the publishing process militates against real collaboration. It would be (and is, in most cases) more like post-laboration, where the illustrator comes into the process last and tries to add what he or she can after the writing process is done. Come to think of it, a real collaboration with a real living author might be an interesting thing. . . .

Much to my surprise, the current list of my picturebook titles adds up to nine, with two more coming down the pike. I guess that's a significant number, but, no, I can't say I feel like part of the children's book world. For one thing, as you suggested, I do live pretty far out on Long Island and that certainly does limit my contacts with other writers and illustrators, and with librarians, reviewers, and book people in general, for that matter.

Then too, my work on children's books is more or less of a piece with my other photographic work, so I tend to identify myself more as a photographer than as a children's book author. There is one important difference, though: The sustained and focused nature of the visual essays I do for my books forces me to be a bit more organized than I am generally. Of course, the work I do for exhibition is sustained in the sense of being an ongoing preoccupation, but it's not very focused with regard to subjects, which change as my whims change. And my commercial work is narrowly defined by the client as to subject, but all too rarely is it sustained. So when I do a children's book I enjoy working for six months or so on a single subject. It deepens the vision.

Here's a complaint, of sorts: In my experience it seems that American publishers can't find in America the kind of quality they get from Japanese and other Asian printers, at least not at a price they can afford, and that seems to me a shame. I say this not out of any kind of chauvinism, but simply because it is no longer possible for me to be present when my work goes on press. I am not a stickler for accuracy in the reproduction of my work. To me the effectiveness of the image as it is finally printed is the crucial thing, and there have been times when an increase of contrast or a slight shift in color on press has actually improved a particular image. Assuming that I am present to approve the change, something serendipitous can occur—otherwise the best we can hope for is mere mechanical accuracy.

Also, schedules suffer from the exigencies of trans–Pacific shipping, and sometimes the books themselves suffer, too. Two years ago Viking accepted a shipment of my books that had spent some time under extremely humid, if not to say moist conditions, possibly dockside or in the hold of a cargo vessel. Every one of the book cases warped, and the returns are still showing up on my royalty statements. Generally, though, I've been pretty lucky with the production work that's gone into the making of my books.

With rare exceptions the format of an upcoming book has been settled upon well before I begin making final prints for a book. Sometimes, not always, considerations of design or cost require that a particular photograph be reproduced a bit smaller than I might wish, but in the main my work is the same for reproduction as for exhibition.

You asked if the reviewers have been more receptive to the special qualities of photographs than they were five years ago. Well, the answer is that I don't really know. Mostly, I only get to see reviews of my own books and at that only the ones that my publishers forward to me. And, of course, it's mostly the trade media that review children's books. One doesn't pick up *Newsweek* or the daily *New York Times* and see much in the way of children's book reviews unless a record amount of money has been paid to the author. But I must say I think I've been treated pretty fairly by reviewers in general, and quite generously by some (not excluding yourselves). Some, it's true, are not very sophisticated or knowledgeable about photography, but they are generally very accepting of it.

—*1990*

Twenty-Three

Tony Ross

A Sampling of Works in Print

The Boy Who Cried Wolf Dial, 1985.

Don't Do That! Random House, 1991.

Earth Tigerlets As Explained by Professor Xargle translated into Hyman by Jeanne Willis. Dutton, 1990.

Foxy Fables Dial, 1986.

Hansel and Gretel Random, 1990.

I Want a Cat Farrar, Straus, 1989.

I Want My Potty Kane-Miller, 1988.

I'm Coming to Get You Dial, 1984, 1987.

Lazy Jack Dial, 1986, 1988.

Michael by Tony Bradman. Macmillan, 1991.

Mrs. Goat and Her Seven Little Kids Macmillan, 1990.

The Pop-Up Book of Nonsense Verse Random, 1989.

Super Dooper Jezebel Farrar, Straus, 1988.

This Old Man Macmillan, 1990.

The Treasure of Cozy Cove Farrar, Straus, 1990.

The Treasure Sock Dell, 1987.

Well I Never! by Heather Eyles. Overlook, 1990.

We did not venture out to his home in Devon, but met with Tony Ross instead at the Chelsea Arts Club, a rustic casual contrast to the usual British clubs seen on film and TV. A lawnmower added to outside noise, as we chatted by a fountain. Inside, billiards tables are by the bar, and the men's loo is where the extra beer kegs are stored. The cat in the window of the dining room is Orlando. He actually is a member of the club. "He's been one longer than I have," says Ross. Whistler's self-portrait on the wall adds another incongruity to the scene.

Were you really the son of a magician?

Yes, but not a traveling one. We didn't move about in a caravan or anything like that. He just went where the jobs took him.

Do you think that had any influence on you?

184

Tony Ross

That's hard to say, isn't it? My mother did a bit of stage work as well. And my grandfather was a professional musician. Somewhere in the family was an engraver for Charles Dickens, so there was a lot of artistic background. I grew up thinking that doing something in the arts was the norm, and I'm thankful for that.

Some influences that have been suggested in the writing about you have been Rackham, Shepard and Ardizzone. Were those important to you as a child?

Not so much as a child. They passed in and out. I liked *Winnie the Pooh* very much, as did most children my age. But I started to look at these books much more technically, of course, when I went to art school. When I was a kid I liked the stories, and the illustrations were just there. I don't think it ever dawned on any of us that anybody "did" them. They just happened.

How about Gustav Doré, who has also been suggested as an influence?

My grandfather collected illustrated books. I've forgotten what age I was, but I was ill, I'd read everything, *Rupert* and everything else that was lying around; and I found a huge *Don Quixote* by Doré. I took that to bed. I didn't read it, of course, but the illustrations haunted me: the gaunt knight with the cracked shield, the windmills wrenching him off his horse. From the earliest time book illustration hit me and stayed in my mind. Dore still does.

At this time were you drawing as well?

I can remember very early attempts on slates, where you could draw, erase and draw again, which you can never do on paper. Chalk and slate always interested me. Oddly enough, now I like black and white and I guess there's a similarity with the white on black. When I was little I did play around a lot with every sort of drawing. Of course when I went to school it was about the only thing I could do, along with playing games. At school everybody has to be good at something, and drawing was the one thing I could be the top of the class at, where I stayed until I left school.

Did you do A levels and O levels in art?

No, oddly enough. I took woodworking, because at that time there were one or two things I wanted to make. I wasn't concerned about O levels. I liked the art lessons. I knew I could draw, so I couldn't see any sense in taking examinations in it. I thought I should do an examination in something useful. I did all the usual: French, Latin, math, etc. I took art later, to get into art school.

One of the things I wanted to make was an articulated puppet, which I did. But the woodworking master couldn't help me: He knew how to make stools and shelves. Woodworking was one thing that has been of no use to me. I haven't touched a saw since.

Have you thought of working any of your characters out in three dimensions?

Not in wood. But recently I bought a couple of bronzes. I've heard that Ralph Steadman, Leo Lionni and Fulvio Testa have worked in bronze, so I thought that might be something to take on. I'd like to do small pieces, to give to friends. But I'd have to have them cast.

One of my hobbies is collecting toy soldiers, and I've tried casting some of those, with disastrous results. I never learned the technology.

I'd like to see some of my characters in three dimensions. When I doodle, I like to doodle in three dimensions, to do light falling on things and casting shadows. I think in every book I've done every figure has a light side and a dark side. I think that's why I first took to art designing, because being black and white it could show a moonlit night or a summer morning or a November afternoon and it would all be there just by the use of line, tone and hatching.

Maybe it's a byproduct of teaching as well. It's one of the first things you have to teach, to lift the flat image off the flat page, and make it round. It's not inborn, it has to be taught; you have to know where the light is coming from. I remember I was taught this to an excruciating degree at art college, where the classic exercise was to shine a strong light through a spiral staircase on the floor. I think that there in art school was the first time I learned anything that was really of use to me in life, except for Scouts. There we learned to tie knots, and I've always been able to tie a parcel ever since.... Even when I travel, and I go all over the world, the better bits of French or German that I know and use I learned from the French and Germans, not in school.

In Liverpool did you do specifically an illustration course?

Yes. But in those days we were also taught some typography. I also did a little bit of sculpture, pottery. You got a taste of everything and chose what you liked.

I don't know quite why I chose illustration. I was interested in the graphic area. I liked doing lithographs, I liked doing design very much, I liked typography. When I left college I was a designer, a typographer, an art director in an advertising agency. I was happier with design work, especially with the money it offered. Illustration seemed to offer practically nothing. In fact being taught illustration was like being taught jousting.

Do you still do some free-lance work in advertising?

I try not to. It has to be a very good offer. I don't like the advertising ethos. I don't mind if people want to relieve the gullible of their money. I just can't be bothered with the people who want me to do a tiny illustration of a kipper and think they have to brief me for 10 days on how to do it and go to meeting after meeting about it.

So how did you get from advertising to children's books?

At the same time as I was art director I was also doing cartoons, as were others, like Michael Foreman and Ralph Steadman. We all seemed to pop up in the same journals, like *Punch*. Then I took a job at the Polytechnic School of Art teaching advertising. They had a group of illustration students about with no teacher, so they said, "You draw a bit, don't you? Why don't you be the teacher?" So I thought this is ridiculous, I'm in advertising. I'd better see what this is all about if I'm going to teach it. I tried illustrating a book and sent it to a publisher. It was published, and there I was, a published illustrator. I thought maybe I'd do one or two more and call it a day. Somehow it grew, and took over.

You obviously take pleasure in it or you wouldn't do it.

Frankly, I wouldn't swap it for anything. It's a way of life I have no complaints about at all. Perhaps a film star would be better....

Do you think the years in advertising added to your sense of humor in such books as those reinterpreting fairy tales and fables? Red Riding Hood or The Three Little Pigs?

No, I don't think so. The agencies tried to squash that out of me. In the 1960s David Ogilvie set the tone in advertising. He said in one of his books: "People don't buy from clowns." My art director kept telling me, "Be serious. Advertising is a serious business." Underneath I wanted to be funny. Perhaps that's why I drew cartoons.

What I did enjoy as a designer was moving elements about the page. So every drawing I do now, although it may not be evident, in my mind is a construction and a design. I like to place things and move things around. When I was making TV animated films I loved being able to move the bits and pieces in the background here or there. This is what I did as a typographer. I was presented with an area and what was to go in it, and I had to find the perfect place.

But yes, there were a lot of things I found funny about advertising, but not in the work. They were in the people and the lifestyle that went with the work.

Does your publisher ever object to the kinds of things you do with your stories?

Not at all, because I have a very good publisher. There's a story I like to tell by Alistair Cooke, about a young English publisher who went to New York, to a publishers' party, where he didn't know anyone. He looked around and said, "Who are these people?" The man with him said, "Do you see that man over there with the snuff stains on his waistcoat? That's Alfred Knopf the publisher. The man over there on the other side is in the book business."

I don't get along with people in the "book business." They say, "I don't think that will sell. Good heavens, I can't publish that!" My publisher says, "If you like that, or if I like it, I'll publish it." He doesn't try to change it. He believes in his artists. He's not frightened of failure. He accepts that to do anything good you may crash occasionally. To achieve anything you have to make mistakes. If you're safe every time you never grow.

In the U.S. my books have not sold well until recently. But now I'm approached by American publishers. I did *Meanwhile Back at the Ranch* which was strange because I know nothing about the American West. I got it all from TV. I had to ask an American friend things like "What kind of toilet paper do they have in America?" I did a couple of books for Dial where I had to ask about things like Apple Jacks.

I've just finished a pop-up book.

Do you find the design problems different for a pop-up book than for a regular one?

It's pretty similar. Although I've done cut-paper animation which is similar to the little pieces for a pop-up, it isn't until you see the whole thing finished that you know whether it actually works. It's a relief when it all fits together.

Do you select your own type for your books?

Not so much any more. I learned in the era of hot type. Now it's all computerized, a different set of rules. But I like to do it now and again. My publisher likes me to do it. I like designing the book. You shouldn't notice the designer; everything should just work together; that's my ideal book. I do like to play around with the form of the book. It's interesting how many people do a book without thinking that it has a physical form. In *I'm Coming to Get You* I have a monster bursting through from the back to the front. That's using the form. In *Lazy Jack* I put a picture before the title page. I'm working on a book now with two covers, back to front and front to back. It doesn't matter which way; it's got the same title, two slightly different pictures on the covers, two converging stories that meet in the middle. Nobody would make a film without considering the form of the film, and the nature of the film, but for a long time nobody considered the nature of the book. . . . There are some obvious things happening, like the holes of Eric Carle. Some Victorian books are marvelously creative in terms of paper engineering.

I make mistakes in my work. I don't know that it's terribly important. It would be if I were an architect, and the building I designed fell down and killed people. I don't treat the book like a scientific exercise. I blaze through it. The pictures and the words come together. And everything is slightly autobiographical. If I were going to clean the drains, like the Fox in *Foxy Fables*, I'd put on my jeans. Most of the animal reactions in these are really me. I'm the one who sits down, but my wife won't let me when things have to be done around the house. But I don't analyze it. On the other hand, in *Admiral Mouse*, which is a highly researched book, you won't find many mistakes.

How about the change in style in Admiral Mouse?

You see, I don't want "a style." I don't like that; I don't want my work so easily recognized. Every text craves different ideas in me. There was something about the story of Nelson that needed the tradition of American marine painting, the great gallery oils of the period. There's no other way to translate it. *The Light Brigade* was the same thing. I collect miniature paintings, and marine paintings. I've always admired them.

Were the illustrations done to size?

Smaller. In the book they are 10 percent up.

Do you use a magnifying glass?

No, that's no use. It magnifies the point of your brush as well. Fortunately I have good eyesight. I've never had a picture that has taken me longer than two days. Most are started and finished in one day, because I can't get up in the morning and face yesterday's picture. So they have to be smallish, to be finished in a day. Those were quite a day's work, especially when you're trying to flick through books to get the details right.

Did you have to do research for a book like Fables?

I did look at other books of fables. I had an Aesop. I called it *Foxy Fables* because they all had foxes in them, except one. But I put that in as a joke. It's nice to have a publisher who goes along. If it had been some other publishers I could name they would have said, "That's no good. This one isn't about foxes."

How did you happen to have the turtle take his shell off?

You've got to undress to take a shower, and the turtle had nothing else to take off. I don't know if the turtle is actually fastened to that or not.

Since we can't see it, tell us about your house in Devon.

The house was built somewhere around 1600. It used to be a thatched roof, but now it's too much trouble finding someone to thatch it. So it's now slate. It's quite big, with typical English lawns and flowers. It's in a hamlet of about 30 houses, no pubs or anything else.

I work in front of a window; it would be terrible not to. It's good for the eyes to keep changing the focus. My father always said, when he had to work with figures, always keep sitting by a window and keep looking into the distance, so I always have.

Do you storyboard your ideas first and make a dummy?

I don't have a working method as such. The bulk of the ideas are in my head. With a very complicated book, like the one that starts at both ends, I have to make a dummy for that, or the publisher won't know what goes where. But most of my books are self-explanatory, a text and a series of illustrations numbered 1 to 25 or so.

And you work to size.

Nearly always to size. It suits me as a size to work to. I like drawing. It cuts out a lot of problems to draw to size and you can visualize how much text goes on a page. My way of working is first to think of an idea and sort it out in my mind. Then I start with the drawing, somewhere in the middle. That way you don't see the drawing any worse in the beginning or the end. As I'm drawing, I get the ideas on how to write it. So by the time I've finished all the drawings, I've got the phrases in my head. I've just been drawing a boy in the dark. He was saying he wasn't afraid. But when he had his "comforting rag," he was less afraid. While I was drawing it I found it quite nice to have him say that when he had it he was "even more not afraid." So I find the drawing a help with the writing. Working that way you're not tempted to write anything you can't draw. If I wrote first I might write something about horses' back legs, and I could never draw horses' back legs. This way when I'm finished drawing the whole thing is already written in my head, and I can tap it out on the word processor.

What happens when you have been given a text that you can't change?

If the author has such strong ideas that he won't change, they can get another illustrator, or do it themselves. I have my own point of view on the story. I've done some of Roald Dahl. If he points out something that's obviously not in the text, well what can I say? I generally find that authors are O.K. They don't give me trouble. But then, I don't go to them and tell them I don't like the way they've ended the story either. We respect each other.

Usually when I'm working on a book, I'll have another sitting there glaring at me; sometimes there are more. It happens that work will pile up;

the cover for a series I've been doing is needed at the same time I'm doing two black and white books and a picturebook of my own. It's a temptation to do a lot of work. You never quite know when the bubble might burst, and you might wake up and nobody will ask you again.

How much time do you spend on a picturebook?

The quickest I ever did was an afternoon. They can go up to a couple of months. It depends on how many other things you are doing at the same time. Sometimes when you do a book everything is crystal clear and you can blaze through. Sometimes there are interruptions and you put it aside.

When you tour, do you keep a sketchbook or diary?

No. I've tried, but always give up after the first page. I doodle on the telephone pad, and I do my books, but nothing in between but an occasional poster. I like to do posters. I like to see things in that size once in a while.

With no sketches, no other pictures to look at, where does a character like the fox come from?

A lot of Aesop's fables are about outwitting somebody, as are fairy tales, and foxes just crop up as wily. He's really just a person in a more attractive skin. I find the drawing very easy; it just comes. I find the writing difficult. I draw a lot of foxes, and wolves. They're pretty much the same, except foxes are red and wolves are gray. I find horses and cows the same; when I draw a cow it's a horse with horns on. It's how it comes, and as long as it's recognizable, any other details are unnecessary. I leave those for the scientist or the naturalist. When Max sails away in the boat in *Where the Wild Things Are*, it hasn't a rig and could never actually sail anywhere, but that doesn't really matter; any more than whether my cow can actually give milk.

In *Admiral Mouse*, the details are there more, but the essential truths are not. Not one of those mice is in fact mouse-shaped. If you stand a mouse on its hind legs, it's nearly all feet; its legs are very short. You couldn't put naval breeches on him. So he's really just a little fat man. If you want to put clothes on a cat, he has to be redesigned. The child knows it's a cat if it has the ears, whiskers and tail.

How do you think the character of British illustration is special?

We sell all over the world, because we are quirky. We see at Bologna others that are so beautiful, so well-drawn. But illustration doesn't exist anywhere else to the extent that we do it. We have the tradition of Rowlandson in the 18th century, and Cruikshank in the 19th. And Edward Lear, of course, who would never understand why he is remembered not for his oil painting but for his scribbles.

Are you influenced by the critics of your work?

Not really. If I were I'd try to make it saleable, make it like a Sendak. But it's not an artist's business to bother about that. I tell my publisher, "If you like it, publish it. If you don't, I don't care. I don't do them for you to publish. I do them for me." Most artists, I think, if they're honest, like most of the things they do.

Do you sell your original artwork?

I used to sell a great deal of it. I only have two from *Admiral Mouse* left, including my favorite: jumping over the cannonball. I regret selling because I've spent the money and I miss having the work.

Is the princess in I Want My Potty *based on a real person?*

Yes. It's my daughter Alexandra. One day when she was on her potty with brow furrowed I asked her, "What's the matter, princess?" She said, "I'm not a princess." I said, "Of course you are. You're wearing a crown." She said, "No I'm not. I'm just a little girl." I said, "It's very rare for the fairies to give out a crown. They only give it to people they feel are princesses. I've never seen anyone get one before. You've got the only one. It's a shame you don't believe it." "Don't be silly," she giggled. "But it's invisible," I told her. "Only if you believe in the fairies can you see it. That's why I can see it and you can't." We spoke like that for a while, until she reached up and began to feel for the crown. When she got ready for bed and I read her a story, before I turned out the light, I saw her reach up and take off the imaginary crown. That's how she became the princess.

Do you write with a specific audience in mind?

Yes. It's every kid I've ever known. They're all different. It's impossible to find a typical child. You'll find one who likes this; maybe others don't, and that goes into the book. But it's not any child in particular. It's sort of gleaned from them all. I've been married three times, and three marriages mean a lot of childhoods. Katy is my newest daughter. Her fingermarks are the end-papers for *Oscar Got the Blame*. I credited her for them. In the book it's not absolutely clear whether the monster is real. I was asked to make it clearer, but I don't really know myself. I'd rather leave that to the readers.

Is I Want a Cat *a true story?*

Yes. Two years ago a sailing friend told me this. He said, "My daughter wanted a cat, and we said we wouldn't give her one. So she made herself cat ears and a tail and said she would wear them forever until we got her one." I asked if he minded if I used the story. The last page, about the dog, was an afterthought.

How about Jezebel?

Yes. There was a girl I went to school with who was like that, just perfect. She was always dressed in white, always perfectly groomed, like an angel, a real irritation to the other children. Always parents would ask, "Why aren't you like her?" I met her when we were grown up and she was just the same!

I wrote the story when one of my daughters was having a bad time at school. *Lazy Jack* has the same theme: Don't worry. Even if you can't do anything it will turn out all right in the end. In *Jezebel* it's: Don't worry. If you're perfect bad things can happen to you.

There are a lot more children out there that add up to nothing much than those who are gifted. I'm interested in those who add up to nothing. All children are interesting.

I talk at libraries, where people attack me for changing fairy tales around and altering endings. I point out the obvious: that these stories are always changing anyhow. There are plenty of the usual ones about. I am interested in minorities. I think it's a very bad thing if libraries become so organized that they have nothing but the "correct" things on their shelves. I always imagined the pale strange boy with a limp who comes to the library looking for something odd. I think there should be something on the shelf for him. Even if a child reacts violently against it, it's good. They shouldn't like everything. Libraries are places with miles of shelves. I think there ought to be a lot of different things there.

In fairy tales, I try to keep the essential things there. Details can be changed. They always have been changed. I was attacked by a critic for *Red Riding Hood* "getting away from the way it should be." Well, the story is a thousand years old and we don't know how it was told in 1100. It changed by the Victorian time. There must be hundreds of versions around the world. If you were living in a cottage in 10th century England on the edge of a deep wood you'd never been in, you had to tell your children something to keep them safely out of the forest, especially the girls, who might not be attacked by wolves but might be vulnerable to other kinds of attacks. So it was good to tell a story like that. But in today's city you've got curb-crawlers in cars like the 10th century forest after all; it's the same place.

I don't write my books for academic circles. The books' function is to give a child a laugh before going to bed. That's why my wolf is not hacked open. I don't want the child who has a dog or cat thinking about them badly hurt or dead. In my new version of *The Goat and the Kids* the kids come out whole.

When I was in advertising, I always believed that there was a way of telling the truth to sell the product. You didn't need to make something up about it, to tell lies. My publisher believes that the most important thing is the book; that everyone should get a fair deal: artist, author, publisher, printer. He'll even negotiate a higher percentage of foreign royalties when I would settle for less. He gets the best print quality as well.

Have you thought of doing lives of artists?

I was asked why I don't do something serious. I said everything I do is serious! I've thought of a biography of Beethoven that cuts out music and stops when he's about six . . . I always wanted to do a film about the life of George Morland, the painter. I work with a film animation company. They're afraid of live action.

You don't want to give young people just facts that terminate every-thing. You want to provoke them. It's the duty of a teacher to say provoking things. "Inspired lies" and intuitive guesses may be better than facts. Shake-speare has been killed in so many schools by teachers of English litera-ture.

Basically when you do a book it's still you and the idea. With each book it's in the lap of the gods whether it's going to be good or absolutely awful. When I did *I Want My Potty* I thought, "That's a bit of nothing." I didn't even have the nerve to give it to Klaus Fluge myself; I sent it with a student who was going to see him. I met Klaus in Australia and asked, "By the way, did you like it at all?" He told me everyone loved it and he was auctioning it. Yet books like *Admiral Mouse* that I feel very proud of really bombed. But if you try to write just to sell, eventually all the books will look the same.

Have you ever been to the U.S.?

Never. Perhaps I used to upset more people there than I amused. I took enormous pleasure in that. I always do. I feel quite proud when some-thing I've done offends somebody. I feel I'm doing something right. I've won awards in other countries, but not here. Artists like David McKee, Michael Foreman and I started our creative careers during the age of rebellion in the U.S. and here. We still feel that sense. But recently there was a list of "approved writers" for the schools, and we were all on it! We were shocked to find we've become part of the Establishment!

— Summer 1989

Twenty-Four

Amy Schwartz

---

*There's nothing tricky or trite about the stories Amy Schwartz tells with her words and pictures. They emerge from a life experience that seems to be archetypal of all Western people, softly humorous with a focus on human relationships and matters mundane but very close to our hearts. Sara (*Begin at the Beginning*) has had a hard day at school and now must paint a "wonderful" picture for homework. Her struggles are ignored by the family until a knowing mother sets Sara in her lap and lovingly helps her understand that "wonderful" begins with the simple things. Indeed, whether illustrating her own stories or those of others, Schwartz makes sure that we understand the significance of those simple things that create our environment: the cafeteria workers' hairnets; a mother reading while her youngsters play in a park's sandbox; the jumble of papers and stuff on a tailor's desk. Such attention to details combined with her intuitive trimming of text produces books that trigger delight in youngsters whose own experiences are*

Amy Schwartz

empathetic with the girls who star in them. She maintains the same concern for the details of place in her pictures for the stories of others. One may only wonder to what extent her childhood, nurtured by a close-knit minority community in San Diego, plays a role in her evolving style where humans are all rounded and soft to touch, where scenes are set to emphasize the human scale. Her apartment in Brooklyn, New York, with its comfortable ambiance exudes a personality through its collections of personally acquired things, that convinces us that Schwartz remains the sensitive storyteller of her childhood.

How did you get into children's book illustration? Did you have any special art training when you were growing up?

I think that my present career grew out of an early involvement with both books and art. My parents' influence was more important than any specific art training when I was young. My father ran a printing shop and he's now a writer. My mother, a chemistry professor, has always spent time drawing and painting. These interests were passed along to me. I received books as birthday gifts, was taken to story hour at the library by my grand-mother, and, later, to check out books with my mother. My parents were always reading; there were always new books coming into the house.

I also spent a lot of time drawing and painting, which gave me a great deal of pleasure. My parents enrolled me in weekend art classes at the museum and at the zoo, and certainly encouraged me in many ways.

What books do you remember in particular from your childhood?

Blueberries for Sal, Lentil, Andy and the Lion, the Little House books. I remember reading *Little Women* abridged, over and over and over. I had three sisters and no brothers, so you can see the appeal.

I was involved with books in a way which I don't think will ever happen again. Though I think I knew stories in books weren't "real," I could easily decide to overlook that knowledge. I remember a period when I made great efforts to keep one foot on an item of clothing as long as possible when I undressed for a bath, so that if the powers that be picked that particular minute to whisk me away to Narnia, I wouldn't have to endure my adventures totally unclothed.

You studied art at the California College of Arts and Crafts, in Oakland, California. Did you have illustration in mind when you started?

No, I didn't. I was a drawing major. I never took illustration courses; I found them too intimidating. At that time the school didn't offer any courses in children's books. I didn't have any idea that illustration could be a personal experience, originating with my own ideas. My favorite classes were in life drawing.

I kept sketchbooks at home. After graduating, I disciplined myself to keep up my drawing and painting on a daily basis. My drawings became more involved and unlike anything I had done in school. It was a relief to not have to try to outguess an instructor. I drew portraits of my friends and family and interiors of my home, working within a very small world that had personal meaning for me. And it was around this time that I began to be interested in illustrating children's books.

How did that come about?

I had started doing some freelance illustration, and was realizing that this was a possible way to earn a living. At the same time I was becoming more and more interested in children's books. I found myself spending a lot of time in the picturebook sections in bookstores and libraries. My childhood love of picturebooks had resurfaced. I enrolled in a children's book illustration class, which at that time was difficult to find in the Bay Area. I learned that picturebooks were 32 pages, and a little something about designing them, and decided to come to New York to find work. I came East with a good deal of naiveté, without which I don't think I would have been brave enough to make such a move.

Is Begin at the Beginning *autobiographical?*

Yes, it is. It was the first children's story I ever wrote. Shortly after I'd moved to New York, I signed up for a children's book writing class. At the first session we were given the assignment to write a story. I went home, sharpened my pencils, laid out my notebook before me, and sat down, and sat there, and sat there, and sat. I got up, got something to eat, sat down, got up, brushed my hair, so on and so forth. Finally, just to be writing something, I wrote in my journal about how hard it was for me to get started writing, and why I thought that was so. I also made a list of all the ridiculous procrastinatory activities I was engaged in to avoid having to get started. This journal entry eventually became *Begin at the Beginning.*

Do you think that children have such problems?

I know that I certainly had work anxieties, and expected great things of myself when I was growing up, and many parents and teachers have told me that they see this same dynamic in young children.

Did this story go through many revisions?

I am a very slow writer, and most of my stories are written over a period of years, with extensive rewriting. I find that having a story idea is one thing and taking a reader gracefully through that story is quite another. The most difficult part in *Begin at the Beginning* was coming up with a solution to Sara's problem. For one thing, I was better acquainted with the problem of procrastination than with its solution! And I had to figure out how to have Sara verbalize her realizations, but not have it all sound overly moralistic. With the help of my editor, I tried to make Sara's problem, and its resolution, both concrete and a little poetic.

How much of Her Majesty, Aunt Essie *is real?*

The actual characters and events portrayed are fictional, but the theme is real. When I was a child I had a very active fantasy life. Like many other kids, I had dreams of a grander and more dramatic life, with several versions of how this was to occur. Growing up in the age of the Cold War and TV shows such as *The Man from U.N.C.L.E.*, at one point I decided my grandmother was a secret agent, with a two-way radio hidden perhaps under the nylons in her dresser drawer. I also envisioned a life in the White House, like little Caroline, and would calculate how many years my father had to organize his campaign in time for the next presidential election. These daydreams were the basis for *Aunt Essie.*

I wrote the book soon after moving to Brooklyn, so it is my Brooklyn book as well.

How did the manuscript develop?

The story began as essentially a collection of one-liners. It was funny, but rather empty. I added Maisie-next-door, and the extravagant bet between Ruthie and Maisie. This gave the tale more of a plot and more warmth. It brought out Ruthie's personality, her bravado, and her vulnerability.

Do your books require much research?

That varies, of course, from book to book. If the book is set in an historical period, such as Amy Hest's stories, which take place in the 1940s and '50s, and in very specific places, a good amount of work is involved. And it's often unexpected details that are difficult. For *Fancy Aunt Jess*, I had to track down photos of trains, buses and subways from 1940s New York. My first attempt to ask a butcher to let me take pictures of his shop for an illustration in the book left me in tears. I think he thought I was a spy sent by a rival butcher. I had better luck on my next try.

For *The Purple Coat* my agent and I went searching for a tailor shop in the garment district. We finally found one we liked. The shop had the glamorous name of Pierre's of Paris, but the name on the proprietor's business card was Mr. P. Papadopoulos. I had phoned Amy Hest and asked her for a description of the tailorshop she remembered from her childhood. She kept saying it had been very large, but I realized that this was only because, at that time, Amy herself was very small.

The research which I did for *Yossel Zissel and the Wisdom of Chelm* (Jewish Publication Society, 1986) was very moving to me. I went to YIVO, an institute devoted to the study of Jewish life in Eastern Europe. I looked through a very old book of photographs of shtetl life, the pages literally crumbling in my hands. While I was looking at woodcuts from that period in YIVO's basement, an older woman came in. The archivist told her that I was researching a tale from Chelm, Jewish mythology's town of fools. She began excitedly speaking to me in Yiddish. When the archivist finally got her to speak English, I found out that she was telling me that she was a native of the actual town of Chelm, a town which no longer exists. For me it was an incredible melding of the real and the unreal, the past, and the present.

Would you talk a little about your new Mother Goose collection?

Mother Goose's Little Misfortunes, on which I collaborated with Leonard Marcus, is a collection of Mother Goose rhymes in which calamities occur, some major and some miniscule. The idea for such a collection was Leonard's, and the theme appealed to me very much. There are many elements that make Mother Goose rhymes so much fun, their rhythms, their quick rhymes, and the satisfying mischief of saying things that one would not ordinarily be able to get away with under normal circumstances ("I do not like thee, Doctor Fell").

In choosing the poems, we followed our own tastes and intuition as to which to include and which not. There were a few rhymes which we did find too disturbing. In others, the tale might be one of disaster, but the nature of the language prevents one from taking it all too seriously ("Here lies old Fred. It's a pity he's dead").

Since working on the book, I've become very aware of other Mother Goose collections. There have been a few recently which seem to miss the point. I've come across at least two collections in which the author saw fit to supplement the original poems with additional verses which undo the intent of the rhyme: Humpty Dumpty gets put back together, and so forth. I can't lay my finger on exactly why I'm so bothered by this, but there seems to be something a little frightening in an adult's inability to relate to Jack and Jill in a lighthearted manner.

The style you used in illustrating this book is quite different from any you have used previously.

This was a very different kind of project. The rhymes seemed very graphic to me. Their form and content are unified, both hitting you at once with equal force. I thought my illustrations should have some of that same quality, rather than simply being narrative.

I originally envisioned this book as being quite tiny, but then decided on a tall and narrow format. This fit the column-like shape of most of the rhymes, and also accentuated their eccentricity.

Did you encounter any special problems in illustrating the misfortunes?

Yes, I did. It's one thing to relate a calamitous event in playful, poetic language, and quite another to visually depict that same action. "Here lies old Fred" presented that problem. My early sketches were of wakes and funerals, pretty serious stuff. Finally I hit upon the solution of having the poem appear as an epitaph on a gravestone, which stressed the language of the poem as much as the situation. I added the despicable relatives crowding around the top.

Corporal Tim, who "had a fight," and "died of fright," was difficult also. After many, many sketches, I at last realized that the corporal's vanity, and not the means of his destruction, was the core of the rhyme, and I painted a portrait which I hope reflected that.

How did Annabelle Swift, Kindergartner *come into being?*

Annabelle started with a story my sister Joan wrote when she was in the seventh grade, about a precocious kindergartner. I was in the first grade then, and Joan's story made quite an impression on me. As an adult, I reread the piece, and it became the starting point for *Annabelle.*

I worked on the manuscript over a period of several years. I knew I wanted to write a kindergarten story, using the idea from Joan's story of a classroom outsider recovering her dignity through her prowess with numbers, but I was quite stuck as to a real heart to the tale. I didn't want the teacher to be an adversary, nor the other students. When it hit me to have a sisterly relationship be part of the book, and to have Annabelle's conflicts take place mainly within herself, I had found a meaningful core for the book.

I am the third of four sisters, and I used childhood feelings, if not specific experiences, in *Annabelle.* I played many games with my immediate older sister, Debbie, when I was young, in which Debbie played a role similar to the role that Lucy takes with Annabelle as they play school. I thought of Debbie as the big, confident kid, while I felt much more vulnerable and confused. I suppose many younger siblings feel that way. When I drew

Annabelle, I thought of my little sister Becky, small and sweet, and quite a tough cookie underneath.

Your stories all seem to have a cultural bias of deep, positive, loving, caring, human and family relationships. Do you feel your family background or experience has influenced that?

Recently I was asked about the fact that most of my books were about relationships, and my first thought was, what an odd question, what else is there to write about? Then I realized that there were other options, and that this was indeed my orientation. I gave some examples earlier of working on stories which felt quite empty until I added the dynamic of a relationship. Even in *Mrs. Moskowitz and the Sabbath Candlesticks*, I had to add Fred, the cat, to give Mrs. Moskowitz someone to talk to, a way in which to amplify her experience.

I like to spend a good deal of time alone, which is part of the reason I am an artist, but I define what's important in my life by my close relationships. I grew up in a household of seven, with every family member closely involved with one another, and, yes, I do think this has helped shape the stories I write.

—*Fall 1988; updated 1990*

Twenty-Five

Posy Simmonds

A Sampling of Works in Print

The Chocolate Wedding Knopf, 1991.   *Lulu and the Flying Babies* Knopf,
Fred Knopf, 1988.   1989.

---

*Before we went to England for interviews, we knew Posy Simmonds only
from her two delightful picturebooks,* Fred *and* Lulu and the Flying Babies, *and
guessed she was just a beginner with an amazing sophistication in her drawing.
We did pursue the fact noted on the jacket flap, however, that she was also a cartoonist. This produced the revelation that she was well-known not only in the
bookstores but to the general adult population of England from a long-running
series of cartoons in the Manchester* Guardian *that might be compared to an
amalgam of* For Better or Worse, Sally Forth, Doonesbury, *and* Cathy *played
by the cast of* thirtysomething. *Collected in a series of books, they reveal life of
the yuppies of England over the past decade with sometimes gentle, sometimes
sardonic, biting humor. So by the time we met, we knew Ms. Simmonds to be more
than the neophyte picturebook artist that we had originally imagined or that she
appeared on the surface. She has a house in Cornwall, where she spends part of
her time. Her London apartment is really part of a house, reached through a gate
and a separate entrance. Although it is in a busy tourist area not far from the
British Museum, the immediate neighborhood has its own small shops, a hospital,
and a sense of isolation from the hordes of tourists only blocks away.*

Why don't we in the U.S.A. see your cartoons?
They tried them in *Harpers* a few years ago, but they didn't go over.
People kept saying they were too British.
*What's a nice girl like you doing in a job like cartooning, one so few
women succeed in?*

People are always asking me why women aren't funny and why there aren't more women cartoonists. I actually don't know.

What led you to this kind of work?

I guess I've always had the interest. As a child I was very realistic. I always knew when something was going on; why someone was crying. I also like making people laugh. I drew a lot as a child, but the people always had balloons coming out of their mouths. I did comics very early. I come from a big family, and part of it was making my brothers or my father or whoever laugh. I didn't do them on purpose to be outrageous or precocious, but one knew from the response. So it's something I've always known.

You were raised on a Berkshire dairy farm, and started cartooning about age 8. Did you go to a local school?

No. I went to boarding school. I studied art there and did A levels and O levels.

What childhood reading influenced you?

I read so much as a child; the house was full of books. I read bound copies of *Punch*. That's how I learned to read, partly from reading the captions of cartoons. This was pre-school. I went to school when I was three, at the Vicarage school, where we learned to read by the time we were four, but this was unusual at this little school with a dozen children. I liked the copies of *Punch* from the '30s especially, where there were cartoons that you didn't need to be able to read. We didn't have many comics. But there were some American children in the village whose parents were stationed at the nearby air base. They had comics I'd never seen. I was fascinated by Mickey Mouse, and Casper the Ghost, and Superman. They used to give us their old ones. As for books, I had Beatrix Potter, and Orlando and all the usual. There were also a lot of Victorian books from my grandmother, which I used to like when I wanted a good cry: *Froggy's Little Brother,* and stories of children dying of cholera; terrific stuff, chapter books, not picturebooks. They would have about 12 pictures. I liked fairy tales. I didn't like Rackham's drawings as a child, only later. They were not real enough. I loved Sheperd and Beatrix Potter. I read *Alice* when I was seven, but didn't like it until much later.

How do you feel about all the new illustrations for the classics?

I think they're very brave to have a crack at it. I don't think I'd try *Alice*.

Were there other influences?

I liked Rackham, Dulac and Tenniel only later; not as a child.

Are there other favorite visual resources that recur?

Ucello, Piero della Francesca. Hogarth, Rowlandson, Brueghel, Ronald Searle, Giles of the London *Express*. My childhood was very happy and I remember a lot of that. I was very lucky.

Were you the oldest, youngest?

I was the third of five, two older brothers, a younger sister and brother.

Self-portrait by Posy Simmonds

When you were entertaining your brothers with stories, were they long stories?

I used to write out long stories.

But you haven't been interested in writing long stories commercially?

Not since then. I've worked it out in pictures. The longer book I'm working on currently has more text and I find that difficult because I'm so used to blends.

Then you went to the Sorbonne to study painting?

No, I studied French there, and did a bit of life drawing at the École des Beaux-Arts. I thought I was going to be a painter. But I always wrote. After all that drawing, I never did get into painting. So I came back to England to study graphic design at the Central School. It was a four-year course. There wasn't much drawing; it was mainly typography. But I was very bad at all that; I'm no good at anything that comes between me and the pencil and the results. Because I was clumsy at setting type, I used to draw my own lettering. I had a good time, though, so I stayed the four years.

What other courses did you take in art school?

Designing book jackets, different techniques like silk screen printing, and research. I really learned to use the library.

You wrote as well? Yours is a narrative art.

The words are first, really. The pictures carry them.

Do you see a similarity to Raymond Briggs in your work?

Yes, but when I began *Fred*, I wasn't thinking of Briggs at all. I began it and designed it just like my strip, because I had been doing strips for 10 years. I wasn't consciously influenced by him. I had been drawing for 20 years in more or less the same way. But one review mentioned "a ghostly echo of Raymond Briggs in the sleeping scene in *Fred*." I think there is a tradition of that kind of realism in other cartoons here. As a child I liked them because they had real people and streets, with recognizable real details. There were a lot of cartoonists here who drew things as they were, in *Punch* and other places.

Do you see specific British characteristics of picturebooks?

I think something has to be true at its core. Then you can have all kinds of fun and fantasy. But it only works if it's basically true. The bland, straight truth can be very boring, flat, but it's the way you address it.

How often do your cartoons appear?

I used to do one every week, but at the moment, I'm just working on books.

How did you get from cartooning to children's picturebooks?

I think it was my publisher who said, "What are you going to do next? Why don't you do a children's book?" So I thought I'd have a go. But I couldn't think of anything at all. Then I went to Cornwall. I'd been to a funeral in London, but hadn't been to Cornwall for a while. All the local cats had been using our garden in a rather terrible way. So I drew a cat as an undertaker in my sketchbook. I hadn't done color, because I had been working in black and white for so long. I found it terribly difficult.

You aren't confined to boxes or the page; you're not afraid to go across the gutter. . . . Was a designer involved?

It's all mine. But I think I know the rhythm from doing the newspaper work: If you have a long shot, sooner or later you must have a close-up or you get it all looking the same.

What is the role of the editor?

I wrote the story out and took in a few sketches, and my editor at Cape said, "This is much too long" and "You said this twice"; and was very good at trimming and suggesting I find another way to get them from this situation to that. I found that very helpful. Then it was just a matter of doing it spread by spread. I did a rough dummy, to scale.

Do you have a cat? The cats in your work are so real.

No. I like them, because they don't care. Dogs do. But it's hard to have one living in two places. They'd like it in Cornwall, but they wouldn't like it here. We had cats at home, and friends have them.

Do you feel there is a Tiepolo and Ardizzone influence in Fred?

I like them both, and I like their drawing especially.

Since you don't have children around, how do you draw such realistic kids?

I know a lot of children. I also have step-children. And there are always children playing outside here.

Where did the idea for Lulu and the Flying Babies *come from?*

I had been drawing cherubs in my strip, so I was in a cherub mode. I was doodling in my sketchbook, and drew a child. Then I began doodling scenes that I saw in my head. They could be any painting. Then there was the child in the museum, with "Don't touch" signs, and a man telling her off. From the afternoon doodle I got carried away. I decided it would be winter. I knew the babies would talk to her. I knew she would be angry. It was all like thinking with a pencil. The speech pattern I took from listening to kids.

How did you get that two-page scary woods picture?

It's from Casper Friedrich, a German painter from the 19th century. He's very dramatic. *Monasteries in the Mist.*

Did you go to any particular museum?

Actually I did. Having always done things in boxes, when I have a full-page spread, it terrifies me. Where does it end? Am I above or below it? The museum spread took me a long time to do, because I wanted to have so much in it.

You did the calligraphy in both your books?

Yes. I even put names on my typefaces, and the little one with serif I call Anal Retentive.

What media do you use; watercolor, pen and ink?

I use all kinds. The cartoons are done in black and white only.

What is the next book you are working on?

A chocolate book. I'm a chocolate freak, but only certain kinds. There are mice in it. The girls eats too much chocolate. She gets sick and can't be a bridesmaid. She cries.

What would your editor get?

He gets the sketches, and a little dummy, and scribbles on what she might be saying. Then if he likes the idea he'll tell me to make the real dummy where I work it all out.

You convey truth in such a few lines. . . .

I sometimes think that the rough sketch is better than the final, because you do it all at once, and I do it bigger.

Do you go out to talk to groups about your books?

I've done autographing on Saturday mornings in children's book shops. It's nice, but the children always say things like "Draw a tractor" or something else I can't draw.

Do you sell your artwork?

I've actually stopped selling things. Readers used to write and ask for a particular strip, and I needed cash. But because I only did it once a week, I began to have no good ones that I really liked left. When I had exhibitions I had nothing to show, so I sell very few now.

Is there a scorn here in the U.K. of illustration?

It's thought to be a poor relation of "real *art*" and when you tell people you do cartoons, they say "What else do you do . . . ? Have you ever thought of doing any serious work?"

Do you do any of that?

If I really wanted to I would make time to do it. I do a lot of sketching, but not a lot of "real drawing." I get as much out of doing a cartoon. The Renaissance artists were certainly illustrators. They were film directors as well, casting, using props, writing, using storyboards. . . .

You are not writing specifically for children?

No. It's the story that counts. I'm quite interested, later, after it's done, in how it's read by adults. There's not much text, so the parents have to work very hard, and the story is a little different every night. The child may complain that they're not doing it the way they did it last night. Some children have written that they've done *Fred* as a play. They've sent very touching pictures, where they've made little cat masks . . . it works quite well as drama.

Do you know the work of other picturebook artists?

When my step-sons were little, I used to read to them, so I knew some then. But as they grew up, I stopped. I don't actually buy a lot. If I'm writing something I won't look at any, because it gets in the way. I start remembering how Dulac drew. I find the same thing with cartoons. I would want to see how Ronald Searle drew shoes, or dogs, or how Steinberg did cats. It would become an amalgam.

Are your pictures from memory, or do you do visual research?

I can draw figures doing almost everything freehand. But if it's an object like a car I'll go and look at it in the street or look it up in a photograph. Objects that I want to look real and I can't remember what they look like have to be researched; in *Lulu* things like the stand where they sell cards, for instance, or plinths.

So the life drawing is in the hand, from experience and training?

Yes. I think the life drawing is like grammar; you learn it and forget it.

When I first started drawing the cartoons it was almost like doing little life drawings. I didn't develop my kind of language for a bit. I'm really glad I did life drawing so I know how to exaggerate an elbow, or make someone run.

Do you feel a relation to cinema? In the way you develop scenes?

Not consciously. But I think if I had to analyze it, that is what I do. It's a design thing in the strips. If you're describing a person you might do a close-up for the details: clothes, earrings, whatever. The long shot shows who's there, what kind of furniture . . . . Usually I'd find that two long shots shouldn't be together, unless something was happening to compare the two. A change of scale was always good. And I knew I'd need in the right-hand corner on the top a solid black area and another one on the bottom to weight it. In the middle row you'd need another bit of black. It's just how it looks. Someone who is a television director talking about *Fred* said where they first meet the cat, "That's what I would do. I would do them side view, and then the camera would go around so you see them front view." That made me think about it that way, that you are a director. I can remember doing a spread in *Fred* that was far too blue, where all the cats come into the garden. So I gave the cat a torch (flashlight) because it needed the yellow. That's the same sort of thing that I would do with a strip, give it more black to weight it. My editor at Cape said, "You've got to make every spread a surprise" so the child reading it won't know what to expect. In 24 pages it's very difficult.

I've enjoyed doing the picturebooks as a change, and especially not having to do them in a week! And using color; I learned a lot.

— *Summer 1989*

Twenty-Six

Peter Sis

A Sampling of Works in Print

Beach Ball Greenwillow, 1990.
Follow the Dream: The Story of Christopher Columbus Knopf, 1991.
Going Up Greenwillow, 1989.
The Midnight Horse by Sid Fleischman. Greenwillow, 1990.
More Stories to Solve: Fifteen Folktales

from Around the World told by George Shannon. Greenwillow, 1990.
Rainbow Rhino Knopf, 1987.
Scarebird by Sid Fleischman. Greenwillow, 1988.
Waving Greenwillow, 1988.

Peter Sis has come to the U.S. from Czechoslovakia via England. In fluent English he explains his recent move to a high-ceilinged, brightly lit, modernized apartment with skylight and stunning view of lower Manhattan as a lucky find, even if it is around the corner from the famous Bowery and on the scene of more New York action than he really wants. Some of his works, not book illustrations, are framed on the white walls, and his fascinating small surreal sculptures are on the bookshelves. The large drawing table in the corner is clear and ready for new work as he returns from having mailed off his most recent job for Time. *He is clearly excited by the news from his homeland, which now he is able to visit, and he can also now have his parents visit him.*

What books do you remember from childhood?
Many different ones, some of them in English, because my mother was here as a child. My grandfather came to this country in the '30s to design railway stations in Cleveland and Chicago, so my mother grew up here for a few years. He was very organized, and collected the comic strips from the Chicago papers, with Orphan Annie and Krazy Kat, Katzenjammer Kids. So

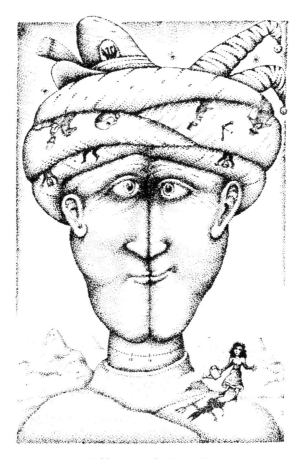

Self-portrait by Peter Sis

as a small boy I could look at that huge book of wonderful pictures. But I
didn't have the other things in my childhood that you take for granted here,
like *Leave It to Beaver*, *Star Trek* or *Velveteen Rabbit*.

*Did you become involved with illustration as part of your Czech training
before you went to England?*

Yes. I was with Trnka [well-known Czech illustrator, animator, pup-
peteer, filmmaker]. He was my professor who selected me. Everyone in my
family, father, sister, brother, all are in film, and I wanted to be too. But at
that time Trnka was upset with film, and became a professor of illustration.
I wish now that I had been able to learn more about graphic techniques
from him. I got more into it with Quentin Blake in England, especially the
thinking process. The Anglo-Saxon way of thinking, of approaching a problem, was a revelation. In central Europe there was the tradition of the

Academy where you would ask questions and get answers, and were supposed to follow a certain path. In England, I remember when I would finish something I would ask, "Should the background be red or green?" Quentin would say, "You know what the background should be. You're just asking me to be sure."

They would invite someone who might be a graduate of the school who would be famous, and someone who might be living in obscurity, then someone in fashion, and then Michael Foreman, and we could see all these different possibilities.

How did you happen to come to the U.S.?

I went to Los Angeles to work on a film, but I also needed to sell my other work. I got in touch with Maurice Sendak who after seeing my work told me there were only a few really good children's book editors. He also gave me an introduction to them while I was in Los Angeles. I was lucky ALA was taking place there. Ava Weiss from Greenwillow looked at my portfolio and books, and that was that.

The first book I did for Greenwillow was *Bean Boy*. When I came to New York from California I realized I could not pay the rent here with just the money from the book. So I began to do my work for magazines. That was also the beginning of my editorial work for *The New York Times*. There were other publishers who were trying to get work for me. I did *OAF* for Knopf about the same time as *Whipping Boy*, and I felt a bit bad because Greenwillow had given me the chance, and it was like a big happy family there. But they said they didn't want to "chain" me. I had done a book for Margaret McElderry then because I had known her from Europe. And I have done a few for Harper.

I had met many children's book editors when I first had the story for *Rainbow Rhinoceros* and was taking it around. I met nearly every editor who would tell me what he thought about it. I found out whom I liked and whom I didn't. I can see the flaws in the story now. But Frances Foster at Knopf worked on it with me, published it, and that was the first book that was both my text and my illustrations. Now with all the response I'm getting I feel that I ought to have publishing continuity, so I'm working on a book about Columbus with Knopf, and two others for Greenwillow. I am trying to make an animated film at the same time, for which I need at least six to seven months. In the beginning I would take anything just to keep working. Now other publishers are calling and offering me very tempting projects, but I can't do it all. I feel the time has come for me to be loyal. Greenwillow has said I can bring over anything I want to do, which is wonderful to me. I've come from a country where everything was under one publishing house and you had to work for them and nothing else.

The decision between children's books and the editorial work is very hard to make. It's a great pleasure to do children's books, but it is a lot of work. And the magazines pay you so much more money for one picture. But of course your work comes out one week, and next week it's old news. Right now because of the political developments in Czechoslovakia, there was a request for a drawing this week. At the same time, I'm running late with illustrations for the new Sid Fleischman book. I always try to imagine myself about 13, on vacation and reading it. It's a good story, like *Whipping Boy.* But I think I will be doing this less and less. I find it much easier to work for myself. If other people write "The forest has spruces all around" it can be hard to draw. I can write what I like to draw, like one tree.

I have been told that I made a poor choice in having two "quality" publishers and no mass-market publishers who make money for you. But I didn't approach it from that perspective. I did films, and I also did children's books. In Europe it was much easier to be an artist and do whatever came up. Here especially in New York I am in that box of "illustrator," so if I paint a painting they say, "You can't do that, you're an illustrator." If I say I am working on a film, they say, "How can you as an illustrator be working on a film?" This is the first year I have slowed down at all since I came to New York in 1984. I used to have one or two books on the fall list and one or two on the spring list every year.

How long does it take you to do a book?

A lot of time, especially since I'm doing a lot of editorial work as well. At first I wanted to show what I could do for people who don't know me, like the high-wire act in the circus. I would work in black and white, and in color. I didn't get a chance to do color in the beginning. When *The New York Times* gave me the first job for the *Book Review,* I felt that I had to make it, there was no going back. I had few styles, one with the dots that was very time-consuming; no one else did it. So I thought if I used that I would be sure of getting more work there. Well, that was it. I would get calls and they all wanted that style. And I was stuck with those dots. Whenever my friends would call me to go to a ball game or something, I couldn't, because I was sitting there making the little dots. Now that is a problem I have to deal with, because I have new stories and ideas, but with the time-consuming technique they have to wait.

I was brought up to concentrate on one project at a time. Any of these projects could take a year to live with it, concentrate, do all the research until one morning I would wake up and it would all fall into place and do it, and then you relax a little before you start another. But here there are so many things going on, books, editorial illustrations, films, posters, all in the same time. So I'm trying to cut down. I've got an agent, and she's supposed to say, "Sorry, he can't do it," but still some people like *Time* magazine call, and I think I can work that in. And if I'm concentrating on something like the Fleischman book and I squeeze in one story for this magazine and one story for that magazine there's constant interruption. It's nice just to do the children's books, but I don't know if you can survive in New York that way.

You might get as much for magazine work as for a picturebook?

Yes, and more. You get the advance for the picturebook. But you have to wait to see about the royalties. You make mistakes. I didn't ask for enough for the poster of *Amadeus*, for example. But I didn't know.

For a story, the pictures are adding texture to the plot. But when you begin with poetry, which is supposed to be using language to paint pictures, what role has the illustrator in relation to the poet?

That is the most challenging and satisfying work. With the poem as inspiration I try to come in from a completely different angle. It's like two different things coming together. For *City Nights* it would be interesting for you to see the dummy. I had a lot of different ideas. Then it built up from the San Gennaro festival. That was my first full color book for Greenwillow. The one before, *Three Yellow Dogs*, was interesting for me, not having grown up in this country. It was just lines of words, and I was very proud of having come up with a story for it.

In *City Nights* first there was a cat who ran away, but then it was much more visual to incorporate the bird. In other books, like Fleischman's, it doesn't leave me with very much to invent. The author describes a lot of it. But I remember how I loved Jules Verne's books. When you opened them, there was a quotation and some pictures to see what might happen. That was what I like about these other books. I get a feeling of being on vacation with grandmother in the country. It's illustration in the traditional sense of serving the story and maybe picking up the dramatic situations that would be the most interesting to do. The picturebooks give me more challenge; I like the thinking process. It takes a long time to negotiate what we don't talk about in the text. In *City Nights* there is a secondary, almost a third story in the pictures, a building up and then the quieting down, like going to bed. That's the same thing I was trying to do with *Scarebird*, but unfortunately the gutter divided the pictures, which were much stronger when I had them spread on the floor.

Are you just having fun when you put in characters or animals that aren't in the text, as in City Nights?

It's more the capturing of the feeling of when you go to Mulberry Street for San Gennaro, everything condensed together rather than spread out as it is in California.

I met Eve Rice only after the book was completed. She was the first author I was allowed to meet! Then I met with Sid Fleischman finally on a trip back to the coast.

Did you work directly with Ava Weiss [Greenwillow art director]?

Yes. I was concerned with the layout from the beginning, as I always am. I like working with her because it happens right away, like Denise

Cronin at Knopf. At some other houses it goes to a large art department and it takes weeks of meetings before they come back with suggestions. When I talk to Henrik Drescher, Lane Smith, or others in New York, I think the situation is better. But when I go out to the supermarkets, or watch the animation on the Saturday morning cartoons, or see the children with the "He-Man" characters, I see the danger. The special quality bookstores and the parents who select only the best for their children and deny them "McDonald's" may have children who develop a craving for that. It's like a Thomas Mann story about a dog who has only the best to eat, but then goes out at night looking for garbage. We need to find something in the middle. What I deplore are the people who are prepared to do anything to make money on kids. It seems to be the name of the game, unfortunately. I don't want a totalitarian government to say "Stop that!" But there should be something like common decency.

The contradiction for me is that I'm coming from art schools in Prague and London where the books are very artistic, you are happy to make them that way; people would say that's your responsibility. Sometimes you might want to make it simple. I thought it was great here that I could go from *Rainbow Rhinoceros* to something like *Waving*. I found it difficult to come up with the simple illustration concept for just a little anecdote. I found the story in the paper, about how in New York, where no one says hello to you, a woman waved at a cab and someone waved from the bus, then people in the outdoor cafe waved, and finally a whole block was waving. It was not a deep story. It's a little thing that could happen any day, for little kids, and I didn't feel like doing it in my painstaking style. It needed to be bright and sunny. I would try watercolors washed together, and Ava would say it was still too European. I was getting more bright colors, which I never did before, but I thought it was serving the story; I wanted to get the message over. Of course when the book came out (and I'm quite happy with it even if it is different from what I had done before), people from Europe would say they had seen *Rainbow Rhino*, and "That was art that you could put in a exhibition. But that *Waving*; man, you're becoming Walt Disney with those bright colors."

Unfortunately what is happening here is that the level of the mass market is so low that anything above it you can call art. So then it's very hard to differentiate what is very good. You can go to specialized bookstores, but how many people can afford to spend that kind of money?

I can see what's happening with kids in the inner city. All these things should be available to them somehow. But do they want to deal with dreams or reality? When I came up with a story about street people, or a bag lady, I was told that children don't want to deal with that. It's depressing, of course. But at the same time, when I am in the subway I see little kids asking who is that man in the plastic bag. I realize that people in Michigan don't know about this. But it's definitely an issue. I was accused of prejudice in *Waving* because I made the Asian children yellow. It was never my intention. I grew up in a country where there was very rigid censorship. I was called in to the Ministry of Information on a record cover where the wind was blowing and they were concerned about whether it was blowing from the right or the left, and whether that was the political "left" and "right" or whether it was from East to West on the map of Europe. Then I came here and have been constantly running into things like books that might be Bibles and landscapes that might be people, and lettering that after printing might look like something else. In Eastern Europe you learn to live with that and work around it. It becomes a constant problem to give the message without really telling the message. But here you expect to be free. Until I got the letter about the Asians, I never noticed if they were yellow or not. I just had all these colors in the book. In my next book I will be watching everyone very carefully, or try to avoid all of them. Maybe I will stay with animals. In a very fine review in *The New York Times*, Karla Kuskin said she only wished I would have equal numbers of women in *Waving*. So I counted and it was something like 45 to 11. I looked to see where I could have. It depended on the language I used. If I said "six waiters" they had to be men. But I could have made half of the musicians women, because in English the word is the same. But somehow I was thinking of "musicians" as masculine, as it is in French. If I do an editorial illustration of a corporate meeting, I must do equal numbers of men and women, blacks and whites, and have someone in a wheelchair. So I'm still learning. I can't wait to see what will happen with the beach book. It is a very simple book, like *Waving* and *Going Up*, about a mother and daughter who go the beach. The beach ball flies away and she chases it through the pages, one of which would be letters, one shapes, one colors. Each page has lots of people on the beach. It was a great idea, but then I had to do it, with all those people.

What kind of visual homework do you do (aside from the National Geographics *you have mentioned before)? Do you sketch people from the books?*

It depends on the project. I realized when I came to New York that for the books and the editorial work I was doing much more homework, even in the sense of traveling to look at things. I do as much as I can. I can rely on books. I might approach friends who had a child of a certain age. I realize I can only go so far. The idealistic story I am thinking of about the whale should be just an average whale. I went to California to see the whales, to Hawaii, to Florida. . . . The best were in Massachusetts, where we got really close. Now I know my whale is somewhere between a pilot and a humpback. All of a sudden I know too much. The story is really very simple, based on a true story from public television, about a whale that grew up at Sea World. When she became too big, they released her with a radio and expected she was intelligent enough to join the other whales. I was coming from the premise that she doesn't know what the other whales look like, because she didn't grow up with them, so she's going to be looking for what a whale is. This book will have to wait, because I have to get started on my book about Columbus. I was surprised that it was almost like magic: He had three brothers, he had three audiences with the king and queen and three ships going west. But he is not my first-choice explorer, because from the books I've read he was not such a wonderful person. I wanted to start with Marco Polo, but because the Columbus anniversary was coming up . . . . I plan to do stories on explorers, people who wanted to leave tradition for the unknown. But then I am afraid I might be stuck for the next 20 years doing explorers.

Do you work to size?

Most of the time.

Your blues are exceptional.

Yes, they are very blue, and plentiful in my pictures. They told me after the Fleischman book, "No more blues and greens please."

Did you have a particular kid in mind to model the boys in Whipping Boy *or* Bean Boy?

No. I sort of invented them. With *Bean Boy*, I used to do sketches with a little black dot for a nose, and Susan Hirschman would send it back to California and say, "Too European. No pointy nose." It was hard, because I knew what the original illustration will look like, but of course she couldn't know. It was our first project.

What is the market you see for the animated film?

I think for the future in communications, books will still be here. But it will help to do things like Weston Woods is doing. Only they are doing them when the books become successful. But if I have *Columbus* as a book I could have lots of things explained on a tape that went along with it, or a film could be complementary with the book. Lots of people are getting into this sort of thing, and it's getting very heavily commercial, which is unfortunate. Some film companies talked to me, and said that I couldn't choose what to do because they have to be geared to the average in this country. This is going to be the danger, because nobody wants to take a chance. I thought it might be nice to take a chance and do something in the form of book and film at the same time, but people don't want to put money into that. I would have to do it independently or more for the European market.

That has been another problem. When I first came here everyone said, "That's too European! Too whimsical." But now when I was trying to take some of my books to Europe they would say, "That's too American!" I don't feel that is the case.

You seem to be particularly disturbed by American film offerings for children.

I have noticed that every spring since I came to this country there has been a conference concerned with the content and quality of Saturday morning television for children. But nothing seems to happen because there's so much money behind it. What I find so insulting and vulgar and awful is that all of it is commercials for toys. It's like brainwashing.

I went to see *The Little Mermaid*. I came home depressed. They had to change the ending into a happy ending.

How much talking about your books in schools do you do?

I didn't even know it existed. Friends upstate invited me, and they took me to a lot of classes. I enjoyed it, and then I found out I was supposed to get a salary for it. I do it occasionally. I find it inspirational in first and second grade. But when they get older they have become infected by the popular culture that I did not grow up with. I like to go to a school where the kids couldn't care less. They will tell you they didn't like your book and why....

I'm also very comfortable with art students who are curious about their future as professionals. I realize that through that, going to Athens, Ohio, or Kansas City, or Oregon, is a way to get to know the country. These are not the usual places to go. I talk about my work, show my films, we have workshops. In Athens there was also an exhibition. So I'm trying to do more. Now I have admiration for teachers, because I never realized it was so exhausting, not just teaching but talking about the stuff.

Twenty years from now do you think you will still be doing some picture-books?

I hope so. I can see that sometimes a child will look at a page for 20 minutes or so. But I also begin to see in certain sequence patterns of the pages another dimension in the building of the story. I hope to have some children of my own. I would like to get inside more; not think of it just as an assignment, or lose that fear that I'm taking pictures to an editor or reviewer, but feel that I'm getting looser about it. I have what I think are some pretty nice dummies, but I tighten up along the way.

Right now the question is how much I have to be in New York. I think there is a limited time that you can stay sane here. When I was down and out and on the first floor in the West Village I was much more in contact with life. Now I am in a sort of ivory tower, and when I come down I am in "Crack Alley" and bump into real life. Up here I am trying to create beautiful pictures. I don't want to run away, but I can see that the people who have moved out of the city have more integrity. They come in to deal with what they have to and then go back to the place they want to be. I was always landlocked in central Europe, and now I can go anywhere I want to be, Mexico or upstate New York.... A lot of the people doing children's books seem to be in Vermont or some other peaceful place where they have a garden....

—*October 1989*

Twenty-Seven

Ralph Steadman

A Sampling of Works in Print

The Jelly Book Scroll, n.d.
No Good Dogs Putnam, 1983.
No Room to Swing a Cat Random, 1990.

That's My Dad David and Charles, 1987.
Two Donkeys and a Bridge David and Charles, 1987.

After a short drive from a bustling shopping town in Kent, down a hill to the end of a suburban street just this side of rural, behind a gate and up the drive to an impressive three-story rambling house, we encounter a statue of a large horse. And peering around the rear of the animal, straw hat on his head, is Ralph Steadman, being photographed for a Sunday Telegraph Magazine *article. There is time to explore the extensive gardens with their casually cultivated flowers, fruits and vegetables; to watch the sheep cropping the grass, while wandering past the swimming pool to the barn/garage that Steadman has gutted, breaking through gabled roofs for skylights to create a studio. The drawing table with pens, inks, stains and watercolors handy takes up only a small area; the rest contains paintings large and small, graphics, old typefaces, a picture file, and toward the back an incredible collection of machine and furniture parts in reserve for future sculpture.*

When you were young, did you want to be an artist?
No. I wanted to be an aircraft engineer. And I wanted to be a manager at a Woolworth's, a bank manager, a pilot. I was a swimming pool attendant, a rat catcher, gardener, all in North Wales.
You went to a technical college?
For aircraft engineering. I think it was when I started drawing things

Self-portrait by Ralph Steadman

in columns there was a need in me to push them a bit, to twist the engineering drawing slightly. I think I have retained that; I use the straight line and the compass a lot. The machinery is there, and I find that it goes very well with freedom. I like the work of Yves Tinguely, the wonderful works that explode.

I've drawn to make a living, so I guess my stuff is marketable.

You left Wales after college?

I went to do my National Service in 1954. In 1956 I came out to London. I got a job as a newspaper cartoonist trainee. I started doing nine ideas a day, to go out to the different papers in the group. About three years gave me grounding. At the same time I was learning to draw. I was going to college part time, five nights a week life drawing, Saturday morning life drawing . . . Victoria and Albert Museum twice a week drawing from the antiques for seven years. This started getting in the way; I could no longer do just the little cartoon in the newspaper. I realized there was more to it. I was still telling jokes; perhaps I could tell them a little more eloquently if I could draw. You'd chuck the comedian off the stage if he told the joke badly even though the joke was brilliant. I thought even a poor joke can be told well. So if you find a way of drawing that can be combined with telling stories, the better you can draw, the better it will be.

Were there any special teachers or tutors?

I've only had two, both really good ones. One was Stanley Squires. He made me aware of the esthetic quality of line, of paint, of anything, even a wall. And Leslie Richardson, who taught both me and Gerald Scarfe. I introduced Gerald to him. Gerald was doing mail order catalogs, and he said he liked my line. The three of us used to get together and talk a lot about the connection of everything: photography, drawing, sculpture, architecture, politics; it's all a part of the same thing, and you can't separate art from it and make it a precious item. It isn't; it's very much a part of life. Unfortunately what happens in school is that they try to separate art and make it the kind of thing you can do if you can't do Latin or Greek. Then you're either alienated from it, or you're an artist and one of the dummies. They devalue art in school, they discourage it. In a way art is a kind of troublemaking process; it's a kind of anarchy. All those things are a danger in school where they wish to control people, to prepare them for adult life. I think that's a terrible mistake. I think that art should be such an important part of any curriculum, whether you're going to be a scientist or an accountant or anything. Think of the unemployed. If they had an interest in something they could pick up later . . . . You can teach children anything. Certainly you can teach them to be open and aware of all possibilities. I find myself saddened by that; that art is something we can accept only if we turn it into some sort of a commodity that's worth a lot of money. Then we start looking at it again; we reassess Van Gogh when his work sells for millions. This makes the man in the street take notice. And they're even more fascinated when they realize that he never sold a painting in his life, died penniless. That's even better; that's what art's about.

Did you ever want to teach?

I have done a bit in a technical college in East London. I did it for three years in the '60s, stayed with them through the course. I started an illustration course and did a bit of design, etching, printmaking. Then, when they came to leave, I said I would too. "Why should I stay here while you go out and get all the jobs?" That was the last time I taught properly. I've done a bit here and there since. I was artist in residence at Exeter where I put on my operetta. I've also visited the hospital children's ward, and talked and drawn with them. I went to the art college and gave a life class, where I got them all to draw the figures from the feet up. They had a helluva job. For years they'd been starting from the head. I said, "I bet hardly any of you ever got to the bottom before the lesson was over. You're always up here. So you're never realizing it in three dimensions; you're never breaking the surface of your paper. Why not start from the floor where the feet are? Let's try to realize they are describing a flat plane. Imagine it's a statue that has fallen over, and put the pieces back one on top of the other." I also gave a lecture there, with slides. I talked about life, and politics, and philosophy.

Do you ever go out to talk to kids?

I hate talking to kids . . . I've had five of my own.

The Jelly Book *was done for Children's Hospital?*

Yes. I did it when my daughter was in there. I have three daughters, and the second eldest, who's 25 now, when she was 2½ had a perforated stomach wall. She was bleeding internally and had to have an operation. The stitches broke and she had to be in for another month, right over Xmas. So I thought I had to do something for them. I went in and painted *The Jelly Book*. Because all I ever saw in the hospital was jelly (jello) and ice cream. I thought they must like that. (We really ought to republish that book; I rather like it.) The drawings were just splashed up for the kids; and it went around the wards. I was going in every day. There's nothing worse than going to visit in the hospital, and just sitting there. That book was done the right way, thinking what kids will like and not what will sell.

If you get more ideas, will you do more children's picturebooks?

I try not to say I'll do one every year, but if I get a nice idea. . . . Right now I have a lot of drawings of splashes that look like creatures. I thought I might make one of that. *Splashy Creatures* or *Something Went Splat on the Page*. . . .

Do you work with a particular child in mind?

I think if I got enjoyment from it someone else will. Otherwise you torture yourself trying to think of someone.

Do you think some concept books don't need stories?

That's the way I wrote *That's My Dad*. I was in the hospital when I thought of that. Seeing people's limbs up in the air here, something done with an eye here, or a nose there, gave me the idea. Another was pills for everything, for a bad toe, a funny knee, which would give me the opportunity to do a really big ear. I made a list of them. Kids will accept all that. If you can come up with the unexpected, when you don't even know what it is yourself. Kids say, "No he can't. . . ." But also the repetition, as in Freud's "compulsion to repeat" even rude words. It's the reestablishing the familiar before moving on.

How do your children's picturebooks relate to all the other work you do?

I don't like illustrating other people's stories anymore. The last one I did was *Treasure Island*, a wonderful classic. But I like to write my own if I can. I have one about a beaver and the intensity with which he goes about building a dam that I wrote in the '70s and never got around to illustrating. It's called *A Saga of Wild Ambition*. It's a children's book, because they're all animals. There's a little marmoset and a talking worm who tells jokes, and a sloth who talks very slowly. There's a dead village in it. I wrote it in France where they were beginning to sink a lot of villages to make a reservoir, while we were watching it rise up. We could see a village half in the water and half out. I was thinking of this for older children, a sort of *Lord of the Rings* saga. The books I do for younger children are really very simple. Children like little surprises, very simple surprises. I think one of the best people to do them is Maurice Sendak.

Books are all right, but publishers are getting so rubbishy. They're all being taken over. If you stay in the same place you get published by everyone. You never know who your editor is either. Just when you find you've developed a relationship with someone, you find you're dealing with a complete stranger and you have to start explaining everything. I used to think it was a wonderful, romantic area to be involved in. Now I just think it's a business, and it could be sausages I'm doing. It's a sad reflection on America that among all those millions of people you can sell only 3,000 copies of a book.

Tell us about the new edition of Alice in Wonderland.

Those were published in '68 and '72. Then they wanted to republish it as one volume with the *Hunting of the Snark*, but they wanted color. And I didn't see color. So what I did, as a sort of compromise, was to lay the originals out on the floor. I borrowed a wooden box camera, Japanese made; got some lights, and lit my pages like a theater stage, in colors. I didn't touch the drawings; I colored them with lights and photographed them for that edition. I didn't want to just fill in the areas; I just wanted to give them a tinge of color. *Alice* is a very Gothic tale; a dank thing. I felt there was something damp about the story. It's not a color book, and it's not for young children. I did it as a vehicle for my own expression. Which is how I like to illustrate books anyway, as a springboard for my own thinking.

How much control do you have over the binding and what happens in the gutters?

I never bother about the gutters. I'll start drawing a picture to incorporate the gutter in such a way that somehow you have a neutral break in the picture even though you don't want one. So I can't worry about it. I draw for the picture more than anything else. I don't like it sometimes when you get it right through a face. But in the end you start designing just for the book and not for the pictures if you worry too much. Occasionally we have shifted things to one side or another, but sometimes I don't allow enough space for that. I'm not very professional; if I get too involved in the technical side of it I find the light goes out of it.

Does the publisher determine the size of the picturebooks?

We talk about it.

So these pictures (on the wall) would be considered larger than what is in the book?

I always do them large. If they were designed for the book I think they would lose a lot of the gutsy feeling, the essence.

Does I, Leonardo *have an actual historical basis?*

I went to all those places. I sat a whole day in the little house where he was born. I walked down the hill to the little village of Vinci. I walked up the hill to where he used to play as a boy. I went around Florence and Tuscany. It was a beautiful thing to do. To get my whereabouts straight, I jogged through Florence with my tape recorder. There's also a film about my doing the book, for which I used the tape. We sat out in the garden and I played it while we were filming. I couldn't believe I could hear Italian traffic in my garden. It took me four years to do the book. [The new book on God, *The Big I Am*, took three.]

For the book on Freud as well, I went to Vienna to soak it up. I decided to do it in black and white and halftones, like old photographs. I could put Freud in situations that might well have happened. And if I draw well enough, if I make it believable enough, then that's how it was. It brings a sense of authenticity, which it had from what I read about him. I even lay down in his first consulting room. They let me in there; it's below the museum. The cover of the book is Freud looking down on me.

It would be nice to do a children's book that exercised the intellect as well, that is, that I got something out of doing it the way I did with *Freud*.

With I, Leonardo *and your admiration for Picasso, I could see an* I, Picasso. *Can you?*

I have 380 Picasso-esque drawings I did for a ballet last year. They are all done on graph paper in his methods: three musicians cubism, minotaur sequence . . . I spent two months doing them. I kept referring to his work generally to keep the mannerisms. We projected them onto ballet dancers dressed in white. A guitarist played flamenco while the images kept changing. Maybe I will use them for a book. "I don't seek, I find," Picasso said. He enjoyed himself.

Do you work with inks?

Yes, I like inks. I can see the iridescence through them. If you lose your line, something's gone out of it. I found it a bit difficult sometimes with paintings to keep that linear strength. I've found myself going back to linear with very direct drawing.

At the moment I'm doing a book called *Wonderful Characters*, "good old boys," wonderful freaks. They've been around a bit: the Fasting Woman, the Man Who Tried to Crucify Himself, the Man Who Would Do 1,000 Gallops on the Mechanical Horse Before Breakfast, the Astonishing Pedestrian—sort of like *Ripley's Believe It or Not*. They're going to be black and white. I thought it would be nice to do a black and white book again, because I've been doing quite a lot of color.

There's a series of paintings I call *Heads of State*, which is a series of portraits of peculiar characters from whatever I choose to do it on. If I take a piece of magazine to use as a face or the beginning of a face, I paint the picture around it. It's just a series I wanted to do, since I have all these canvases I want to use. Otherwise you have a canvas sitting there staring at you;

it's terrible. The longer you leave it there the worse it gets. It's the fear of the white space; you just start painting.

Things in my life are changing. I'm not doing so much with books at the moment. I've just written an operetta which was performed at Exeter Cathedral with the Welsh Cathedral Choir, John Williams the guitarist, Ian Holm the actor; Richard Harvey composed the music, full orchestra. I had my images projected onto a 30-foot circular screen. It's called *The Plague and the Moon Flower*. There were only two performances but now it may be performed at St. Paul's Cathedral in London in September.

How long has music been an interest?

It's just the idea of doing anything in a different dimension. I wrote a musical around my book *I, Leonardo*. I wrote the lyrics and started writing guitar music for it. I can't arrange or orchestrate. I can do chords and melody, to get the spirit and feeling. I do listen to classical music while I work, but sometimes I don't want anything, just the wind or the birds.

Do you have an interest in hand calligraphy?

Not copperplate. I like the way a line becomes alive, some wonderful shape. But it must come off the top; I can't design it and then draw it, or it will just go. It could be very large, but sometimes I do it tiny. Drawings are generally done large and then reduced. I'm in sculpture also. I hate being pigeonholed, which is why I try a broader sweep of things. I believe when I do a piece of sculpture I'm still cartooning in three dimensions, I'm thinking in a cartoon way. I think Picasso is the perfect example of someone who saw in a cartoon way. He used the cartoon method of drawing, of faces. It was a sort of leap of faith, reaching out to find the unexpected. Many of the painters, Goya, Daumier, were cartoonists. I would say that Leonardo was a cartoonist. He invented the Renaissance face, the one we all know. It's obviously not a real face; it's a stylization of a face; it's a caricature however slight to achieve an ideal.

I believe that the cartoon is the basic impulse for all creative activity. The impulse to express is the basic design of any cartoon, the unexpected surprise. I'm trying to get people to give cartoonists the benefit of a little more status than they're usually given. I would consider all drawing that is not slavishly realistic to be cartoon, because it has to be expressive, his own response. It really began in the caves with the cave painters. They would draw a line around the woolly mammoth to encapsulate their fear, to cancel it out. I think it's the same impulse the cartoonists use to hit politicians; they draw a line around a politician to exorcise that fear. I think that all creative expression is a form of exorcism. That's my major thesis. So when you ask about my bridging the areas between picturebooks and the other media I work in, it's really an attempt to take the cartoon into different areas.

How does your engagement with music relate to this?

I suppose you might say it's the sense of fun in music. But it's not funny music, because it's also sentimental. . . . I'm a Welshman, and all Welshmen are sentimental; they like to sing and they get all weepy. English don't; they're cold. I think you might say that in his way Stravinsky early in this century was adopting the cartoonist's approach to music, of reaching out to surprise and shock musically, in sound. If we had a classical approach to music he and Shostakovitch and Schoenberg would then choose to try to caricature music to change it, to alter its nature and total range, different scale. John Cage is another example of a cartoonist. People say a cartoon is a cartoon. But I'm talking about the impulse behind the cartoon, the impulse to express, the need to twist, to push, to reinvent. When you draw someone's face and you caricature, you are in a sense reinventing it and finding ways to express it in a number of marks. Those marks are your invention or device by which you capture somebody's appearance. Michelangelo's people are not real people. They are muscle-bound faggots, not real people, idealized, cartoons. I suppose I'm changing. I was losing interest in just the cartoon, the drawing form and what I can do with it. I won't say, "I'm not going to do it anymore, I'm now going to be an Artist (capital A)." That's rubbish. I have an impulse to be a cartoonist type artist. So I'll just rationalize and say I'm doing them (cartoons) in different form.

Three-dimensional work as well?

Yes. I have to use all those pieces I've collected; I can't bear to throw them away, so they'll all be turned into sculpture. The only way I can clean that room up is to go through it and make something. If one day I'm lucky enough to find some gallery to cast them in bronze. . . . It would be lovely. I can't weld, so I put them together with plaster, etc. . . . I like the idea that while it's still wet I can do a bit of drawing so to speak, like Daumier's wax work. Plaster and mechanical bits make beautiful objects. With the cartoonist's quaint quirks in them here and there they'll be engaging. I have a chair with a Michelangelo foot on it. That's the kind of thing I'd like to do more of, with humor.

All your work is equally fun?

Not always. Sometimes I find I've taken on a job and then I'm bored and I wish I hadn't.

Is something missing in the work you haven't enjoyed doing?

Without a doubt. I've done things I've really hated. It comes out ugly, wrong; it comes out as if I can't draw. Recently someone wanted a beautiful catalog of a new architectural scheme on the river. They asked if I could do something with it in the style of Leonardo da Vinci. They would have paid lots of money, but I just couldn't do it. It wasn't Florence, it wasn't Tuscany, it wasn't my love of the things. There are cartoons for newspapers I might have done 20 years ago, but won't do now. I don't want to do a political slot any more; I've stopped drawing political figures. I think every cartoonist in the world should stop drawing them. If we ignore them, they won't go away, but we can at least hit them where it hurts the most: in their ego. No figures in our society are more personified than the politicians. We indulge them with our skill and wit and every form of humor, and they love it. If we get vicious they love it even more. So if we must do political cartoons, we should just do the issues. Because they're all petty bureaucrats; there are no men of vision around. If there's anyone good around, they shoot them. We have 10 years left to the millennium. We are going to have to make way for the Third World in the 21st century. They are growing all the time, full of desire for all the things we have. I sense a shift, adapting attitudes in order to survive. I mean by that we have to change our point of view.

—*Summer 1989*

Twenty-Eight

Ed Young

A Sampling of Works in Print

All of You Was Singing by Richard Lewis. Atheneum, 1991.

Cats Are Cats Nancy Larrick, comp. Philomel, 1988.

Eyes of the Dragon by Margaret Leaf. Lothrop, 1987.

Foolish Rabbit's Big Mistake by Rafe Martin. Putnam, 1985.

The Happy Prince by Oscar Wilde. Simon and Schuster, 1990.

High in the Mountains by Ruth Radin. Macmillan, 1989.

I Wish I Were a Butterfly by James Howe. Harcourt, Brace, 1987.

Lon Po Po: A Red Riding Hood Story from China Putnam, 1989.

Moon Tiger by Phyllis Root. Holt, 1985.

The Other Bone Harper, 1984.

Up a Tree Harper, 1983.

The Voice of the Great Bell by Margaret Hodges. Little, Brown, 1989.

Yeh-Shen: A Cinderella Story from China by Ai-Ling Louie. Philomel, 1982.

Ed Young came to Columbus for a children's book conference, but also to see again after many years a local resident whom he had known as a child in China. Having been impressed by his versatility as well as his obvious ability to design pages and tell stories with his pictures, we were fortunate to be able to meet with him. But he is not only articulate about how he works. He has also obviously given much thought to why he works the way he does, and about the world in which he works.

What did you read when you were young in China?

As a child I read a lot of Chinese fairy tales and legends, historical novels, stories that were also in Peking opera. A few Western stories were translated into Chinese, but I didn't know them in Western titles. Now some of them ring familiar bells to me, because I have read the Chinese translations somehow there.

How did you come to the U.S.?

I came to study architecture. But in my three years in Illinois I found that I thrived in my drawing courses and returning to beyond simply architectural things. I loved to draw buildings, but I didn't want to do that forever. So I took a summer course for the eight weeks which became three years as it turned out to be exactly what I wanted. I left my things in Illinois, and never returned. It was the Los Angeles Art Center School of Design. I didn't know what advertising design was. It was just another name to me. But it was exciting to me; using visual means to communicate with the viewers efficiently and effectively.

Then I went to New York to work in advertising. But my heart couldn't get into it. I didn't like a relationship where consumers are treated like people with no minds of their own. Some people suggested that I should try children's books since I love animals. I had drawn cats all the time, and went to the zoo a lot. I had a lot of sketches on paper napkins and little scraps of paper left over from jobs at the advertising studio. I put a whole stack of these in an A & P shopping bag, and made an appointment with Harper and Row. The doorman sent me to the freight elevator and the secretary told me to leave the delivery at the desk. But I said I was there to see Ursula Nordstrum. When I was admitted to her office, Ursula went through all my sketches patiently; she pulled open a drawer and took out the manuscript of *Mean Mouse and Other Mean Stories*, which turned out to be my first book. I didn't want to do it at first because there were animals doing non-animal things like shoving one another around or standing on two legs. But she said take it home for a week, and if you still don't like it send it back.

In advertising, I never got to see a product from beginning to end. This was my chance to see how a book got printed, trimmed, bound, etc. So that was going to be my first book and my last, just to see how a book was made. It won a prize and an agent called to represent me. That's how I got into children's books. But it wasn't until eight years later that I began to say, "Yes, I guess I'm a children's book illustrator." I was always doing the books for the child in myself who would love to be told these stories with those images. I never liked being patronized by cutesy words and things. I like children to be exposed to things that adults are because they are capable of understanding too. But the scope of my work evolved through the years. By the time *Bo Rabbit* came to me as the stories were so good, all I wanted was to tell them. When the book was published, I suddenly realized that the things I had objected to in doing *Mean Mouse*, with animals talking to each other and doing human things, were not really an issue anymore. I had

Self-portrait by Ed Young

told them all and thoroughly enjoyed it. So *Foolish Rabbit* came very easily for me. It was no longer important for me to do animals only as animals, because they have integrity as animals anyway.

Do you work to size?

Yes, the final art usually is. First drawings are made on the manuscript itself, as soon as I read it. They are thumbnail sketches. They look like smudges to you, but I see them in my head. In time they become more visible to others, and I know what I need to find out more about. It demands more; it says, "You must put down what I am fully, not just my spirit." So I go deeper. Often it evolves into a color study. It's like composing music, balancing it between tension and relaxation, changing moods. It seems that each round the story demands more. In the end the book ought to feel to me like it is one indivisible whole: all the pictures and words linked together with a rhythm of sound and silences, as with music and lyrics. And when you put it away you should have that music continuing in your head, and if it is any good it will last. It must be so believable that you can actually taste, see, hear or smell it on other levels.

Are you satisfied with the reproduction of your art?

Not always, but one must live with limitations. Publishers are generally very conscientious and responsible. *Cats* is an example. We are changing the color of the thread in the second edition, for example, because the white color is too jarring on some pages.

Sometimes economics, but more often human inner and outer conflicts, get in the way. Then time, energy, and money are wasted; inferior work comes with little love to give people. I don't like to work that way—no love means no time.

You work for several different publishers?

Yes, since I get offers from many good publishers. Each publisher has a different personality. You find kinships and develop friendships but that also changes as companies evolve with time.

Some of your books use a Chinese seal. What do they mean?

Basically, it's a signature. Sometimes, for me, it's the title of my book. The title of *Eye of the Dragon* is also a Chinese proverb. The story on the copyright page is another version of the same story. In other books I use my name in the design of a seal. I had a seal made with a cat on it for *Up a Tree* and a dog for *The Other Bone*. At first we had the title of *Cats Are Cats* in red, but later it was changed to white so we used the red seal instead.

How did Lion and Mouse *get started?*

A British publisher wanted a lion story, and sent me several versions. I chose the best version, and spread it across the pages like a wordless book. This whetted my appetite. I found out it's not so easy to tell stories without words, because words are so easy for one to run to for an explanation. When you look at pictures you have to arrive at your own meaning. Kids love that. Some adults like to tell the children what it all means. When I show wordless books to adults there is often a feeling of uneasiness. So with a book like that I show it to children, or to adults who want to play. I say "Tell me the story," by these pictures as by then I am too subjective. If there are gaps in what it conveys, then I see where I have failed. So it's really a participational process with people who read it. Every time there is a new audience they may tell me a slightly different interpretation and I can see whether it's getting close or not, so I'll follow what I hear by doing another round. Finally it will say completion for itself.

Is the Red Lion *Persian with Chinese technique?*

I really cannot tell if I have a Chinese accent as I speak or as I draw. What impressed me in the Persian art style was that in one picture you can have several different time sequences happening at once. I was struggling with that problem because I had done long scrolls of the story. Those pictures wanted to get into the book but there was no place for them in 28 pages; they would be squeezed out. You have to put them into panels, like *Yeh-Shen,* or you do little friezes. I utilized their way of doing pictures to get it all in. With *The Girl Who Loved the Wind* I became more of a student of Persian painting. I went to the curator at the Metropolitan Museum Moghul painting show and asked her to show me anything that was wrong with my interpretation of telling the Persian tale because I wanted to be as authentic as possible. She pointed out that everything was following the 12th century style, so why had I put an 8th century painting in among them?

So I removed it as a result. But there is one two-page spread that has a great deal of space not in the Persian mode. That is my Chinese self in there, I suppose, who just couldn't stand all that clutter any more, and I had to open up for some room somewhere in the composition of the book.

Did you develop that versatility in advertising?

Not there as there is never time for growth in that way. My art training was in Los Angeles and mostly on my own, outside of schools and the advertising field.

Would you describe how you went about creating some of your books?

For *The Emperor and the Kite* I wanted to try the cut paper technique to see how it works. I even did some pages several times. What's exciting about it is when you lift it from the paper and see the shadow of the kite or people really moving. We wanted them to reproduce it as close to three dimensions as possible. That's also why I want to do a film with shadow puppets where you can move something on a screen. In a book when you make a shadow sometimes it just looks like a misprint or off registered. So it became two-dimensionally flat again. I realized there was no more reason to do it in cut paper; somehow one could paint it just as well and save some time. I learned how to do play with cut paper and that was good enough for me already.

Later in *Who-Paddled-Backwards-with-Trout* I wanted to do a shadow play. That's more complicated because you have to cut it out first, then get a photographer and shoot it on a screen with a light behind. The screen changes as you tilt the cut paper; it adds dimension. It needs no color. The story itself is elusive and so I wanted to do it this way. I had a photographer friend shoot the whole thing to show to my editor. I said when it was finished it will not be my cut paper art but the shadows of the paper-cut will be my finished art. She could choose which version she preferred. In the end we didn't use the shadow-play pictures. I myself had mixed feelings about it. The deadline was too short. If I had to work with someone else to do the photography, I would be working for a long time with a process I know very little about. And I could not guarantee the effect. It is more experimental, therefore risky. So if she wasn't excited that way, I might as well do it another time. With the shadows you would have seen a lot more that isn't there. You could have seen branches, and felt the rustling of the wind. It brings dimensions on other levels. The shadows themselves are forms and realities we tend to neglect.

How did you come to do Bo Rabbit Smart for True?

At a celebration of a local gallery show opening, someone said to me, "Ed, you've got to hear these great stories." Priscilla Jacquith had just translated them from a telling recorded in Gullah language. When I heard her tell them I decided I wanted to do them with her. It was done at a time when I was doing a lot with graphite pencil art work.

Does your style relate to the media you are working in?

One's style grows out of the media, and one's media grows largely out of the content. Yes, until their limitations can't serve the story any more. I know what I want to do, and that will be the kind of story I like to tell. I find those challenging ones that I can really play with. In other words they promise some growth in me.

For *The Girl Who Loved the Wind* I started with designs for woodcuts, while the story was in Japan. I could see the castle by the sea. But when I got to the tropical garden, it didn't fit any more, so I had to move to a different place and thereby medium. I tried so many my studio was filled with different things, each for a few pages. The story moved to Tahiti, then to Southern France, to South America, and the architecture and everything changed. I had asked Jane where this girl is from, and she said, "You name it." After going around the world a few more times I ended in Persia, where the fruit and vegetables and architecture worked, and everything fit. She agreed, and found another name for the girl. But the trade-off is you don't get the dramatic impact I wanted with Persian miniatures. In the scene where the man is whipped I wanted the master looming on top of the staircase looking down. In Persian miniatures you're not there to dramatize with perspectives. I learned a lot making that story work within the Persian format.

Each book I make is somewhat like giving birth to a child. The author inspires my imagination. I was involved with finishing *Foolish Rabbit* using pastels for the first time. I started in gouache painting but it made the paper curl and warp. So I rethought out the whole process. *Moon Tiger* became an experiment with colors in the nighttime as opposed to *Foolish Rabbit* which was daytime—throughout the day. Together they gave me a chance to see what pastels could and couldn't do.

Up a Tree started off from a magazine story I read of a cat caught up a tree in a small midwestern town with a town square. The fire department was called and all the traffic stopped. When I was young I had a similar experience trying to save a cat from a cat and dog fight. I wanted to write that story. I kept trying but I couldn't get what I wanted. But I kept getting fewer and fewer words, until I finally had no words at all. I decided that if the story could be told that way why bother with words? But I didn't want it in a particular time or place, because it's a universal story; as long as there are cats there will be this story. So I moved it to the Middle East, where people's clothings haven't changed for centuries. Then I couldn't remember just how a cat came down from a tall tree. You know cats never perform when you want them to. I waited for a cat to come down so I could see. Finally I saw a raccoon come down. They do a flip-flop. That was how I did the research.

I usually do not work from models; I work primarily from my experience.

Nancy Larrick had a collection of mice poems which I received as a manuscript before *Cats Are Cats*. But I was having a problem finding a way to do that book. People's relation to mice is profoundly different from that with cats. Not everybody has a warm feeling toward mice as toward cats; they are rodents, meanwhile they can also be very lovable. I didn't want to use mouse caricatures as an easy way out. I couldn't make them huge and overpowering by filling out the spreads the way I did the cats. I felt you would have to live intimately with one every day, where he would come out and have his breakfast and then go back into his hole, and you could keep a journal of him. I was struggling to find a suitable style, when Nancy's cat collection came along. In view of public sentiment and my knowledge on cats already available I thought the latter offer would be easier. That's how *Cats Are Cats* came first. I'm still looking for something comfortable for the mice. Still *Cats Are Cats* was not an easy book. You must know the moods of a cat can be from cuddly to very fierce and independent. I didn't want the book to feel spotty and unconnected as if there is no continuity from one poem to another. Nancy Larrick had an idea of how the poems were ordered, but pictorially it was difficult for me in colors and moods, so I suggested a new arrangement as some authors are more protective about their work than others and Nancy was open-minded to entrust it all to me and said, "I guess you know best." Then I researched to find the image I wanted; for instance, what kind of cat in what kind of pose would suit which poem. Then I arranged them along the order of outdoors to indoors and night into day.

Still, I missed some kind of a cat story. So I made up a simple story from the cover by having a cat sneaking up on something. And I carried that through the table of contents to the first poem, and then the footprints at the end, like the actors coming onstage and then leaving the stage at curtain.

Red Lion came to me while I was visiting Italy, in a collection of fairy tales from Persia written for adults; pages and pages of endless description. I loved the story. I went to Ann Beneduce, who published almost every book till then. She said just edit it. I rewrote it, and found out how difficult it was to tell a story that way. I went through many formats such as comic strips with balloons to house for the words; I also did a scroll about 40 feet long with collage. I was trying to squeeze words out of the pictures but no matter how hard I tried it simply would not appear. When I went to Bologna I received many other offers, but I was so stuck with this one that I didn't feel like accepting any more. It felt terrible. So I went back to Ann and said, "I've got to get this out no matter who writes it." I showed her what I had. By this time the art was done in Persian miniature style, with just a little rectangular space where the words should go. 28 pages. Who could and would do words to fit the pictures? Finally Diane Wolkstein came to mind.

I called her and she accepted the challenge. Somehow she got the words to fit the space.

When the book came out we celebrated. We invited her to come to our local library to tell the *Red Lion*. We made a Persian setting for her, with rugs, and she wore robes. She told *Red Lion* as it should be told. Then she told *White Wave* and said, "I want to give something back to you. You gave me the pictures for *Red Lion*; now I give you the words and you will supply the pictures." That's how *White Wave* was made.

How does Eyes of the Dragon *relate to* Pied Piper?

As I was not brought up in this country, I am not familiar with the children's literature in the West. I only came across *Winnie the Pooh* less than 10 years ago, and the *Pied Piper* only last week on television. Margaret Leaf, Munro's widow, found this story in the Boston Muesum. Dorothy Briley of Lothrop sent it to me, and I asked if she was flexible. Since I know China, I am particular about Chinese tales, for it had to feel like China to me; otherwise however wonderful it is I couldn't do it. I know that tale from my own background. So I put that version in there too, on the copyright page in small type. There were other difficulties. The wall to go around an entire village had to be so long, it would take years before he could finish the wall painting so time must be compressed and made believable. There were questions about what kind of a dragon? We worked it out so it could satisfy both the Chinese and American ideas of the magical creature.

Yeh-Shen was based on research of a tribe on the Vietnam border, the Hmong people. When Ai-Ling Louie first claimed that the story was told to her by her grandmother as a version of the Cinderella story, I wasn't especially interested in adding just another Cinderella story unless it had some authenticity to it. When she told me that there was a Chinese version in Chinese, I asked to see it, and thought it would be the end. As fate would have it, she sent me one version written in the Tang dynasty and edited in the Ming dynasty as a legend that actually happened in China. I include that in the first few pages of the book.

The first problem came when I found that the people of this story didn't wear shoes. I knew I was in trouble. I didn't want to invent a shoe just for the story. So I was stuck. I was sent to a library collection of Chinese books and objects. On leaving, I thought to ask whether the librarian had anything on these people at that time. As a matter of fact, she had some wood engraving made at that time. There for the first time I saw shoes that they wore. I kept collecting anything I could find about these people. I was also looking for an image for my Cinderella, a beautiful girl by their standard as well as ours to be the central figure of the story.

I did the whole book in one continuous image, but still had many questions about how these people lived. The book was really stuck. I wrote some in Chinese, and tried to incorporate the images. It became vertical. *Yeh* means leaves, and you can see that in the old character. A flagstaff with banner sticking out means location, and there is an eye with two legs meaning a person turning around and looking. That's the character Shen, meaning leaving; a person who has reached a border. Together it means tenderness, the tip of a leaf. I was trying to squeeze images out of that, and did a whole series of characters to play with bringing them in.

Meanwhile Ai-Ling Louie was eager about her story. To help me along she would call me to tell me about a show or book about these people. I found an exhibit from a community of Hmong when I was doing a workshop in Boulder and could sketch the jewelry and patterns of colors of clothing. My family in Beijing helped by sending pictures and descriptions. I had a Japanese print of a fish on my wall all the time as inspiration for the fish in the story. When I did a scroll the format began to take shape. I did the cover before the book was finished. I have always resisted that, because the cover should represent everything that is inside. I tried to get the shimmer of the water, but then you could not read it. Even with embroidery, but you still couldn't read it. Finally it was done by a superb calligrapher.

Foolish Rabbit was initially sketched out on old IBM cards. It was hard to get the lion right. When it was about done, I felt that I didn't really have the spirit of the story. The story didn't feel happy about its presentation. It didn't have enough drama, make enough noise and fury. So I asked for more time to do it all over again. When I was given the extension it was ready to explode into the present mode of expression. When I had to do the lion's paw, I went to look at the most available one. But for all my research, it didn't turn out correctly. This paw is from the lion in front of the 42nd Street Library in New York City. It stayed very still and I sketched it from the front. But later I found that thumb part actually goes higher up on the leg when the lion stands up. I was amazed to find out how easily a mistake can happen when one does not think or understand the most basic things about anatomy or his characters.

Jim Howe, the author of *I Wish I Were a Butterfly*, happens to live in the same town that I do. It was through the publisher (HBJ) that we found ourselves living in the same town. I didn't have much problem with the story. I was familiar with all the subjects of the story. Jim was reluctant about one of the pictures in the sequence, the frog, looming on that spread. When I showed the sketch to him and the editor, he said, "I didn't think it was going to be this big!" I assured him it would be all right when it's finished. That input was important to me, however. When the book was finished, the frog was still the same size, but he could hardly be seen behind the foliages. Still it was a threatening presence. Jim said when he saw the book that same size frog was no longer a problem for him! That's how it works from one stage to the next.

Do you usually have contact with the author?

Since *White Wave* I make a point to connect with the authors. Up until that point the editors had kept author and artist apart. I had accepted that as the way things were done. It is simpler that way, to avoid the stake of clashing egos, perhaps. But at the time of *White Wave* I decided that if I put my energy into making anything worthwhile the publisher ought to give me limitless time, and I will give anyone on the production a chance to give input of ideas or feelings while in process; even the printer is invited to participate. So a book takes much longer to do. I feel that this way the book has a chance to mature in a way I couldn't have done by myself. Everybody's input enriches the final product.

For "Birches" by Robert Frost, of course, there is no flexibility on the other side. Generally I would like the author to be flexible about the text if the pictures no longer need the words in that particular telling to produce the optimum effects. It's like throwing a ball back and forth between words and pictures. It takes longer, but at one point the text is strong by doing what the pictures cannot do and the pictures are strong by doing what the words cannot do and they feel as if they are locked in and you can't change anything any more, and that's what a good picturebook is.

What next?

A biggie for me. My first 30-minute television film of *Sadako and the Thousand Paper Cranes*, with Liv Ullman's narration. A bit frightening for me. Seven hundred frames—it's like 20 books within one year. Now all my book projects are on the back burner. Wonderful story on hope and courage, but I turned it down the first time I read it. There is a lot of dialogue with nothing to show it seemed in pictures. When I went to see the producer in Santa Cruz to return the manuscript and turn down the book, he let me hear Liv Ullman's narration. There it came alive for me. Since then it has become a different thing for me altogether. Images came like magic. She pours possibilities of symbolic images into my head for this to be an animated film. The film business is different from publishing. When you have a deadline there are no "buts" about it because of the mixing of all aspects on the media involved. So I will be buried someplace, with maybe a trip to Japan in the summer/fall to see what Hiroshima looks like. August is the hottest time in Japan, so it will be interesting. Right now I'm thinking of the film in black and white with occasional colors. I have missed that in books, because of the printing process. I want to explore possibilities with sounds, play with pasting it together. You don't have pages to play with any more; and it is more continuous. You can choose what you zoom in on the screen and to phase out. It's very different, very exciting, and a bit unnerving. I have six other books waiting on the back burner, for 1992 and onwards.

How do you feel about the Caldecott? [Young was awarded the Caldecott Gold Medal in 1989 for Lon-Po-Po.]

I suppose it would be important, as it is important for many people in the field. It is a celebration of quality books and my own appreciation for those who share that view behind my work. It is good for business, of course, but my reward is not in the prize for I am where I love to be without the limelight. I am happiest in my studio even though I enjoy meeting people and sign books occasionally.

When working I feel in touch with the world in a deeper way than signing my books. Shaking hands is one way of touching. Showing it on paper is another way to show how people can be touched. If we touch each other it's not always visible. It's something magical and miraculous; it's chemistry that I can't describe but I know exists between people. No words can describe that. This is what fascinates me about stories: how deeply you can reach with a story to touch another person. Without that I wouldn't be in this business.

Do you think about the child as audience?

No, I just do it for my world which includes all humanity. I believe that in each person there is that child that is in me. That child needs to be addressed for this particular story, to feel the excitement that I feel in myself. If the child in me is excited, I trust that somebody else will be too. The universal quality I catch in the tale is there for everybody. When I visit schools it is reaffirming to see how the children respond. They are very honest and to the point; I have immediate feedback.

What is your studio like?

It's an old barn set apart from my house. It goes through a tremendous chaotic period when everything is all over the place as I struggle to get a book right. Research material keeps coming in. Nobody would believe I could find anything in that jumble. Then I have to clean all that up before I do another book. Nothing much is left from the earlier books. Nearly everything was piled up, thrown away and burned. It's clutter I don't use. It's difficult to throw things away because one had happy memories with them. But after it's gone, you don't miss it. I gave some research and sketches from *The Emperor and the Kite* to the Kerlan collection.

What do you teach your students (in workshops)?

There are several important things other than drawing and design. One is that your heart has to be connected with what you do. If the work is worthwhile, give it time, let it mature. If you compress it into a contract with a deadline, the story suffers. Find something else to support you, and do the illustration for pleasure. In the end it pays off, because you get the story you want to do and you can be at your best. When you're grounded properly, it will support you.

For me, there are two needs; they are complementary. One is the physical, that is that roof over your head, all earthly provisions must be served. Yet the value of a person as an artist is on another plane: the inspiration, the heavenly side; your own vision of how the world can become by way of your talents. Those are the areas a person can hope to grow into, the ultimate potential as an artist. Without the first need being fulfilled you can never get into the second. But without the second the first will be utterly meaningless. For the artist the most important thing is to free oneself so that the person can grow and serve to the fullest potential. You don't have to scrape too hard; you can enjoy that part of life, you just have to know what limit you must set in order to be free to grow. Many people lose track of that. They expend the just living part and then they are no longer free as an artist in their own way and freely give to the society at large. And they wonder why.

My first taste of this was in advertising. I could earn a lot of money there. And on weekends I could go out and do some painting. But that is a trap. Because you are falling into company and a living style which generally is for people who don't want to do anything for anyone else. But you could also be on the other end, and starve in the poorhouse like the stereotype of an artist. Somewhere in between one must continually discover that place where it's feasible, and that place changes as I grow. So a young artist has to be aware of the two aspects of his needs. One is to grow as an artist, and the other is to maintain oneself as a whole person, living healthily to maintain that balance while still having the free time to grow as an artist. I have learned from the artists of the past. They were not just scraping along, but also freeing themselves so that they could grow. A person does not really have to suffer to be a whole person. But he ought to be in that place where his struggle is understood and accepted as an ingredient in life. In stories that I illustrate often there's a character who suffers if you could understand just how it feels by putting yourself in his shoes. If you've had a good life all your life, you tend to be an outsider to the less fortunate side of life. It makes a limited artist as well.

Do you feel you are in balance?

Sometimes. Enough to know when I am not. I learned discipline by my experience in advertising, and what I was capable of. Visual language is potent, and can reach deeply into the emotions of people. That can serve the highest in people by inspiration, or the lowest of wants to serve oneself alone. I can continue to learn from the business. And I lead occasional art workshops, and Tai Chi. Tai Chi is where I got my personal grounding, and with it I find my own base by the way I wish to live.

I am not that different from people born and brought up here. In the U.S. everybody, except for Native Americans, is from somewhere else, and is cut off from his roots in ways that they can never retrieve fully. I am not unique. I am simply expressing it in my own way. It's an acceptance of a particular predicament of me being neither fully Chinese nor an American. I don't know what being an American really means. I think that the sense

of being cut off from roots is in almost everybody here. Even the very middle American still has the feeling "what is us?" Two hundred years isn't a
long time to connect with one's roots. I go to Tai Chi often or the Chinese
language for these roots.

Even in China I was brought up with missionaries so it wasn't until I
was in America that I looked back to see what I was missing. It became apparent that I was a Westerner even before I came here. All was in the sub-
conscious. I am surprised when people told me about some early work of
American stories that it was apparent that I was not really American. (The
Bicycle Rider was done without thinking of anything Chinese.) It's like the
way I speak. I always think I talk like everyone around me, but when I listen
to myself on tape, I can hear not only the Chinese accent, but particularly
the Shanghai accent. So there must be something ingrained in my character. I may believe I'm an American like everyone else, but actually cannot
change the fact that I'm of Chinese descent, and people catch that accent
in my art as well. I often don't see it myself unless I look for it.

When you feel good, you feel you can be a bridge between the East
and the West, but when you don't feel that good, you may feel like an island.
By the same token, one may at times feel neither here nor there. In one's
age, I feel that way too. I'm not an old person, nor a young person. It could
be great; it could be that you can understand and appreciate both sides and
be a bridge to pull it all together. In that way, everybody is a bridge. But
at times, you would like to be a bridge, but you are cut off. You feel isolated.
It would take a long time and a lot of work to be that kind of bridge.

What would you choose to say about yourself?

I am not fully committed to any one field of endeavor, because each
is only one aspect of a life that can be expressed in so many different ways.
Film is one way. Teaching is another; relating to you across a table is
another. It's all the same. My expression simply looks different. To me what
is most important is not the medium or the skill alone per se. The intent
and content of what you write or the music you compose can be just as
beautiful because it is the best you can do. Whatever a person chooses to
do to be involved fully in the process regardless of the pain, there is the
promise of transcending. When I talk about my books now, I am no longer
the same person as the one who did them. Although I have my memory of
the process of doing the book, I don't care whether they are liked or not
because that is finished for me. When I am asked which book I like best,
obviously it's the one I am working on. It's still mine in the process. But
there is nothing to go back to when I'm done; it's finished unless I have
reason to pick it up for revision or for another reason.

I wish everyone could find that place. When I teach illustration we
sometimes don't do much illustration, as we search for that place by way
of illustration. Even in a nine-to-five job it can be something valuable there

for us. The higher one goes up the field, the more power one gets, but the more restricting it is to our boundary in some other ways. I am aware of what I need to be aware of as I am moving up. I'm remembering my childhood, my roots, and remembering where I am now.

—*February 1989*

Twenty-Nine

Paul Zelinsky

A Sampling of Works in Print

Hansel and Gretel by Rika Lesser. Dodd, 1985.

The Lion and the Stoat Greenwillow, 1984.

The Maid and the Mouse and the Odd-Shaped House Putnam, 1986.

Rumpelstiltskin Dutton, 1986.

The Story of Mrs. Lovewright and Purrless Her Cat by Lore Segal. Knopf, 1985.

The Wheels on the Bus Dutton, 1990.

> *Born and raised in a quiet suburb of Chicago, Paul O. Zelinsky now lives in New York City. To visit him you must first endure the physical affront to the senses generated by the subway: a clattering cacophony amplified by the long tunnel under the East River, odors to make you gasp, and the shrieking intimidation of the spray-painted graffiti. The climb up into the light and air of Brooklyn Heights is a spiritually cleansing experience that brings you onto narrow streets lined with old but apparently well-maintained apartment buildings. You turn onto his street and are suddenly confronted with lower Manhattan's skyline almost within reach across the active harbor. Zelinsky lives in a modest brick apartment building with a very alert, vocal, active, and adorable toddler named Anna and her alert, active, and charming mother—a full-time music teacher and part-time graduate student. We entered a multi-purpose living room obviously very much lived in. A piano, harpsichord, shelves of books, and paintings competed for space with the more typical social furniture. After the usual greetings we asked him more about his work.**

What are your early memories of picturebooks?

*Originally published, in an earlier form, in The Horn Book Magazine, *May/June 1986.*

Self-portrait by Paul Zelinsky

The Little Golden Book *Tawny Scrawny Lion* with Tengren's illustrations. And I liked *The Story of Ferdinand*. It wasn't long ago that I looked at it again, the first time since childhood, and saw the corks hanging from the cork trees. I never knew that was a joke! I liked Margaret Wise Brown's *The Color Kittens*. I don't have a very complete recollection of the books from my childhood.

Then how did you start doing children's books?

I would look at them in stores, but it didn't occur to me that I could create them for a livelihood until I took a course at Yale with Maurice Sendak, a seminar initiated by a student who had convinced him to teach it. He seemed to be making a living at creating books. At that point I had already decided to be an art major, so I figured I'd need a means of making a living. I thought that making picturebooks would be something I could do.

You were more levelheaded about your future than many young art students we know. But how did you go about breaking into this competitive field?

I have an uncle who works for *The New York Times*. He suggested I show some of my drawings to their art director. Because I was an art major and did real paintings, I didn't feel as if my ego was at stake. I showed drawings to the art director. He liked them, and I went home with an assignment. The real possibility of a career in illustration fell into my lap, more or less.

I went on painting and thought I might teach. Then I got my master's in painting, and got a short-term teaching job. I found out that I was a lousy teacher and that teaching wasn't what I wanted to do. In the meantime I had been visiting publishers with a portfolio, feeling all the while that I didn't have anything personal at stake because I was really a painter. In my art education the word "illustration" had been a term of criticism. I was embarrassed to tell my painting teachers for some time what I was doing. I was actually taken aback when I found that William Bailey, one of my favorite painting teachers at Yale, had seen some of my books and thought they were *wonderful*—a word he used for almost nothing.

When we see the illustrations in your books, it's clear that your approach to the way you depict characters is so varied. Is there a Zelinsky style?

Instead of a style I have a chain, a continuous chain, of ways that I work. I try to make the pictures talk with the same accent as the text and not worry about whether they are in my style or not. (I've had this line quoted back to me and it struck me that it sounds significant but means absolutely nothing.) In different books, I may have covered the range that I can work in: from extremely detailed, rounded images in real space, such as the almost photographic images in *How I Hunted the Little Fellows*, to *The Maid and the Mouse and the Odd-Shaped House*. It seems to me that everything else I've done fits somewhere on a continuum between the two.

I would worry more if I were doing what my art school training taught me—to do one thing again and again, hone in on a particular image. I get a kick out of doing each book differently. I've been pleased that people like the fact that there's a lot of variation in what I do, because I expected to be called on the carpet for not having a style—the pictorial equivalent of a voice for an author. I figure a style will come on its own if it wants to.

I was first given *Emily Upham's Revenge* because there was something in my portfolio that looked Victorian. When I did the *Little Fellows*, which is set in the 1890s, I got worried that I would be typecast as working in the 19th century style. I guess I didn't really want to be pegged. I would never want to do any book in the same style. Different books offer different things. I have a lot of loyalty to the text. I don't think any book is a "Zelinsky." When I look at a text, I don't usually know how it should look right away, but I often know what it shouldn't look like, and that's enough to start with.

I often find myself thinking of periods or individuals from the history of art when I'm working on a book. Sometimes I'll copy a painting or a drawing — not to use in my illustration, but to get a feeling for a certain kind of shape, or the use of space or light. With *Hansel and Gretel* I hope it was clear that I was looking at Dutch genre paintings. But for Beverly Cleary's *Ralph S. Mouse* I actually just wished I was Garth Williams.

The Maid was our introduction to your work, and her depictions immediately challenged and amused us. Where did she come from?

The text came from my editor, Donna Brooks. Her grandmother had been a teacher, and this poem was among her teaching notes. Donna's mother found it in an attic. It was pretty crude and dated and took a lot of changing. It sounded like an 1890s idea of a funny rhyme. From the start I thought of the book as a sort of board game, very flat and ornamental. At first I thought I was inspired to know just what period to set the book in, but later I realized that I was just thinking along the lines of Mother Goose, that is, 18th century England. I didn't know where the look of the old maid came from. I tried lots and lots of maids. I had just recently looked at Sendak's *Hector Protector* and saw the incredible size of the woman's bonnet and her period costume and realized there's almost no limit to how far you can exaggerate. So my maid grew pretty thin, with quite a bonnet of her own. The editor later thought she looked like the old maid character in the card game. I do remember that I played Old Maid. She could have come from there.

Do you work in sequence?

I try always to work out of sequence because I tend to learn how to do what I'm doing as I make the book, and the later drawings are generally better than the first ones — if not esthetically better then technically more facile. So the book would start out crude and become facile at the end if I didn't jump around.

How do you decide on the particular scenes in a story that you want to illustrate? Do you have them all in mind before you start creating anything on paper?

If a picturebook is an art form, the art happens at the stage when you are choosing what you will illustrate. That's when the rhythm is set and when the emotional impact gets set up. Choosing the scenes to illustrate is the first thing that I do. I start out knowing the number of pages and with a text that seems to break in certain places. Maybe a surprise in the text really needs to be accompanied by a visual surprise with a page turn. Sometimes an image demands to be a double-page spread or a single page. Just dealing with the text from the beginning sets a lot of constraints on what is and is not going to be pictured.

Telling the story through the pictures means: how do you get from one picture to the next in a visual and logical progression? There may or may not be changes in the scale or format. Selecting the pictures is making the whole book into what you want it to be.

What made you choose such a demanding visual setting for Hansel and Gretel?

From the time I started illustrating children's books I've always wanted to do *Hansel and Gretel.* I was disappointed that everyone else was doing it, too. I hadn't seen any *Hansel and Gretel* book that expressed the story for me, that seemed remotely right. The story is very serious. I don't mean that it's not happy. But it's deep; it's rich emotionally and deals with very basic fears. It's about how infants become their own people, how they come to realize that they're not an outgrowth of their parents.

Many people's main association with the story is the witch's house. My basic image of it is the children lost in the woods: how big the woods are and how small the children are. The idea of thousands of birds in the vast forest eating up all the crumbs is an operatic idea that I responded to when I first heard the story as a child.

Did you choose a winter setting to make a more compelling book?

I thought about the fire the father builds; it's not very warm out. Actually my vision was affected by the painting my great-grandmother did of *Hansel and Gretel.* My great-grandmother started painting when she was in her mid–70s, like Grandma Moses. I showed her painting, the painting I grew up with, as a tapestry on the wall in the witch's house. It has a glowing, light greenish, creamy white roof and a very intense blue sky with black trees against it. The whole thing has a glow to it; the light doesn't seem to come from anywhere. I suppose that's why I would think of the glowing light on the book's cover that illuminates the house and the children and not the woods.

Did her painting or other factors lead you to a kind of pastiche of 17th-century painting styles?

I was looking at 17th-century Dutch genre paintings—like Steen's—that are full of characters in the Metropolitan Museum of Art. (Nobody offered to pay my way to see the paintings in Europe.) Genre paintings don't have the kind of emotional distance that some other classical paintings have. You can look at them more for their subject matter—really look at the people, get involved in what they're doing, be amused by them, and not have a layer of Great Art come between you and the painting.

Rika Lesser's text was almost finished by the time I started the pictures. Then Rika actually did make some changes based on the pictures, which is a nice way to work. I don't know if there was any idea of tradition in what I was doing, when I selected the scenes to illustrate. I hadn't looked at other picturebooks. It might just be the way the text is; you're left with certain necessary ways of telling certain scenes. Sometimes the text might dictate a certain composition.

Do you do items more for illustration purposes than for painting design—such as the chamber pot in the bedroom scene?

I hope that they come together in their purpose. The fact that there's a chamber pot does fill out the world of that household. They would have had a chamber pot. But also the scene of the parents in bed is a one-page picture, and it's difficult to fit objects into such a vertical shape. The very large footboard of the bed would have left a lot of dead space below it, and the cut-off chamber pot does bring the footboard closer to the reader and does make the base of the picture more alive. The curve in the handle refers in some ways to other curves in the picture: the curve in the brim of the man's hat and also the shape of the woman's nightcap.

Did you do a dummy first?

I did pencil drawings which I tore out of the sketchbook as I did them, so I could flip through them. The drawings were fairly detailed. Because of time constraints, I ended up taking slides of those pencil sketches and projecting them onto stretched paper. Then I could make changes. The dummy had been done before I knew the exact proportions of the book and how much space the text would take. With the slides I could project the drawings onto the paper at an angle and change their proportions, squash them sideways. In the first forest scene the trees are actually a lot thicker than in the sketch because there was more text than I had anticipated. I wanted to make the woods very big and the children very small. I had to keep exerting an effort because the children get bigger and the woods smaller. I went walking in the woods of western Connecticut, near the house of some friends, for woods research. Without those walks, I wouldn't have thought to paint the large fallen trees on the forest floor.

Where did the witch come from?

I think I made her face up. She doesn't really remind me of anything outside the book. The picture where Hansel is sticking the bone outside the cage was one of the first ones I did. Afterwards, when I was visiting my grandmother in Florida, I suddenly realized that the witch's costume—the whole picture and composition—was snitched from a little bronze tableau that she had, a scene of Persian shoemakers about four inches high with their turbans and robes, working in their workshop. It had a little light bulb inside it and when I visited my grandmother as a child, I would have her turn it on, and the fantasy of it would turn me on.

Suddenly it was time for Anna's nap and for us to walk several blocks to Zelinsky's "safe house," a studio on the second floor of a somewhat seedy old building on a store-lined street. On the way Zelinsky told us about his notebook full of story ideas and his possible interest in doing board books now that he has his own customer for them. "I wouldn't if Anna hadn't come. The idea of books that are like catalogues with a word and an object are not that interesting for me. I would like to do a board book if I could do more that just a catalogue. I do my books mainly for myself. It seems to work that way. If the narrative has a childlike feeling, it should come through."

Upstairs, beyond the multi-locked door, were the room and work tables. While not chaotic, the scene gave no evidence of the kinds of order found in Zelinsky's paintings or drawings. Tubes of paint reminded us that before the printed illustration there was a hand-produced object.

Are you satisfied with Hansel and Gretel *as you look at it now?*
The longer I spend without looking at the originals, the more satisfied I get. The second printing was better. The book was printed in Hong Kong with nobody from the publisher there. I don't know if the artwork could have been reproduced better. The sense of light is vastly changed.

We noticed when comparing one of your paintings with the printed version that some parts of the original were cut off. Were you consulted first?
No, I wasn't. That's the way the book came back from the printer. There were all sorts of little disappointments and mistakes. There always are. The pictures were many different shapes. I tried to do them all in exactly the right proportion, but a couple of times I miscalculated or was given the wrong figures. Generally I don't like to publicize the flaws.

But we see only the books, not your artwork, and reviewers respond to the pages produced by your printer. How do you handle reviews?
I use them to decide what I think of the reviewer. There's a lot of reviewing that could be done on a higher level of intelligence. Sometimes reviews, such as some of *Hansel and Gretel*, seem to be negative for reasons that are personal to the reviewer. Something about the book really sets them off, so much so that I can't believe it's just the book. I must have hit a chord with that person.

Clearly he had hit several of our responsive chords. But it was time to return to the streets and to retrace our steps to the subway and the return journey to Manhattan. Somehow we didn't seem to notice the dirt and noise as much this time as we reflected on the hours we had filled listening to this quiet artist and gentle father tell us about his books.
—1986

Update

It's nice to be given the opportunity to add to our 1985 [sic] interview and bring it up to the present—that is, the summer of 1990. The birth of our daughter Rachel has been the biggest event in the Zelinsky household. She is now a two-year-old rascal with more charm than a button is cute, who speaks a language that is finally beginning to resolve into English. Anna, now six, is becoming a reader, which is almost as exciting for her parents as it is for her. She is just finishing kindergarten in our local school, the same one into which her mother managed to transfer as a teacher before Rachel was born. Our existence is becoming increasingly convenient. Last summer we finally moved from our overcrowded apartment (which, by the way, I thought was nifty and elegant; it had a view of trees and Manhattan reflecting in the East River, if you looked out from the right spot in the bedroom) and into a bigger one in the same neighborhood.

When you came to Brooklyn, I was, if I remember right, in the early stages of work on *Rumpelstiltskin*. I should have been much farther along. If the work did not speed up, I imagined, Dutton would simply reschedule the book beyond its slot on the fall '86 list. This turned out not to be possible, for a variety of reasons, and the work did not speed up. But paintings were coming out that surprised me, pleasantly, with the various qualities. So when I learned that my promise to deliver finished art in time for fall publication was one I would have to deliver on, I felt I had no choice but to shift into high gear the likes of which I hope never again to experience. The eight months that followed combined 16 months' worth of work with a decade's worth of personal bad luck and disasters, topped off with some serious bad health. The only pleasures I recall from this period arose as the pictures for *Rumpelstiltskin* came to completion one by one (and not in the order of the book). Since finishing *Hansel and Gretel* I have planned to try my hand at three Grimm tales at least, and it has taken me until now to bear the thought of starting another one.

It was a full year after *Rumpelstiltskin* was finished before my efforts on the next book bore any kind of fruit. The job was not helped by my loss of the lease to my cherished studio (one of the blows of the *Rumpelstiltskin* year) at a time when space in New York was at a premium. The best I could do to replace my studio was a mile away in a depressed manufacturing district—a room in an old paint factory that now houses several artists' studios. Where my old studio had been matchless for people-watching, here the windows, alas, were frosted. I languished for a while; eventually, several pounds of book resulted: *The Random House Book of Humor for Children*. An anthology of fiction for a wide range of ages, it took practically an age to illustrate. Much of the slowness came from my need (granted by R.H.) to lay out the entire 320 pages of typeset text in order to ensure that the pictures I wanted to draw, in the places and proportions that I favored, would have available spaces in the text in which to fit. I drew the pictures on a frosted Mylar "paper" in black Prisma-color (i.e., in colored pencil on plastic), aiming for a nice, strong range of tones from black to white, and a feeling something like a lithograph. Neither of these came through in reproduction. Still, even without texture and much of a tonal range, much that is in the drawings remains visible in the book. Especially, I hope, the humor.

By the time the humor book was done, *Rumpelstiltskin*'s success had afforded me the opportunity of moving my studio back into my home neighborhood. My new studio is a studio apartment halfway between our home and the public school. It is on a quiet block, without much people-traffic, but my windows look out on a lovely churchyard full of flowering trees and shrubs, with a beautiful iron grille gate. (Last week it was transformed for one day into a playground for shooting one scene in the movie *Three Men and a Little Lady*; if you see the movie, you will have shared my view.)

I think some of my pleasure at being back, in a couple of ways, went into the painting in *The Wheels on the Bus*, which will have come out before the printing of this book. I learned the song from my wife; it seems I was one of the few people in this country who did not know it already. And the idea came to me immediately that I would like to see a book in which the actions of the song take place literally on the page: the doors opening and closing, the windows going up and down, and so on. The book was somewhat involved in the making, but it was all a pleasure, as bright a project as I have yet known. With one more Grimm tale on the horizon, darker visions may be looming, but *The Wheels on the Bus* is still making me smile when I look at it, and I'm having trouble waiting until its publication. I need to know that it's not just me who smiles.

—*1990*

Bibliography

A list of sources before 1987 appears in The Art of Children's Picture Books: A Selective Reference Guide *by Sylvia and Kenneth Marantz, Garland, 1988.*

Some recent publications about picturebook artists:

Annual ('87, '88, etc.): *Illustrators of Children's Books.* Picture Book Press, yearly. Annual catalog of the juried Illustrator's Exhibition at the Bologna International Children's Book Fair.

The Art of Babar by Nicholas Knox Weber. Abrams, 1989.

Behind the Covers, Vol. 2: Interviews with Authors and Illustrators of Books for Children and Young Adults by Jim Roginski. Libraries Unlimited, 1989.

Bill Peet: An Autobiography by Bill Peet. Houghton Mifflin, 1989.

Caldecott & Co.: Notes on Books and Pictures by Maurice Sendak. Farrar, Straus, 1988.

Jessie Willcox Smith: American Illustrator by Edward D. Nudelman. Pelican, 1990.

Meet the Newbery Author: Arnold Lobel rev. ed. (filmstrip) Random House/Miller Brody, 1986.

Robert McCloskey by Gary D. Schmidt. Twayne, 1990.

Something About the Author: Autobiography Series continuing publications from Gale.

The Telling Line: Essays on Fifteen Contemporary Book Illustrators by Douglas Martin. Delacorte, 1989.

Note: Interviews with illustrators appear frequently in periodicals such as: *Booklist, Horn Book, Teaching K-8.*

Index

DUE